Psycho
and Beyond

Psychoanalysis
and Beyond

Charles Rycroft

Edited by Peter Fuller

A TIGERSTRIPE BOOK

CHATTO & WINDUS

THE HOGARTH PRESS
LONDON

A TIGERSTRIPE BOOK

Published in 1985 by
Chatto & Windus · The Hogarth Press
40 William IV Street, London WC2N 4DF

British Library Cataloguing in Publication Data

Rycroft, Charles
Psychoanalysis and beyond – (A Tigerstripe book)
1. Psychoanalysis
I. Title
616.89'17   RC504

ISBN 0 7011 2971 9

Photoset in Linotron Sabon by
Rowland Phototypesetting Ltd
Bury St Edmunds, Suffolk
Printed in Great Britain by
Redwood Burn Ltd
Trowbridge, Wiltshire

Contents

Introduction

In the 1950s and early 1960s, Charles Rycroft's work as a
writer, therapist and organization man was well enough known
within the psychoanalytic community. Between 1947 and 1961
he sat on numerous committees of the British Psycho-Analytical
Society, and, as he has put it, 'held several offices and wrote
numerous "scientific" papers'. Although the latter received
'polite, sincere, but often uncomprehending praise', however,
he came to feel that his voice carried little weight in the Society's
affairs and that real power belonged to those of whose values
he did not approve. His eventual departure from the Society in
1978 can have come as a surprise to no one, least of all himself.

As he makes clear, Rycroft left the Psycho-Analytical Society
after deciding not to try to change it from within. Why did he
take this option? As the essays in this book demonstrate, he
was not short on compelling theoretical arguments. But the
weight of orthodoxy was such that any open confrontation
with it inside the Society would have dragged him into precisely
those rituals of polemic and pronouncement of anathemas
that he was seeking to reject. In effect he wanted to see the
emancipation of psychoanalysis from psychoanalysts. He could
not, therefore, put himself forward as yet another spokesman
for an alternative, schismatic, therapeutic 'school'. He went
quietly.

But his silence was meaningful. Indeed, he elaborated its
meaning in his work with patients and the articles he continued
to write for a 'lay' public, whom he addressed through news-
papers and non-specialist journals. The position he elaborated

is nothing if not clear. Nonetheless, its impact has been dispersed through a plethora of publications. I hope that this book will both clarify and terminate the silence surrounding Rycroft's departure from the organized institutions of psychoanalysis. If Rycroft is right (and I believe he is) the arguments he is seeking to advance have considerable importance, not just for psychoanalysts, but for all of us: they constitute a major, innovative contribution to our understanding of ourselves and our species.

The reception accorded to Rycroft's first major paper, 'Symbolism and its Relationship to the Primary and Secondary Processes', presented in 1956, helps to illuminate his originality. At that time, the accepted psychoanalytic theory of symbolism had stood unchanged for forty years. In 1916 Ernest Jones, Freud's leading British disciple, had delivered his authoritative paper, 'The Theory of Symbolism', which drew heavily and uncritically on Freud's own findings.

Jones had sought to reserve the concept of 'symbolism' for a very narrow area of mental functioning. He insisted that the process of symbolization was invariably carried out unconsciously: the individual who made use of the symbol was not aware of what it symbolized. 'Only what is repressed is symbolized,' Jones wrote. 'Only what is repressed needs to be symbolized.' This, he said, was 'the touchstone of the psychoanalytical theory of symbolism'.

For Jones symbolism had a special, indeed an exclusive, association with the 'primary processes', or primitive and maladaptive modes of thinking characteristic of the unconscious. Symbolism, according to Jones, 'always constitutes a regression to a simpler mode of apprehension'.

When Rycroft turned his mind to symbolism, however, he took a very different view. His concern was to rehabilitate the concept of symbolism; he presented it not as a regressive or defensive phenomena, but rather as 'a general capacity of the mind' which could be deployed in manifold different ways. In his view, symbolization had no particular association with the repressed, nor with primitive or unconscious modes of thinking. Rycroft argued that words themselves were only a special kind of symbol. ('Classical' psychoanalytic theory had seen verbalization as the hallmark of conscious, 'secondary process' thinking.) Indeed, Rycroft insisted that 'unconscious symbolic and imaginative processes underlie the development and maintenance of a sense of reality just as much as they do neurosis'.

In putting these ideas forward, Rycroft took care to declare his 'immense debt' to Jones's classic paper. But twelve years later Rycroft himself was to criticize the tendency in psychoanalytic writing to make appeals to authority in order to legitimize the ancestry of theories, or to ward off charges of unorthodoxy. The truth is that Rycroft's paper is not so much an extension or revision of Ernest Jones's as a reversal of its principal insights and arguments. The two papers take up mutually exclusive positions. If Rycroft's conception of symbolism is right, then Jones's is wrong, and vice versa.

How was Rycroft's revolutionary communication received by his psychoanalytic colleagues? There was a certain amount of pecking, scratching and fluttering of the wings in the theoretical dovecots of the Society, almost all of it designed to protect the orthodox position. Meanwhile, Jones wrote to Rycroft saying, 'You are of course right in pointing out that my use of the word "unconscious" has since been superseded, and that my formulations need bringing up to date in the way you have excellently attempted.' But then the awkward matter was largely forgotten. To the best of my knowledge, Jones never publicly acknowledged that his 'classical' theory of symbolism required a revision, or even a defence.

Nonetheless, I think that most of those outside the psychoanalytic movement who read both Jones and Rycroft on symbolism today would concur with Jones's privately expressed view that Rycroft had got it right. Symbolism is such a pervasive characteristic of human psychological and cultural life that Jones's attempt to restrict the concept to a very particular usage seems arbitrary, even perverse. Similarly, experience indicates that symbolism is intimately involved in the 'highest' (e.g. aesthetic, religious and scientific) as well as the 'lowest' (e.g. instinctual or sexual) modes of thought; nor can we really believe that its use in the latter is always unconsciously determined. It is not just that Rycroft appears to have logic and common sense on his side: his way of discussing psychoanalytic ideas renders them compatible with insights arising from quite different kinds of discipline, and, indeed, from the experience of life itself. Nonetheless, this incident epitomizes Rycroft's relationship to psychoanalytic orthodoxy.

For example, his most recent, and in my view his finest book, *The Innocence of Dreams*, is a thorough-going reversal of Freud's pioneering classic of psychoanalysis, *The Interpretation of Dreams*. Indeed, Rycroft's arguments against Freud's view of dreams are similar to those he put up against Jones's concept of symbolism. For Rycroft, dreams are not *necessarily* disguised expressions of repressed wishes, the royal road to the unconscious, nor analogies for psychopathological symptoms. Rather, he sees them simply as the way we think while asleep. Characteristically, Rycroft's conception of dreaming, unlike Freud's, is in keeping with contemporary non-psychoanalytic thinking on the subject.

Rycroft's work on symbolism and on dreams alike shows that he has done something rather more radical than making adjustments and additions to an accepted core of psychoanalytical knowledge. His writing is refreshingly free of that self-abasing piety with which even Freud's most radical critics within the psychoanalytic movement approach the temple of the Standard Edition of his works. He has even gone so far as to suggest that the development of psychoanalysis is a process by which Freud's 'private, introspective hunches' have been sifted clinically by himself and his followers, some becoming accepted, public concepts, while others have had to be discarded. Rycroft has challenged the nature of psychoanalysis as a discipline – a challenge made all the more authoritative by his long clinical experience, and his involvement in the movement. He has consistently raised awkward questions about the way in which its findings are arrived at and the sort of language in which they are cloaked.

Rycroft's concern about the way in which psychoanalysis deployed a confusing terminology, seemingly derived from an inappropriate model drawn from the natural sciences, led him to compile what has become his best-known book, *A Critical Dictionary of Psychoanalysis*. In the introduction he emphasized that although psychoanalysis was formulated *as though* it was based on the objective and detached scrutiny of isolated examples of *Homo sapiens* by a totally uninvolved spectator, in fact its insights 'arise out of the relationship that develops when two people are gathered together in a psychotherapeutic setting'. He expressed the radical belief that psychoanalytical theory would eventually have to be reformulated as a communication theory, and that it would have to reflect, honestly and conceptually, the source of its own data.

Culturally, stylistically and temperamentally, Charles Rycroft does not have much in common with the dominant psychoanalytic schools. German abstract and 'dialectical' thought has never meant much to him. He once asked, 'Why did Freud assume that there were two groups of instincts and not three or four, and why did he assume that they were opposed and not complementary to one another?' He gave the answer himself in the form of another question, 'Was it really because the clinical facts compelled him to make these assumptions, or was it perhaps because linguistic habits of thought impelled him to follow Hegel and Marx and to construct a dialectical theory which came naturally to him but which seems alien to those who have been nurtured on the English language and English empiricism?' 'Hegel and Nietzsche,' he admits elsewhere, 'are not in my bones.' Similarly, he is impatient with French over-theorization. Of Jacques Lacan he has said, 'Apart from the single fact he would like psychoanalysis to be rewritten from the point of view of linguistics, I found his writings a real load of rubbish.' And the jargon of the American psychoanalytic fraternity has always been alien to him.

Rycroft's writing strikes a tone which is rare in the psychoanalytic tradition. He is often ironic, self-deprecating and humorous. He is always sparing and precise with his words and concepts — to the point of verbal parsimony. His style is studiously empirical, sceptical and cultivated. His customary restraint is sometimes punctuated with indignant outbursts of moral approbation, or ruffled common sense. In 1980, he wrote:

My attitude to analysis is really determined to a large extent by the fact that my intellectual loyalties and allegiances have . . . been to a tradition other than that of the analytical one. Mine has been derived from my family background, education at Cambridge, and at University College Hospital. All the time, I have been in pursuit of a way of viewing human nature acceptable to that tradition.

He felt his *Critical Dictionary of Psychoanalysis* showed this clearly. 'In that book, analytical concepts are defined and commented on from what is actually a peculiarly English point of view.'

And yet, of course, Rycroft's Englishness is of a peculiar, indeed an *exceptional* kind: it is, perhaps, only *half* Englishness. With few exceptions, the English intellectual tradition which shaped and formed Rycroft has been hostile to and dismissive of psychoanalysis, even in its critical and dissident varieties. Perry Anderson was right when in 1968 he acknowledged that the British school of psychoanalysis was 'one of the most flourishing' in the world, but pointed out that its impact on British culture had been virtually nil. Here in Britain, Anderson argued, psychoanalysis 'has been sealed off as a technical enclave: an esoteric and specialized pursuit unrelated to any of the central concerns of mainstream "humanistic" culture'.

This singular fact, I think, goes a long way towards explaining just why Rycroft's challenging work has not yet received the recognition it deserves. Within the psychoanalytic movement, as Rycroft himself once wrily observed, Englishmen do not cut much ice . . . *especially* if they are inclined to question Viennese dialectics. Within British culture as a whole, however, psychoanalysts do not cut much ice . . . *even* if they question Viennese dialectics.

And yet what Rycroft has to say is important: more important, I would suggest, than the bogus 'scientism' of traditional psychoanalysis, or that philistinism which refuses *any* encounter with Freud's great insights into the human psyche. For, in the end, despite all his telling criticisms of psychoanalytic theory, Rycroft affirms psychoanalysis as a therapeutic practice; and, in the best traditions of English empiricism, the authority of his writing springs immediately from his years of experience of that practice.

II

Charles Rycroft was born in 1914 into a uniquely British milieu: his father was a baronet, fox-hunter and country gentleman whose second wife, Charles's mother, was 'well-connected' in the British establishment. As Rycroft explains in the autobiographical fragment printed below (pp. 198ff.), his early childhood was spent in Dummer, a large country house in Hampshire. His father was regarded as 'the local representative of both Church and State', and the young Rycroft's first experience of life was undoubtedly pampered and privileged. But his father died when he was eleven, the offspring of the first marriage inherited the title and the estate, and from then on he, his mother, brother and two sisters lived a life of 'aristocratic poverty'.

Rycroft was nonetheless sent to a fashionable preparatory school in Dorset, and thence to Wellington, a leading public school. Although he disposed of religion at the age of sixteen, and declined to enter the army as had been expected of him, he at first retained the conservative outlook of his social class. After leaving school, he spent the first half of 1933 in Germany, where he quickly became convinced of the inevitability of war. The first political activity he can recall was persuading his brother to cut articles on Germany out of *The Times,* conceal them in copies of *Tatler* and send them to him in Germany, where *The Times* was then banned.

In the autumn of 1933, Rycroft went up to Trinity College, Cambridge, where he studied economics and history. At first, he was a member of the Conservative Association. He was, however, amazed to discover that only the far left seemed aware that the Nazis were bent on war. He involved himself with the Communist-run Anti-War Movement and soon after switched from the Conservative Association to the Socialist Club. In the autumn of 1934, he was recruited into the Communist Party.

Looking back on his Cambridge communism more than thirty

years later, Rycroft characteristically claimed that it did not require any moral courage. He argued that Marxism was fashionable at that time, and that his family thought it proper for young men to engage in political activity: they thought it best for them to start on the left, and move rightwards as they grew older. Rycroft's belief in Russian communism was shaken by the Karl Radek trial of 1935, the year in which he visited the USSR with a party that included Anthony Blunt. On the return journey, he recalls, he spent his twenty-first birthday on a Soviet ship moored in Hamburg harbour. He and his colleagues decided to go on shore to the opera to celebrate. Members of the Soviet crew rowed the party from the ship into Hamburg where their passports were stamped and they were admitted into Germany by uniformed Nazi officials. They watched the opera – *The Meister-Singers of Nuremberg* – and then the uniformed Nazis rowed them back to the Soviet ship. The irony of this situation was lost on the other British Party members; within a few months, however, Rycroft was lost to the Party. He was to remain a socialist all his life, but today he stresses: 'I have come to think of civilization as a much more fragile thing than I did when I was young. It could take generations for a country to recover from violent change.'

Rycroft had not heard of Freud or Jung before he went to Cambridge, but once there he found they were part of the intellectual milieu. When he got a first in Part I of the tripos, the College presented him with ten pounds' worth of books as a prize; he chose Bertrand Russell's *Freedom and Organization*, Karl Marx's *Capital* and Sigmund Freud's *Psychopathology of Everyday Life*. He took to Freud's work without difficulty; but it was still some time before he considered psychoanalysis as a career.

This came about through the influence of Adrian and Karin Stephen, who moved in Bloomsbury circles. But Rycroft says that, even when he eventually decided to apply for training, he had no conception of the nature of the psychoanalyst's profession, nor of the movement itself. Psychoanalysis was just an eddy in the prevailing intellectual climate, a fascinating idea which looked as if it might have a contribution to make to history, sociology and the arts. 'If I had known about the psychoanalytical movement and its quasi-sectarian quality,' he comments, 'I would certainly not have applied.'

But when he was twenty-two, Rycroft was interviewed by Ernest Jones, Edward Glover and John Rickman. In his biography of Jones, Vincent Brome reports Rycroft as having said that Jones thought him an 'upper-class dilettante'. In any event, he was rejected as a lay analyst, but led to believe that if ever he thought of doing medicine, and then reapplied, he might well be accepted. After spending a year in Cambridge as a postgraduate, Rycroft did apply again. He started studying medicine at University College, London, the same week in October 1937 that he began a training analysis with Ella Sharpe, one of the few British lay analysts with a background in academic literary criticism. Rycroft went to work as a house physician at the Maudsley Hospital, which had a reputation for favouring organic and neurological explanations of mental illness. But his teachers were tolerant, even indulgent, of his then psychoanalytic orientation, and he was allowed 'to vanish three times a week' to see his analyst, Sylvia Payne.

It is tempting to suggest that both Sharpe, with her interests in metaphor, language and literature, *and* the Maudsley had a formative effect on the young Rycroft; his own developed ideas have always emphasized *both* symbol, metaphor, 'the literary imagination' *and* a biological approach to the understanding of human behaviour and its difficulties.

After about a year with Sharpe, Rycroft entered analysis with Sylvia Payne. His training was disrupted by the war, which he spent as a medical student. He did not qualify in medicine until 1945, nor in psychoanalysis until 1947. His training analysis coincided with the notorious controversies between Anna Freud and Melanie Klein. Sylvia Payne was in fact instrumental in drawing up the quaintly named 'Gentleman's Agreement' – all the major protagonists were in fact women – which led to an institutional compromise within the Society and the establishment of an A Group (Kleinian), a B Group (Anna Freudian) and a Middle Group (technically, a sub-section of the A Group).

At first Rycroft did not realize the feud was going on: 'I don't know whether it was blindness on my part, or protectiveness on my analyst's part,' he has said. But from 1947, after he had qualified, he could hardly avoid the controversies. He began to hold various offices within the Society. He started to call himself Middle Group: at first he had a reputation for being more sympathetic towards the B than the A Group, but he regarded the whole thing as 'daft'. 'I know I had the idea there was something that could be called "mainstream analysis" and I wanted to represent that.'

Nonetheless, some of Rycroft's early papers showed a certain sympathy to some of Melanie Klein's ideas. Indeed, Klein was impressed by one of his papers and told Rycroft that if ever he wanted to discuss patients with her, she would be 'only too pleased to do so'. Rycroft did not take any notice of this: it did not occur to him that a busy, professional person of Klein's standing could really be bothered with the problems of young, junior analysts. 'But I had misunderstood her approach,' he admits. 'In fact, it was a call. She was hoping to get me into the fold, and I had refused her.'

He says that Klein was 'extremely nasty' about the next paper he wrote for the Society:

She said I would show a deeper understanding of the case if I had, myself, had a deeper analysis. I thought that was bad manners: she was being rude to my analysts. Looking back on it now, I think she might actually have been right. Nonetheless, I didn't think she should have said it. As a person, she was a prima donna: as narcissistic as they are made.

Rycroft's distaste for the way polemics were conducted within the Society only increased as the years went by. He was appalled by the handling of a paper called 'The Concept of Mind', presented to the Society by H. J. Home. This raised a question mark over the whole idea of 'psychic determinism'; Home was ritually denounced by most members present. This was the last meeting of the Society Rycroft attended. Increasingly, he came to realize that behind the 'theoretical' and organizational controversies was an argument 'about what human nature is basically about'. He found it more rewarding to pursue this in his relationships with his patients rather than through public controversy or polemic.

I must at some point have abandoned the idea that there was I, a scientist, observing material presented to me by a patient. I must have gone over from that view (which seems to be implicit in Freud) to the idea that I was having a relationship or an encounter with someone and that therefore the raw material, or basic data, of my science was the relationship I was having with the patient – not 'material' that he was producing. This change happened so gradually that I think, in fact, for a long time my practice was better than my theory. I always did just simply start a relationship with the patient, and explored how that relationship developed. If I wrote something in terms of 'psychic apparatus', I was really only making kow-towing movements towards classical theory. But I think I must have dropped 'psychic apparatus' very early on, as I can remember referring to it as an intellectual masturbating machine.

Rycroft even once sent in his resignation to the British Psycho-Analytical Society, but a senior member was commissioned to take him out to dinner and persuade him to change his mind. He was assured that many people in the Society agreed with every word he was writing, although they felt they could not say so publicly; he was also made to feel he was being 'rather difficult and trying', and was warned about how damaging it would be to the movement to have further splits. And so, partly out of loyalty to those he had trained, and partly out of lethargy and distaste for polemics, Rycroft remained a member of the Society until 1978 . . . when he quietly let his membership lapse without ever sending in a formal resignation.

III

'Freud's writings,' Rycroft once wrote, 'have proved to be more of a quarry than an edifice.' Nonetheless, until the First World War, psychoanalytic theory possessed a coherence it was never subsequently to regain. Freud believed, and in this Rycroft agrees with him, that his most significant discovery was a distinction between two principles of mental functioning which he designated as the 'primary processes' and 'secondary pro- cesses' respectively.

Freud, however, considered these two modes to be antagonistic. He held that the primary processes were characteristic of the unconscious, and characterized by such techniques as symbolization, displacement and condensation. Primary process thinking tends to be 'iconic' (i.e. visual rather than verbal) and to disregard the laws of syntax, time and place. In adult life, it is vividly retained in functions like dreaming. Freud thought that the primary processes were associated with the activity of the sexual instincts, and that they made use of a highly mobile, libidinal energy, which was free and unbound. He held them to be governed by the pleasure principle: in his view, impulses deriving from the primary processes sought constantly to reduce tension within the psychic apparatus through spontaneous and immediate discharge.

Secondary process thinking, however, was for Freud charac-teristic of the ego; he saw it as involving logic, rationality, grammar – and especially, of course, verbalization. Secondary process thinking made use of bound energy, and was character-ized by structure and the activity of the ego-instincts. Freud never described these in much detail, but they correspond roughly to the biological concept of 'self-preservative' instincts. Freud believed the secondary processes were governed by the reality principle, which caused the ego to reduce instinctual tension in adaptive rather than potentially dangerous ways, since, he held, immediate discharge of primary process impulses would be disastrous for the organism.

Freud thought, then, that the mind, or 'psychic apparatus', worked like a machine seeking to reduce the level of excitation within itself and to avoid tension. Its goal was quiescence: or, to be more exact, the maintenance of a low and constant level of internal tension. As has often been pointed out, Freud's model of mind was based closely on the thermodynamics of Helmholtz, whose physics were the inspiration of Freud's teachers, and on physiological concepts, like homeostasis, or rather its conceptual precursor, Fechner's Constancy Principle.

This conception of mind as a 'psychic apparatus' was, as Rycroft once put it, 'the central concept of Freudian metapsy-chology'. None of the 'findings' of psychoanalysis was unaffec-ted by it. One effect of this model was that Freud tended to see the human infant not as a relating person, but rather as an autoerotic isolate, seeking to discharge libidinal impulses. These, Freud held, went through various developmental stages, during which the mouth, anus and genitals, respectively, became the focus of essentially narcissistic pleasure. Freud believed that only at the time of the famous 'Oedipal conflict' did the child develop the capacity for object love. In effect, he conceived of development as the progressive binding of 'polymorphously perverse' libidinal impulses on the part of the ego.

Freud described the developmental process by which 'lower' mental functions became transformed into 'higher' ones as 'sublimation': for him, however, cultural and artistic pursuits were always in some sense suspect because of their proximity to the regressive 'primary processes'. Creativity and civilization itself were, in Freud's scheme of things, necessarily rooted in instinctual renunciation and denial.

Now this set of ideas formed the core of 'classical' psychoanalysis, which Ernest Jones, one of Freud's first and most devoted followers in Britain, sought so assiduously to defend. Together with David Eder, Jones founded the London Psycho-Analytic Society in 1913; six years later, Jones purged Eder and his colleagues for Jungian leanings, and reconstituted a 'purified' British Psycho-Analytical Society. For some years this remained, in the words of one of its leading members, 'a conventional group, undisturbed by schisms and controversies and, for that very reason, rather uninspired'.

By the mid 1920s, however, it was impossible even for the most devoted Freudian to ignore the fact that Freud's own views about the opposition of instincts, the structure of the ego, and the role of aggression, had undergone far-reaching revisions. And it was at just this time that the British Society began to feel the influence of Melanie Klein.

Klein had first become involved in psychoanalysis in 1910, in Budapest; she was analysed by Sandor Ferenczi. (Later, in the 1920s, she went into analysis with Karl Abraham.) Ferenczi was, for many years, among the closest of Freud's colleagues. However, he was also the first analyst to grasp the clinical and theoretical importance of the primary relationship between the mother and her child. As a result, he and Freud went their separate ways. Later, Jones tried to claim that Ferenczi had gone mad. But, as Harry Guntrip put it, 'Ferenczi's concept of "primary object love" prepared the way for the later work of Melanie Klein, Fairbairn, Balint, Winnicott, and all others who today recognize that object-relations start at the beginning in the infant's needs for the mother.'

It is hard to say how much Klein owed directly to Ferenczi. But, as a result of her work with children, she too came into conflict with members of the Berlin and Vienna Psycho-Analytical Societies – in particular with Anna Freud. Surprisingly, perhaps, Jones was protective towards Klein. In 1925 he invited her to lecture in England, where she settled the following year. At first, her presence was relatively uncontentious, but controversy soon began to escalate. As Jones himself wrote in the introduction to one of her books:

In England itself the storm was heightened by the advent of our Viennese colleagues whose life in their homeland had literally become impossible. They added to other criticisms the opinion that Mrs Klein's conclusions not only diverged from but were incompatible with Freud's.

Jones himself thought this a 'grossly exaggerated statement', and continued:

Not that it should be in any event a decisive consideration if experience showed that her conclusions were nearer the truth.

Jones had not always himself proved faithful to such principles. Nonetheless, he continued to do what he could to defend Klein's right to put forward her ideas. Her position was further weakened, however, when in 1938 Jones succeeded in rescuing Freud from occupied Vienna and he arrived, with Anna, to spend the last eighteen months of his life in London.

This, then, was the psychoanalytic milieu which Rycroft unsuspectingly entered when he began his training in 1937. But what were the theoretical underpinnings of this controversy? Freud had put forward his revisions in a series of texts culminating in the publication of his last major theoretical work, *The Ego and the Id*, in 1923. There he proposed a new topography of the 'psychic apparatus' – introducing the terms 'id' and 'super-ego' for the first time. In essence, Anna Freud followed that tendency in Freud's later work which invested a new importance in the development of the rational ego. Her findings influenced American 'ego-psychology', which stressed 'conflict-free areas' and 'autonomous functions' of the ego.

Although Klein could also legitimately claim to have derived her theories from indications in the later Freud, her interests were very different. Like Freud's, Klein's was always an *instinct*-based psychology; but, unlike the classical psycho-analysts or ego-psychologists, Klein took literally Freud's speculative, late opposition of the life and death instincts. In this sense she was, as Rycroft has put it, 'more Freudian than the Freudians'.

Her theory stresses the innate ambivalence between love and hate which, she maintains, derives from this basic opposition. She sees the destructive drives, sadism and aggression of the infant as being a defensive turning away from the self of this inherent, self-destructive death instinct. She focuses on how the infant supposedly copes with its overbearing instinctual drives in relation to the mother and her breast. But, for Klein, the infant emerges as truly monstrous, possessed by 'phantasies' of sadistic destruction directed towards the mother's body.

Whereas Freud believed that the ego becomes differentiated from the id only as a result of the operation of the reality principle, Klein thought a rudimentary ego was innate, but its growth proceeded through a continual process of 'projection' and 'introjection'. The latter is the process by which, as Rycroft puts it, 'the relationship with an object "out there" is replaced by one with an imagined object "inside"'. Projection is the reverse process by which aspects of the self – such as impulses, wishes or internal objects – are treated as aspects of objects in the external world. Indeed, in Klein's writing, the distinction between 'inner' and 'outer' worlds becomes more fundamental than Freud's distinction between 'conscious' and 'unconscious'.

Klein also disposed of Freud's succession of libidinal phases, replacing them with two 'positions' which, she argued, the infant has to work through in the earliest months of life. The first of these was the so-called 'paranoid–schizoid' position characterized by a process known as 'splitting'. Klein conceived of the infant as dividing the representation of the breast into two, the 'good', satisfying, succouring breast, and the 'bad', denying, frustrating breast. Usually, the infant seeks to introject the 'good' breast, and to project his own aggressive feelings on to the 'bad'.

The paranoid–schizoid is succeeded by the 'depressive position' which, as Rycroft has written, 'plays the same part in Kleinian theory as the Oedipus complex does in classical theory'. In working through the depressive position the infant is assumed to learn to accept ambivalence and to acknowledge that 'good' and 'bad' are but aspects of the same 'whole object', the mother, out there in the world, whom the infant *both* loves *and* hates. Klein also improbably came to believe that the infant envied the creativity of the mother's breast.

Although she lacked Freud's breadth, originality and cultural richness, Klein succeeded in giving centrality to the infant's early relationship with the mother – something barely discussed by Freud until as late as 1926. Nonetheless, despite her formal assurances to the contrary, Klein saw this relationship almost exclusively in terms of the conflict of instinctual drives. Or, as Rycroft puts it:

> Kleinian theory is an object theory not an instinct theory inasmuch as it attaches central importance to resolution of ambivalence towards the mother, the breast, and regards ego development as being based primarily on introjection of the mother and/or breast. It differs, however, from the object theories of Fairbairn ... and Winnicott in attaching little importance to the infant's actual experience of mothering, this being overshadowed in the Kleinian view by the infant's difficulties in overcoming its innate ambivalence towards the breast.

A decisive step in the development of psychoanalytic theory was the replacement of a dual instinct theory (whether of the classical or Kleinian variety) by a full object relations theory, in which, in Rycroft's words, 'the subject's need to relate to objects occupies the central position'. This came about in a number of different ways.

For example, many of those gathered around Ferenczi in

Budapest developed his ideas, pointing to all sorts of significant components in the infant–mother relationship (e.g. clinging, clasping and touching) which could not be accommodated in traditional 'instinctual' descriptions. Alice and Michael Balint began to elaborate a radical critique of Freud's theory of narcissism, in which they saw the infant not as simply passive (as Ferenczi had done) but as 'born relating' – even if its mode of loving was egotistic. The Balints stressed the distinction between object relations and erotogenic activities. Eventually they came to live and work in Britain, where their ideas had considerable influence among 'advanced' Kleinians and members of the Middle Group. (Although Rycroft was at first sympathetic towards Michael Balint, he later came to feel there was something inauthentic about him. 'He used to say I was debarred from ever understanding psychoanalysis because I did not know German . . . I now think of him as a bit of a humbug, but that's retrospective.')

Other significant critiques of psychoanalysis were being elaborated *outside* the movement itself. For example, Ian Suttie, who worked at the Tavistock Clinic, wrote *The Origins of Love and Hate*, which was published in 1936; this book provides a systematic account of man as a social animal, whose object-seeking behaviour is discernible from birth. Suttie saw love as social rather than sexual in its biological function; he thought that 'culture-interest' was derived from love as a supplementary mode of companionship (to love) and not as a cryptic form of sexual gratification.

Rycroft does not believe that *The Origins of Love and Hate* was widely read even in the Middle Group in the 1930s, and has no memory of having read it himself. One man who certainly did read it, however, and has acknowledged its influence on him, was John Bowlby, who was analysed by Joan Riviere, one of Klein's foremost followers. Klein herself was one of Bowlby's supervisors when he was a trainee analyst.

In 1946 Bowlby joined the Tavistock without relinquishing his psychoanalytic associations. This, in itself, was an indication of changing times. But Bowlby, like Rycroft, was strongly influenced by the work of the ethologists, especially Tinbergen and Lorenz. This led him to elaborate the most sustained critique of Freudian instinct theory: 'in the place of psychical energy and its discharge, the central concepts are those of behavioural systems and their control, of information, negative feedback, and a behavioural form of homeostasis'.

Bowlby strongly opposed the idea that the infant's relationship to the mother was based on primary need gratification, such as the wish for food. He stressed the infant's need for 'a warm, intimate, and continuous relationship' with the mother 'in which both find satisfaction and enjoyment'. Bowlby held that the 'young child's hunger for his mother's love and presence was as great as his hunger for food'. Rycroft believes that Bowlby's theory is right, 'as far as it goes', though he feels Bowlby understands neither symbolization nor imagination.

But perhaps the critique of classical instinct theory which had the greatest influence on Rycroft was that put forward by W. R. D. Fairbairn, an analyst who, in the middle and late 1930s, was still strongly under the influence of Klein. Between 1940 and 1944 Fairbairn published a series of controversial papers – including 'A Revised Psychopathology of the Psychoses and Psychoneuroses' in 1941 – in which he rewrote psychoanalytic theory 'in terms of the priority of human relations over instincts as the causal factor in development, both normal and abnormal'. Fairbairn described libido not as pleasure-seeking, but as object-seeking; he saw the drive towards good object relationships itself as the primary libidinal need. Rycroft has said:

At one time I might even have said that I was a Fairbairnian, in so far as I ever allow myself to use an adjective ending in 'ian'. I was quite friendly with him and used to send reprints of everything I wrote to him. He would send back long letters about them. He had an intellectual rigour which both Klein and Winnicott were somewhat lacking in: Klein particularly.

But Fairbairn, like Klein before him, was something of a systems builder. Few analysts today make use of his terminology and constructs. None the less, for a certain tradition of British analysis at least, his work paved the way for a full object relations theory.

Rycroft believes that the Middle Group in Britain suffered from its lack of a leader: the man who came closest to fulfilling that role was probably D. W. Winnicott, a paediatrician who turned to psychoanalysis and immediately recognized its potential relevance for the treatment of infants and young children. Winnicott, too, initially gravitated towards Klein's circle; but he soon found he had too many temperamental and theoretical differences to remain there long. In particular, he did not feel the model of madness was appropriate to describe the state of mind of babies; and he did not believe in the death instinct. Indeed, Winnicott emphasized that being came before the handling of instinct, and that healthy being depended on the experience of 'good enough' mothering.

Winnicott thought that the infant made his first simple contact with external reality through 'moments of illusion' which the mother provided: these moments helped him to begin to create an external world, and at the same time to acquire the concept of a limiting membrane, or skin, and an inside for himself. Winnicott defined illusion as 'a bit of experience which the infant can take as *either* his hallucination *or* a thing belonging to external reality'. For example, such a 'moment of illusion' might occur when the mother offered her breast at exactly the moment when the child wanted it. Then the infant's hallucinating and the world's presenting could be taken by him as identical; which, of course, they never in fact are.

In this way, Winnicott says, the infant acquires the illusion that there is an external reality that corresponds to his capacity to create. But, for this to happen, someone has to be bringing the world to the baby in an understandable form and in a limited way suitable to the baby's needs. Winnicott saw this as the mother's task, just as later she had to take the baby through the equally important process of 'disillusion' – a product of weaning and the gradual withdrawal of the identification with the baby which is part of the initial mothering.

Clearly, his conception of illusion had taken him beyond Klein's sharp distinction between 'inner' and 'outer'. As Rycroft puts it:

In Winnicott's view . . . health and creative living depend on the

establishment of a third 'transitional' or 'intermediate' realm, in which
the subjective and objective are fused (or remain undifferentiated). In
this transitional area, objects are felt to be parts of both internal and
external reality, to possess both selfhood and otherness, and activities
are both wish-fulfilling and adaptive. All playing, all culture and all
religion belong in this transitional realm, which only develops in so
far as the mother responds sufficiently sensitively and promptly to the
infant's tendency to hallucinate the objects of its desire, to create for
it the illusion that it has subjectively created objects which objectively
exist independently of it. To the extent that this illusion is successfully
created, and premature disillusionment is avoided, the individual will
feel at home in the world and have a creative relationship with it.

Rycroft believes that this concept of a transitional reality media-
ting between the private world of dreams and the public, shared
world of the environment is 'perhaps the most important contribution made to psychoanalytical theory in the last thirty years'.
Nonetheless, he stresses that it is not entirely original – in that
Winnicott's transitional world is synonymous with what poets
have described as 'imagination', the 'intermediate faculty'
(Coleridge). Despite his great admiration for Winnicott, Rycroft's attitude towards him, as the article below indicates, is
more than a little ambivalent. As he once wrote in a letter to
me, 'You are right in thinking that I use very similar concepts
to Winnicott's, but I like to think that I understand symbolism
better than he did and that I am not so soppy.'

IV

For Freud, then, the human mind was in effect a machine, a
'psychic apparatus'; the analyst was someone who had acquired
a specialist technical knowledge of the workings and mal-
functionings of this machine. The stance he liked to assume
towards his patients was that of a scientific observer. Rycroft
remarks:

When I first became an analyst it seemed to me that the idea of
applying the scientific method to psychological phenomena was a
perfectly straightforward matter and that there were no particular
difficulties about regarding unconscious wishes or infantile complexes
as causes of which present-day symptoms were the effect, or in assuming that if a patient became aware of the unconscious and infantile
determinants of his symptoms, these would vanish.

Gradually Rycroft's view began to change. In this he was influenced by, and also himself influenced, a number of other analysts loosely associated through the 'Middle Group' of the British Psycho-Analytical Society. (These included Fairbairn, Winnicott, Brierley, Milner and Home.) As he explains in his sympathetic review of Roy Schafer's *A New Language for Psychoanalysis*, a variety of factors led to growing scepticism about Freud's mechanistic model of mind: the influence in Britain of Wittgenstein and linguistic philosophy, which questioned the validity of proposing abstract entities and 'forces' as scientific determinants; the rise of existentialism, with its emphasis on the self-as-agent; and the emergence of new disciplines like cybernetics and ethology, which appeared to offer more convincing models for human behaviour than those suggested by physics and chemistry.

For Rycroft himself the strongest influence of all was undoubtedly that of his experience as a therapist. As early as 1958 he had come to the view that 'we are more likely to increase our understanding of the dynamics of the analytical process by viewing it as a relationship, albeit of a unique kind, between two persons, than as a situation in which one person observes another'. As we have seen, he admits that his theory lagged behind his practice. In this he was not alone:

> ... such was the force of tradition and orthodoxy that, in Great Britain at least, every analyst who publicly avowed his doubts about Freudian metapsychology and revealed that he had been influenced by linguistic philosophy, existentialism, cybernetics or ethology withdrew from all further participation in the psychoanalytical movement – and also failed to spell out in convincing detail the full implications of the criticism of Freudian metapsychology that they had made.

He mentions, specifically, Brierley, Bowlby, Home, Lomas, himself and the 'very special case' of Laing; the last had in fact been in analysis with him. But those implications are spelled out, albeit in a terse and scattered fashion, in the corpus of Rycroft's writings.

Once the mind as 'psychic apparatus' has gone, then the principle of 'psychic determinism' is bound to follow; and when that has disappeared the unconscious itself, that shibboleth of

Freudian metapsychology, is clearly at risk. It thus comes as no surprise to discover that, although Rycroft accepts the existence of unconscious mental processes, he now believes that:

> Concepts like the unconscious are unnecessary, redundant, scientistic, and hypostasizing – the last since the concept the unconscious insinuates the idea that there really is some entity somewhere that instigates whatever we do unconsciously, some entity which is not the same entity as instigates whatever we do consciously.

He believes that in infancy the primary determining factor is not the infant's need for instinctual discharge and gratification, but rather the need to relate – upon which the capacity to survive (i.e. to meet instinctual needs) depends. And, he suggests, the case is not so very different in adult life. None the less, he wrote in 1956:

> Even though man is a social animal whose psychical life is primarily concerned with his relations with his objects, each individual is also a separate psychobiological entity with a continuous and independent awareness of self.

And so, he insisted, 'a conceptual framework within which to formulate hypotheses about the intrapsychic processes and genetic development of single individuals is a scientific necessity'. He also emphasized the need for a related frame of reference, arising from the study of 'the interrelationships between individuals and the means of communication between them'. Of course, such communication included words: but Rycroft emphasizes that in life, and also in the analytic situation, it also involves 'affects' (i.e. feelings and emotions) which, following McDougall, he regards as 'communication between two members of the same species'.

Rycroft's view of men and women as separate 'psychobiological entities' necessarily entering into social relationships does not ignore the effects of history. Indeed, more than once, Rycroft has invoked T. S. Eliot's concept of a 'dissociation of sensibility', as a result of which, Rycroft writes:

> ... modern man, unlike medieval man, views reality from two unconnected and incompatible standpoints, one scientific and objective, the other imaginative and subjective.

As he comments in his contribution to *The God I Want*, this 'dissociation of sensibility' compels man to change his stance perpetually and to shift uneasily from participating emotionally in life to adopting the pose that he is above and outside the system he is observing objectively. But, Rycroft warns, the solution of adhering consistently to one stance and ignoring the other involves 'letting more than one baby out with the bath-water':

> Those who adhere to the scientific stance can find no place in their philosophy for art or intuition, those who adopt Eliot's own solution can make nothing of technology, while those who adopt the psychotic solution of jumbling the two stances together become confused, bewildered and incomprehensible to their fellow men.[1]

Rycroft came to believe that the problem of understanding Freud derived in part from his having been compelled, as a scientist, 'to use language which presupposes this split to express ideas which annul it'.

> Since psychoanalysis aims at being a scientific psychology, psycho-analytical observation and theorizing is involved in the paradoxical activity of using secondary process thinking to observe, analyse, and conceptualize precisely that form of mental activity, the primary processes, which scientific thinking has always been at pains to exclude.

Rycroft, in effect, sees Freudian psychoanalysis as contaminated by 'the pathology of the Western intellectual tradition', even when it is attempting to account for those aspects and attributes of mind which are most at odds with that pathology. His revaluation of the nature and interrelationship of what Freud called the primary and secondary processes is at the root of his contribution.

Essentially, Rycroft rejects the way in which Freud *opposes* primary and secondary process thinking, and argues that these

---

[1] It was this latter 'solution' of which Rycroft accused Wilhelm Reich in his telling little monograph about him published in 1971. Reich, Rycroft argues, eventually persuaded himself he had succeeded in reconciling the vitalist understanding of the life principle with the mechanist appeal to the intellect, i.e. his own conception of the nature of human being with Freud's. He did this, however, by the 'discovery' of a substance in which, he alleged, measurable quanta of this life force were embodied. As a result, he was widely regarded as having gone mad.

two different modes of mental functioning are *complementary*; he thinks both are present from the very beginning of life; both are adaptive; and both are necessary throughout life for creative living. Thus he prefers Susanne Langer's distinction between 'non-discursive' and 'discursive' thought to the Freudian terminology of primary and secondary processes. As he wrote in 1962:

In place . . . of the hypothesis that psychic development proceeds by repression of an innate tendency to hallucinatory wish-fulfilment and superimposition of a learned capacity for adaptation, the alternative hypothesis is suggested that the human infant begins life in a state of primary integration in which his expectations (i.e. his capacity to imagine objects providing satisfaction) and his capacity to perceive and signal are in line with one another and both correspond to the possible responses of what Hartmann has called 'an average expectable environment' and Winnicott has called 'an ordinary devoted mother'.

Rycroft points out that one reason why the primary and secondary processes cannot be simply opposed is that the satisfaction of certain wishes (e.g. those produced by oral and genital impulses) requires another person motivated by a reciprocal wish. For instance, 'satisfaction of an infant's oral wishes requires the active participation of a mother who wishes to suckle her baby'.

Here, his debt to both Winnicott and Milner is extensive, and readily acknowledged. In an intriguing early paper about a poem of Leopardi's, Rycroft (still using the terminology of classical metapsychology) wrote of an idea central to their thought, 'the idea that an element of illusion enters into the realistic libidinal cathexis of external reality'. Rycroft incorporates Winnicott's argument that if – to use the latter's phrase – the mother is 'good enough', then that which has been wished for or hallucinated (through the primary processes) corresponds with the real (as experienced through the 'adaptive' secondary processes):

Repeated experience of this overlap or convergence of illusion and reality will tend to attach the individual positively to external reality without disturbances arising from denial, hatred, suspicion, disillusion, or withdrawal. Although frustration may lead to acceptance of reality, only satisfaction can lead to love of it.

Rycroft pointed to Leopardi's disbelief in the possibility of finding joy in life. Leopardi assumed that there was no relation between the products of the rational intellect and those of imagination; he regarded illusions as a necessary escape from joyless reality. Thus whereas he saw poetry as being on the side of life, he equated science with death. As Rycroft put it elsewhere:

> In so far ... as expectations are disappointed and the state of primary relatedness is disrupted, dissociation occurs in such a way that wishful thinking and adaptive adjustment come to operate in different psychic realms. Imaginative capacity becomes disengaged from external reality and operates in a psychic realm in which images cease to *represent* external objects and become instead *substitutes* for them.

Although the illusion that one has created one's objects requires eventual disillusion (i.e. the discovery that one has not), Rycroft argues that in healthy individuals 'the disillusionment will be confined to ... belief in ... omnipotent control of reality, not to reality itself'. In any event, there is the consoling terrain of literary and artistic imaginative activity ...

One effect of the way in which Rycroft rewrites the theory of primary and secondary processes is that he immediately rehabilitates many areas of activity which Freud himself suspected of being regressive, neurotic or analogous to the neuroses. In fact, many of Rycroft's most interesting texts do just that. I have already referred to his early paper, 'Symbolism and Its Relationship to the Primary and Secondary Processes': whereas Freud and Jones had both insisted that symbolization was characteristic only of primary process thinking, Rycroft saw it rather as 'a general tendency or capacity of the mind'.

Similarly, Freud was always trying to equate literary and artistic activity with neurosis and regression; but in 'Psychoanalysis and the Literary Imagination' Rycroft shows how this association was a by-product of Freud's scientific rationalism and his inability to comprehend the role of the primary processes in mature, adult creativity.

As we have seen, for Freud dreams themselves were, like neurotic symptoms, indications of repressed desires: he saw them as the royal road to the unconscious; they required interpretation into rational, verbal, secondary process thought before they could be understood. But, in *The Innocence of Dreams*, Rycroft sees them rather differently:

> The alternative view of dreaming is that visual, symbolic, non-discursive mental activity is just simply the way in which we think while asleep, and that there is no reason to suppose that symbolism is essentially a device by which dreamers deceive and obfuscate themselves, even though it may on occasion be used as such. According to this view dreams are, or can be, true, straightforward messages from one aspect of oneself to another, and dream interpretation is a process of translation of one language into another, a process which requires knowledge of the grammatical rules governing both but does not necessarily involve overcoming the dreamer's waking self's reluctance to accept the truth of the message.

Rycroft also describes dreams as the form the imagination takes during sleep. His concept of imagination differs from psychoanalytic formulations about fantasy, phantasy, hallucination or even the more benign 'illusion' of Winnicott and Milner. Rycroft constantly emphasizes that 'imagination is a natural, normal activity of an agent or self'. As the editors of his collection of papers *Imagination and Reality* point out, his writings manifest 'an acute awareness of the role played by the imagination at every level of mental functioning'. Rycroft stresses that the imagination informs our understanding of the real as well as the fantastic: the writing of history, for example, necessitates a powerfully imaginative response. Although the imagination is a 'negative capability', one which cannot be compelled or commanded, he rejects the idea that there is some determining entity somewhere within the individual corresponding to Freud's 'unconscious'. The fact of the matter, he argues, 'is that we are people who think, imagine, feel and act, sometimes consciously, sometimes unconsciously'.

Rycroft's position raises questions about the role of conscious decisions in determining human actions. (He suggests that consciousness 'transmutes instinctual drives in such a way that the outcome of decision is *not* solely determined by the relative strength of the instinctual forces involved'.) And so, in Rycroft's psychology, issues of human agency and moral choice cannot simply be ushered off the stage as secondary effects. Rather, his emphasis on imagination, as opposed to the unconscious, involves, as his editors put it, 'a shift from considering inner life as a self-sealed unit to that of evaluating the total experience of the patient as a person'.

But Rycroft is not seeking to dissolve the discipline of psychoanalysis altogether; he is insisting that it should be seen as a theory of meaning rather than a natural science dealing with causation, discrete quanta of energy and measurable phenomena. Thus he writes:

If Freud had lived today, he would not, I think, have had to be embarrassed by the apparently non-scientific nature ... of his discoveries, since the emergence of linguistics as a respectable scientific discipline would have enabled him to use that science as a model instead of neuroanatomy.

But unlike many of those who have tried to rewrite psychoanalysis in the light of linguistics, or the new sciences of communication, Rycroft insists that such a project requires caution:

The statement that psychoanalysis is a theory of meaning is incomplete and misleading unless one qualifies it by saying that it is a *biological* theory of meaning. By this I mean that psychoanalysis interprets human behaviour in terms of the self that experiences it and not in terms of entities external to it, such as other-worldly deities or political parties and leaders, and that it regards the self as a psychobiological entity which is always striving for self-realization and self-fulfilment. In other words, it regards mankind as sharing with the animal and plant world the intrinsic drive to create and recreate its own nature.

Throughout his writing Rycroft emphasizes that, although man enters into cultural life, he is also an animal, albeit a unique one, who is the product of the evolutionary processes of nature. As the study of dreams reveals, 'human beings are more preoccupied with their biological destiny than most of them realize'. Unlike many of those (especially the French) who have tried to reformulate psychoanalysis in terms of recent theories about symbols, Rycroft has always endeavoured to relate the findings of psychoanalysis to those of ethology.

This was a concern he shared with John Bowlby. In 1952 Bowlby delivered a paper on 'Instinct and Object Relation

Theories of Zoologists' to the British Psycho-Analytical Society. Rycroft cited this paper in one of his own in 1954, and there are a number of references to Lorenz and Tinbergen even in his writings of the 1950s. He writes:

> Somewhere at quite an early age I formulated the idea that you mustn't make any statements about human beings that you couldn't also make, in an analogous way, about animals. My first wife was very keen on this. She was a doctor, and she had worked looking after animals. And she was always moaning that we analysts don't take any notice of the body, or of animals. I was brought up on a farm, and so I have always taken animals as tolerably natural sorts of things. But most analysts, especially the Viennese group, had quite uncanny views about nature and animals. They just had no idea how animals or bodies work. They would be aghast if a cat brought in a bird it had killed in the garden. Absolutely appalled! But I always took that sort of thing for granted . . . Lots of the analysts seemed to be determined to perform even the sexual act by the use of intellect rather than instinct.

Bowlby was to make a much more thorough and systematic application of the ethological parallel in his theoretical writings than Rycroft; but he lacks Rycroft's insights into symbolization and imagination. Rycroft agrees that if one put together Bowlby's theory of instinct and his own theory of symbolism, then one would have a relatively complete object relations theory. 'I've always had a fantasy that Bowlby and I were burrowing the same tunnel, but we started out at opposite ends,' he says.

In *Anxiety and Neurosis*, however, Rycroft did try to spell out an analogy from ethology in some detail. In introducing this work, G. M. Carstairs wrote, 'Dr Rycroft's book gives hope that by returning to biological principles, students of human behaviour may be able to base our future therapies on a more secure scientific foundation.'[2] Rycroft began by arguing, in

---

[2] This was a characteristic hope of British psychiatric thinking which neither ignored Freud nor incorporated his system *tout court*. As far back as 1920 W. H. R. Rivers had published *Instinct and the Unconscious* which, though sympathetic to psychoanalysis, sought to give a biological view of the psycho-neuroses, 'to bring functional disorders of the mind and nervous system into relation with the concepts concerning their normal mode of working, which are held by the biologist and physiologist'.

opposition to Freud, that anxiety is not in itself a neurotic phenomenon but a form of vigilance. 'The capacity to be anxious,' he writes, 'is a biological function necessary for survival.' Anxiety becomes involved in neurosis, however, because of the peculiarly human capacity for internalization – which Rycroft relates to the long period of dependency of the human infant on the mother. For us, anxiety can be evoked not only by the external environment, but also by those parts of the self which the ego treats as though they were external. Rycroft suggests that even these defences can be classified by relating them to biologically adaptive responses. He draws attention to three different types of defensive response to anxiety among animals: attack, flight and submission. These he correlates with the obsessional, phobic, schizoid and hysterical defences respectively.

Because Rycroft draws these parallels from ethology, this does not, of course, imply that he is in any sense a biological determinist, let alone a behaviourist. His arguments against such reductive positions are made abundantly clear in his essays on Skinner and Desmond Morris. Indeed, one of the most tantalizing implications of Rycroft's work is the idea that it may be possible to elaborate a *specifically human* natural history, a biology of those characteristics man does *not* share with other animals, e.g. a particular kind of imaginative life, affective relationships and a unique capacity for symbolization, upon which the ability to create and enter into cultural life depends. He suggests that all these uniquely human characteristics may have much to do with the long period of dependency of the human infant on the mother. If he is concerned with the continuity between man and the rest of the animal kingdom, he is also concerned with the discontinuity, and with the possibility of describing that discontinuity in a fully secular way.

Nor does Rycroft ignore the effects of history upon man's intrapsychic life and his social relations. He set out to study economics and history, and his early intellectual affiliations were with Marxism. Implicit in his work is the idea that the 'dissociation of sensibility', to which he is constantly drawing attention, has its roots not just in the pathology of the individual subject, but also in the pathology of contemporary cultural life. Characteristically, he argues that the reason the majority of dreams are not understood, or even granted meaning, 'implies that we live in a culture in which alienation and unconscious hypocrisy are endemic'. He insists that the tendency to react defensively to all irrational feeling 'appears not to be a universal characteristic of the human ego but to be confined to Western civilization'.

Thus it may still be possible for the 'good enough mother' to provide those 'moments of illusion' when she meets her child's fantasy with the reality of a nourishing and consoling breast. But, Rycroft implies, there is no longer a continuity between such experiences and adult cultural life. The intellectual tra-ditions, social structures, and technologies of the West conspire to create an external reality in which it is very difficult for us to participate emotionally. In particular, loss of religious faith means that, save in the very special case of the high arts, culture can no longer provide us with consoling and integrating illusions. Higher culture is dominated by a cult of reason which inevitably acquires all the characteristics of unreason; or, as Rycroft describes it, 'loss of contact with the sensuous reality of persons and things leads to the investiture of ideas with absolute and dogmatic value'. Tragically, this has been as true of psychoanalysis itself as of other areas of intellectual discourse.

Predictably, in the intriguing contribution he wrote for the symposium *The God I Want*, Rycroft declared that the God that was really wanted, as opposed to the God he personally wanted, was 'one Who would annul this "dissociation of sensi-bility" by an act of synthesis'. But with characteristic wry pessimism, born of his own secular disillusionment, he went on to say that he doubted whether any self-conscious attempt to synthesize such a deity would be any more successful than those of the God-creating schizophrenics who ultimately assert that they themselves are God.

V

At this point, I feel I should declare an interest. I first met Charles Rycroft in 1972, when I went to see him for a clinical consultation. He advised me to apply to the Clinic at the Institute of Psychoanalysis for a therapeutic analysis. This I did, and soon after I entered analysis with Dr Kenneth Wright. About eighteen months later, my then publisher, Fraser Harrison, submitted the manuscript of a book I had written, *The Champions*, to Rycroft for a reader's report; I also sent him a proof copy of a book called *The Psychology of Gambling*, of which I was one of the joint editors. Both of these were entirely faithful to Freud's system.

I have described Rycroft's responses to these texts elsewhere. Suffice it to say that he wrote to me to explain that I had got myself into a curious intellectual knot because I, an obsessional, was using another obsessional's theories to elucidate obsessional phenomena. He added that I laid myself open to the charge of being a 'paleo-Freudian'.

He went on to argue that the amount of credence one should give to Freud's theory of obsessionality depended on one's view of his 'self-analysis'.

If . . . one allows oneself to query the accuracy and depth of his self-analysis, one has to take seriously the possibility that he was *parti pris* in his formulations about obsessional neurosis, and that you are too in accepting them. If, as I am suggesting is possible, Freud's views on obsessional neurosis, and indeed on human nature in general, contain a defensive element, a function of concealing something that he didn't want to know about, this concealed something must, according to Freud's own style of thinking, be something to do with his relationship with his mother.

He then pointed towards a number of biographical indications that this was indeed so, and went on to say that it was therefore possible that in my two books I was expounding an interpretation of championship and gambling which had built into it both Freud's and my own need 'not to understand something about men's relationships to their mothers and women in general'. Characteristically he apologized for his 'nerve' in writing like this, and 'for taking unfair advantage of our brief clinical contact'.

I wrote back a long, self-critical letter, accepting Rycroft's criticisms and stressing that I had long been suspicious about conspicuous omissions in the biographical and autobiographical accounts of Freud. He replied that he was glad to hear I had perceived the element of suppression of the truth in Jones's and the Freud family's account of Freud, as well as their censorship of the letters.

Presumably the situation will alter when Anna Freud dies. Only in the last five years or so has it become possible within analytical circles to suggest that whole areas of analytical theory may be subtly influenced by Freud's personality; that, for instance, his idea that the aim of all activity is to reduce tension was influenced by his tendency to fainting attacks.

Following this exchange of letters, I continued to correspond with Dr Rycroft, and to meet him socially from time to time. We would have lunch at a small Italian restaurant, not far from his consulting-room in Wimpole Street; he would advise me to read more biology, and reflect with a bemused smile on members of the British Psycho-Analytical Society. And then in July 1975, I was invited by *New Society* to 'cover' the Congress of the International Psychoanalytic Association, held that year at the Dorchester Hotel: ironically, I was a replacement for Rycroft, who had already declined the commission.

That Congress was stamped by the dispute between the 'new' European analysts and the Americans. André Green, from France, gave the inaugural paper in which he spoke of a malaise at the very heart of psychoanalysis:

I think that one of the main contradictions which the analyst faces today is the necessity (and the difficulty) of making a body of interpretations (which derive from the work of Freud and of classical analysis) coexist and harmonize with the clinical experience and the theory of the last twenty years.

Green argued it was no longer possible to think in terms of welding new pieces to an existing theoretical core. He empha-sized that 'the perception of the change that is beginning today is that of *a change within the analyst*'. He explained he had been working with 'borderline' states, conditions which could be classified neither as neurotic nor as psychotic, yet which retain aspects of both.

This work had led Green to a new view both of 'psychic

reality' and of the psychoanalytic situation itself. He suggested the existence of a psychotic core, or 'blank psychosis', within everyone, and saw the defence mechanisms as being mobilized against the fear of madness and self-negation.

Green was opposed by Leo Rangell, whom I described in my report as a die-hard 'paleo-Freudian'. He dismissed Green's work as an 'eclectic mélange' of Freud, Melanie Klein, French existentialism and oriental philosophy. Rangell claimed that though the world was changing rapidly, the 'trunk' of psychoanalytic theory did not need to subject itself to such change, whatever the 'poetic and mystical' activities might be at its periphery. He maintained that 'the oedipal–phallic–castration phase is a hub, a bull's-eye of psychoanalytical penetration'. He seemed upset that some of the most archaic Freudian concepts were no longer in widespread use. 'Where,' he asked, 'are the libidinal phases? Where is all that we learned about the anal phase?' And then, to the astonishment of many, he added, 'So much has been lost in the zealous quest for the first year or months of life. I have a patient for whom to understand her anal phase is to understand her life.'

The fundamental divisions apparent in this opening debate permeated the whole of the Congress. Rangell rightly pointed out that the sharpening polarities within the discipline overrode old distinctions between one group and another: the debate was about what sort of creature psychoanalysis itself was. The Americans were insisting that the old Freudian model, subject to greater or lesser revisions, was quite 'good enough'. But others were pointing out, in various ways, that a causal–deterministic model for psychology was no longer adequate. I ended my report on Congress by writing:

Charles Rycroft is one prominent analyst who is 'sceptical about the validity of applying causal–deterministic principles derived from the physical sciences to the study of living beings who are capable of consciousness and creative activity'. He has argued that psychoanalysis should be regarded as a semantic discipline, more specifically 'a biological theory of meaning'. He maintains that this requires the reformulation of psychoanalytical ideas into terms compatible with communications theory. Above all, he sees no reason why analysts should remain faithful to the principle of psychic determinism. Rycroft remains a member of the British Society, but he was conspicuous by his absence from last week's Congress. If Green's ideas are anything to go by, this formal presence and actual absence within the Congress space might well be read as an indicator of the potential significance of his views. For the sake of psychoanalysis itself, one can only hope that this is the case.

Soon after this appeared, I received a letter from Rycroft praising the article, and saying he hoped it did not just mean that my analysis of the malaise in psychoanalysis agreed with his own.

I must confess that although I was flattered by your last paragraph, it also induced acute existential anxiety in me, as I have a suspicion that your assessment of my role or non-role in British psychoanalysis may be correct, in which case I shall have to decide in the next few months whether to accept the mantle being offered to me or not.

He went on to explain that he had first become fed up with the analytical movement in the late 1950s: at that time, he already decided that he wanted to get out. But, he now wrote, circumstances had changed.

All the elder statesmen and stateswomen have died apart from Anna Freud; it has become possible for a gentile to criticize classical psychoanalysis without being accused of being antisemitic.

Rycroft also said that, despite himself, he had gone on thinking about psychoanalysis, and had, in fact, come round to a concept very similar to Green's 'blank psychosis'.

... and so the possibility, and possible moral necessity, of my converting formal presence and actual absence into actual presence has begun to confront me. But I find the idea of staging a comeback alarms me terribly, as I cannot conceive of my doing so without moral support from others, and where I would find moral supporters, I don't know.

The letter ended suggesting we met on his return to London after the end of the summer holidays. This in fact we did, at the Savile Club. Soon after, Dr Rycroft opted to become less rather than more involved with the affairs of the psychoanalytic movement.

Although I saw less of him in the late 1970s, I found Rycroft's ideas were having an increasing influence on me. One reason for this was my own sense of isolation within the British left –

especially the self-appointed left of the art community. At that time there was a sad proliferation within such circles of Althusserian–Lacanian gnosis. I found Rycroft's work and that of the British 'object relations' school in general provided a healthy antidote to this strange contortion of the mind.

In 1980 I suggested we should do an interview together for the *New Left Review*, and in the early summer of 1980 we taped a long series of wide-ranging discussions in Rycroft's Wimpole Street consulting-room. These interviews never saw the light of publication. Soon after we taped them, it was my turn to enter a state of 'acute existential anxiety' – for reasons quite unrelated to my relationship with Charles Rycroft. And so, instead of preparing the interviews for publication, I began to consult Rycroft once a week as a patient myself. At the end of one session, he asked me whether I would be interested in editing a collection of his essays, lectures and reviews. I had no hesitation in accepting the invitation.

VI

The principal aim of this collection has been to draw out the main themes and emphases of Rycroft's thinking, writing and therapeutic practice, and I hope that it will introduce his radical and independent stance to the wider audience it so clearly deserves.

The first group of writings elucidates his overall attitude towards psychoanalysis. 'Causes and Meaning' was itself originally the introduction to a collection of articles by various writers published under the title *Psychoanalysis Observed* in 1966. (The version printed here, however, contains some additional material written, but not included, at the time.) 'Is Freudian Symbolism a Myth?' is a revised and updated variation of the argument Rycroft first put forward in 1956 which 'liberates' symbolization from its specifically Freudian associations with regressive modes of mental functioning and reinstates it as 'a general tendency or capacity of the mind'.

The reviews in 'Freudiana' clarify Rycroft's attitudes towards Freud – and also towards those who use Freud's theories as a means to 'interpret' the master himself; those in 'Psychoanalysts and Others' are of interest not only for the light they throw on their subjects, but also for the way they help us to 'situate' Rycroft's own work in relation to other members of the British School.

Autobiography is at the heart of the psychoanalytic enterprise: appropriately, this collection includes not just a case history, and comments on the autobiographies of others, but two autobiographical fragments written by Rycroft himself. Other sections are devoted to recurring preoccupations in Rycroft's writing, lecturing and reviewing, e.g. with the nature of human sensation and sexuality. 'Freud and the Literary Imagination' spells out Rycroft's far-reaching objections to Freud's fundamental opposition of primary and secondary process thinking and outlines his alternative view of the imaginative faculties and creative processes. The final section, 'Religion and Morals', contains a paper which confirms that, despite his thoroughgoing atheism and his prolonged encounter with psychoanalysis, Rycroft retains intellectual sympathies with specifically British traditions of moral and religious thought.

In conclusion, Charles Rycroft's thinking seems to me to have a great deal in common with that of one of the writers whom he criticizes in this collection: Sebastiano Timpanaro, an Italian Marxist whost work is also much less well known than it ought to be. I do not expect either Rycroft or Timpanaro to recognize the likeness: their styles are so very different. Rycroft is an English ironist, whose references are to Coleridge, McDougall, Mary Douglas, Gregory Bateson, Fairbairn, Winnicott and Milner. Timpanaro is steeped in the traditions of Hegelian thought and contemporary Italian Marxism: indeed, in his paper on Timpanaro, Rycroft suggests that his Leopardian version of Marxism is strictly not for export. And yet we know from Rycroft's early paper on the Italian poet that his own vision of man springs from very similar insights.

Rycroft, too, insists that we all live our lives within constraints which nature places upon us: we not only enter into social life, but enact our 'biological destinies'. Characteristically, he complained of Reich that 'his writings never touch on such awkward problems for the utopian as the inevitability of ageing or man's awareness of mortality'. Timpanaro has been voicing similar criticisms of the Marxist tradition as a whole. Rycroft's vision, like Timpanaro's, involves a radical critique of classical psychoanalysis – though the way he elaborates it is very different from, and in my view much more convincing than, Timpanaro's. (See below, pp. 81ff.) Against the 'progressive' philistinism prevalent on both the left and the right, Timpanaro and Rycroft stress the significance of continuity in human and cultural life; like Timpanaro, however, Rycroft too retains a sober and tempered belief in the possibility of beneficial social change. Both are materialists, deeply suspicious of those proliferating intellectual theorizations which deny reality to the human subject or the natural world he inhabits. And both are concerned with what Timpanaro once described as 'the importance of the meaning of freedom as the absence of painful constraints, and the presence of all those conditions which ensure the happiness of the individual'.

This improbable similarity emphasizes the fact that Rycroft's Englishness cannot be mistaken for insularity. On the contrary, the positions Timpanaro and Rycroft have elaborated seem to offer the potential for a more accurate emotional and intellectual understanding of the human person, and his or her social relations, than that put forward by traditional Marxism or 'classical' psychoanalysis alike. Such thinkers are intellectually refreshing and invigorating in the stultifying climate of so much fashionable 'post-Marxist' and 'post-Freudian' thought.

Indeed, Rycroft's method of psychoanalysis renders it an intellectually and humanly credible project once again: he offers not a set of abstract speculations, but concrete reflections on his experience of the men and women he has encountered in life, and in the consulting-room. He sees each individual man and woman as a 'psychobiological entity', rooted in natural history and the product of evolutionary process, yet simultaneously capable of achievements unique in the animal kingdom (e.g. of ethical, cultural, religious and scientific accomplishments). These achievements he constantly relates to peculiarly human faculties for imaginative and symbolic thought. Unlike Freud and the 'classical' psychoanalytic tradition, he does not believe these faculties need to be conquered and bound by the inexorable advance of reason or of technological mastery. Rather, like Marx and Darwin before him, he affirms the imagination as being at the very root of that which can be acclaimed as uniquely human. Though he readily acknowledges the imagination can be put in the service of the cruel, perverse and fantastic, he argues that the preconditions for its healthy functioning are an essential component in any 'ecology of hope' – whether personal or social.

Peter Fuller

PSYCHOANALYSIS

Causes and Meaning

When I first became an analyst it seemed to me that the idea of applying the scientific method to psychological phenomena was a perfectly straightforward matter and that there were no particular difficulties about regarding unconscious wishes or infantile complexes as causes of which present-day conscious symptoms were the effect, nor in assuming that, if a patient became aware of the unconscious and infantile determinants of his symptoms, these would vanish; and, indeed, even today I frequently have clinical experiences which can readily be understood in this way.

But, and it is a big but, these experiences only occur with a certain type of patient and under certain conditions. They occur with patients who are basically healthy and whose personality neither the therapist nor the patient feels inclined to call into question, and they occur only if both the patient and his nearest and nominally dearest wish him to lose his symptoms. In other words the patient loses his symptoms only if two conditions are fulfilled; first, that he understands their origin, and, second, that his conscious wish to lose his symptoms is greater than his wish to retain the status quo in his personal relationships. For instance, if a married man is impotent or sexually perverted his recovery depends not only on his understanding of the origin of his disability but also on whether his wife really and truly welcomes his recovery, and on whether, if she does not, he feels prepared to overcome her reluctance or, if that seems impossible, to make alternative arrangements – and whether he does feel prepared to do either will depend on many more factors than the unconscious determinants of his symptoms. It will be influenced by his conscious values, his religious attitudes, his general feelings towards his wife, his assessment of her mental stability, etc.

I am really making three points here. Firstly, symptoms are not solely an individual matter, they have a social nexus and function and change in one person may be contingent on changes in others. Secondly, in patients other than straightforward psychoneurotics, analysis involves consideration of the whole personality, including conscious values. And thirdly, conscious as well as unconscious motives play a part in the maintenance of neuroses.

The last point raises the question as to whether conscious motives can be regarded as causes. Although there are, it seems to me, no difficulties about regarding unconscious 'wishes', 'motives' and 'causes' as synonymous, particularly when the 'effect' being considered is a symptom which is alien to the patient's personality, it is much more difficult to maintain that they are interchangeable ideas when applied to conscious phenomena. Once any mental process or group of ideas becomes conscious it becomes part of the whole complex of thoughts, feelings, wishes, values and aspirations which constitute the personality, and one of the characteristic functions and activities of the personality is making decisions. Although a neurotic cannot decide to become potent or to lose a fear of crowds, and his symptoms are therefore the effect of forces and ideas of which he knows nothing, the healthy person (and the neurotic in healthy and unaffected parts of his life) spends much of his time deciding whether or not to do things that he wishes to do or feels he ought to, and his decisions are influenced not only by the strength of his own wishes and principles but also by his estimate of the likely effects of his actions on himself later and on those around him. It would seem, indeed, that one of the functions of consciousness is to enable decisions to be made, and the idea that all conscious decisions are strictly determined by unconscious forces seems to imply that all deciding is an illusion and that consciousness has no function – which is unlikely. A more probable hypothesis is that consciousness transmutes instinctual drives in such a way that the outcome of any act of decision is NOT solely determined by the relative strength of the instinctual forces involved.

Although this latter assumption is one which could be used to retain the notion of unconscious causation in a psychology which took account of conscious motives – and is indeed so used by the American school of psychoanalytical ego-psychology – it is not in fact the assumption which Freud made when he propounded his principle of psychic determinism. Freud's aim was to establish a 'scientific psychology', and he hoped to be able to do so by applying to psychology the same principles of causality as were in his time considered valid in physics and chemistry. As a young man his own teachers in physiology had held that it was inadmissible to explain the working of the human body by reference to principles other than those which could be derived from physics and chemistry, and as a result they rejected all vitalist biological theories. Freud's grand design was to adopt the same attitude towards the working of the mind, and he believed that his discovery of unconscious mental forces made his project attainable. If, he argued, all mental activity is the result of unconscious mental forces which are instinctual, biological and physical in origin, then human psychology could be formulated in terms of the interaction of forces which were in principle quantifiable, without recourse to any vital mental integrating agency, and psychology would become a natural science like physics.

However, the principle of psychic determinism remains an assumption, one which Freud made out of scientific faith rather than on evidence, and I know of no instance in Freud's writing of his claiming to have predicted in advance the outcome of any choice or decision made by a patient. Indeed, when describing the causes of neuroses, he more than once repudiated the idea that it is possible to predict whether a person will develop a neurosis or, if he does, what kind of neurosis it will be. All he claimed was that in retrospect it is possible to assert that such-and-such an event or situation in childhood had been the cause of the neurosis; a procedure which is more reminiscent of a historian than a scientist.

He did, however, claim, and claim successfully, to be able to demonstrate that choices made by patients are not arbitrary and that they can be understood as revealing and characteristic manifestations of their personality. For instance, in his *Introductory Lectures* Freud describes how he asked a womanizing male patient to tell him the first female name that came into his head. The man did so, producing a name which was not that of any of the many women he knew, but was very similar to Freud's nickname for him. Now, Freud does not claim to have predicted this name – indeed, he describes himself as having been as surprised by it as the patient was – but he saw immediately its similarity to the patient's name, and this did not surprise him, since he had already appreciated that the man was not a great lover of women, but a narcissist.

What Freud did here was not to explain the patient's choice causally but to understand it and give it meaning, and the procedure he engaged in was not the scientific one of elucidating causes but the semantic one of making sense of it. It can indeed be argued that much of Freud's work was really semantic and that he made a revolutionary discovery in semantics, namely that neurotic symptoms are meaningful, disguised communications, but that, owing to his scientific training and allegiance, he formulated his findings in the conceptual framework of the physical sciences. In some aspects of his work Freud saw this clearly himself. His most famous work he entitled *The Interpretation of Dreams*, not *The Cause of Dreams*, and his chapter on symptoms in his *Introductory Lectures* is called 'The Sense of Symptoms'. He was also well aware that many of his ideas had been anticipated by writers and poets rather than by scientists.

The idea that psychoanalysis is not a causal theory but a semantic one is not original. It has been propounded in America by T. Szasz in his *The Myth of Mental Illness*, in which he argues that the idea that the neuroses are diseases with causes is a social fiction. It is also held in different forms by the existentialists. But it is not orthodoxy and the majority of Freudian analysts disclaim it entirely. They thereby lay themselves open to attack from critics like Professor Eysenck who see quite clearly that psychoanalysis cannot satisfy the canons of those sciences which are based on the experimental method but who believe that if they can demonstrate its inadequacy as a causal theory they have proved that it is nonsense. To my mind, one of the merits of the semantic view of analysis is that it completely undercuts the Eysenck–Psychoanalysis controversy by showing that both parties are not only, as Eysenck himself has said, arguing from different premises but from wrong premises. The analysts are claiming that analysis is what it is not, and Eysenck is attacking it for failing to be what it has no need to claim to be. And both parties are assuming that it is only the natural sciences which are intellectually respectable. It is perhaps relevant here that, for very different historical reasons, both psychology and medicine are faculties which suffer from an inferiority complex in relation to science.

Recognition of the semantic nature of psychoanalytical theory would also undercut the tendency of analysts to engage in futile controversy as to whether the cause of neurosis is to be found in the first three months or years of life, or whether the fundamental cause of neurosis is constitutional envy of the mother's breast or is to be found in the Oedipal phase of childhood or in the infant's sensitivity to environmental impingements, and enable them to concentrate on improving their techniques for getting into communication with those who have become alienated.

There is, of course, one type of neurosis which undoubtedly does have a cause, and this is the traumatic neurosis which occurs after a totally unexpected shock. But this is precisely the neurosis which does *not* fit into psychoanalytical theory, and one of its symptoms, the traumatic dream in which the shocking experience is relived, provides the one example of a dream which is not amenable to analytical interpretation. Freud evidently regretted this, since in his last book, *An Outline of Psycho-Analysis* (1940), he wrote of the traumatic neuroses that 'their relations to determinants in childhood have hitherto eluded investigation'.

It does, of course, remain possible that all the neuroses might be explained as similar to the traumatic neuroses, in that they could be seen as responses to specific pathological and unsatisfactory childhood experiences, though it is worth noting that

Winnicott, the English analyst who has been most persistent in tracing the origin of neuroses to environmental failures in early childhood, has also found it necessary to introduce the distinction between a 'true' and a 'false' self. But 'true' and 'false', like the 'authentic' and 'inauthentic' of the existentialists, are semantic and evaluative concepts, not scientific, causal ones. Perhaps the principle of psychic determinism applies to the 'false self', while the 'true self' has free will.

Preoccupation with the idea of causality has led analysts into the position of giving advice and making recommendations about matters on which, to my mind, they only appear to be experts. If, the argument runs, neurosis is the result of infantile traumata and deprivation, then it could be prevented by parents caring for their children better, and analysts have therefore come to regard themselves, and to be accepted, as experts on the upbringing of children. Both in this country and more particularly in America a literature exists which contains advice on such matters as how and when infants should be weaned, how the births of children should be spaced, when and whether they should be punished, and even on how parents should love their children, the authority for such advice apparently deriving from psychoanalysis. Now although much of this advice is probably as wise as advice emanating from other sources, it tends in fact to derive from paediatric and child-guidance experience, and much of it is open to objections of three kinds.

First, the idea that children should be treated lovingly and humanely is one that does not require any scientific, medical or psychological backing and can be arrived at without reference to psychoanalysis or, indeed, any other body of knowledge.

Second, loving is not an activity which can be engaged in on advice, since its essence is sincerity and spontaneity.

And thirdly, much of the trauma and suffering endured by children is unavoidable. It is really no use saying that children should not be separated from their parents and need their full-time love and attention up to such-and-such an age, when the facts of human existence are such that no parent can guarantee to remain alive for the requisite number of years after becoming one, or even that he or she will go on loving the other parent for so long. As a result, much of this sort of advice is both sentimental and perfectionist and may even, on occasion, be harmful, since it may encourage parents to be insincere out of a sense of guilt or duty. It may also induce a sense of guilt in parents who, through no fault of their own, have to bring up children under difficult and unsatisfactory conditions. Many of our patients are the offspring of tragedy, not of faulty child-rearing.

The idea that neurosis is caused by lack of love in childhood can also lead analysts into priggishness. If neurosis is the result of parental deprivation then perhaps analysis is a form of replacement-therapy and the effective agent in treatment is the analyst's concern, devotion and love. But this view of the matter leaves unexplained why the analyst should consider himself to be the possessor of a store of agape (caritas) so much greater than that of his patients' parents. Analysts who hold that their capacity to help patients derives from their ability to understand them, and that this ability depends on their knowledge of the language of the unconscious, are really being more modest. The claim to possess professional expertise does not contain a concealed claim to moral superiority over the laity.

If psychoanalysis is recognized as a semantic theory not a causal one, its theory can start where its practice does – in the consulting-room, where a patient who is suffering from something in himself which he does not understand confronts an analyst with some knowledge of the unconscious: that is, someone who knows something of the way in which repudiated wishes, thoughts, feelings and memories can translate themselves into symptoms, gestures and dreams, and who knows, as it were, the grammar and syntax of such translations and is therefore in a position to interpret them back again into the communal language of consciousness. According to the scientific analyst this can only be done by elucidating and reconstructing the history of the illness and of its infantile origins, but even he agrees that this is useless unless the analyst has made contact (rapport) with the patient, and it seems to me that it makes better sense to say that the analyst makes excursions into historical research in order to understand something which is interfering with his present communication with the patient (in the same way as a translator might turn to history to elucidate an obscure text) than to say that he makes contact with the patient in order to gain access to biographical data. In the former he is using the past to understand the present, in the latter he is using his biographical research to legitimize his rapport with the patient by formulating it in terms of a theory about the causes of neurosis. Furthermore, as the conditions of analytical work make it inconceivable that any analyst, or even group of like-minded analysts, will ever encounter a representative sample of any particular neurosis, and as, indeed, the validity of particular neurotic diagnostic categories is open to doubt, since neuroses are in a sense personal creations, such research is in any case methodologically suspect.

There is, however, a form of research which not only can be done by analysts but is indeed done by all analysts regardless of whether they consider themselves research workers or not. This is research into the private languages of patients and of the ways in which their cryptic and disguised utterances and gestures can be understood and translated back into common and communicable language. This is research in exactly the same sense that linguistic research is. An analyst encountering a new patient is in a position surprisingly similar to that of a linguist who encounters a community which speaks an unfamiliar language. To get his bearings he explores how much language they have in common, listens to him and by locating the contexts in which initially incomprehensible utterances occur and referring back in his own mind to other languages he knows, he gradually learns his patient's language, and makes himself familiar with his imagery and style of thought and feeling.

If he is not theoretically minded he will leave it at that, in the same way as some people who have a gift for languages may learn to speak them without ever acquiring an interest in grammar and linguistic theory. His research will then increase his own insight and clinical competence but will not be communicated to anyone who does not come into direct contact with him as patient, pupil or colleague. The late John Rickman, who would, I suspect, have agreed with much of this essay, often used to remark that much that is valuable in psychoanalysis is handed on not in learned papers but by verbal tradition.

If, on the other hand, he is theoretically minded, he will formulate the language-patterns he has learnt, will relate them to those he has previously encountered or which have already been described in the literature, and will write clinical and theoretical papers. To continue the linguistic analogy, diagnosing a patient as suffering from hysteria or obsessional neurosis is like locating a language as belonging to a particular family, while general analytical theory is analogous to general language theory. The basic principles of the language theory applicable to dreams, verbal imagery and physical gestures have already been formulated by Freud in his *Papers on Metapsychology* where the grammar and syntax of the unconscious is stated in terms of the primary processes (condensation, displacement, etc.) and in the analytical literature on symbolism.

Here again I must disclaim originality. The idea that what Freud described as characteristics of the unconscious or id is better thought of as the grammar of an unconscious, non-verbal language is to be found in, for instance, Erich Fromm's *The Forgotten Language* and Tauber and Green's *Prelogical Experience*, though neither of these are books which I would endorse in their entirety.

The statement that psychoanalysis is a theory of meaning is incomplete and misleading unless one qualifies it by saying that it is a *biological* theory of meaning. By this I mean that psychoanalysis interprets human behaviour in terms of the self that experiences it and not in terms of entities external to it, such as other-worldly deities or political parties and leaders, and that it regards the self as a psychobiological entity which is always striving for self-realization and self-fulfilment. In other words, it regards mankind as sharing with the animal and plant world the intrinsic drive to create and recreate its own nature. Part of the resistance among analysts to the idea that psychoanalysis may be a semantic theory derives from the fact that the concept of meaning is felt to have religious and political overtones. Freud himself dismissed the problem of meaning by asserting that anyone who questions the meaning of life is ill. By this, I think, he can only have meant that living itself gives meaning to life and that this is doubted only by those who have become to some measure self-alienated, and that as a result recourse to religious or ideological theories of meaning as a 'secondary construction', an attempt to restore the lost sense of meaningfulness by deriving it from some source external to the self. This was, I suspect, the real basis of his antagonism to religion. For him, religion was a cosmology, its central notion being a God who was outside the universe and who had created it. As a scientist, he realized that the traditional Judaeo-Christian cosmology was no longer tenable, and he therefore interpreted religion as an illusion which those who needed it created for themselves in order to preserve the childhood illusion of being absolutely protected and loved by a father. However, in interpreting religion as a neurosis, as a defence against anxiety and feelings of helplessness, he was himself applying a theory of meaning, since he made sense of it to himself by ascribing to it a function in the lives of those who believe it and one with which he could himself empathize.

Recent developments in theology, however, make it very doubtful whether cosmology can be regarded as the central religious idea or whether belief in a God 'out there' is the essence of the religious attitude. Although we can have no idea of what Freud personally would have made of Bonhoeffer's 'religionless Christianity', or of Zen Buddhism, or of statements like Guntrip's 'the fundamental therapeutic factor in psychotherapy is more akin to religion than to science, since it is a matter of personal relationship ... religion has always stood for the good object relationship', there would seem to be no necessary incompatibility between psychoanalysis and those religious formulations which locate God within the self. One could, indeed, argue that Freud's id (and even more Groddeck's 'It'), the impersonal force within which is both the core of oneself and yet not oneself, and from which in illness one becomes alienated, is a secular formulation of the insight which makes religious people believe in an immanent God: if this were so, psychoanalysis could be regarded as a semantic bridge between science and biology on the one hand and religion and the humanities on the other. This was what I had in mind at the beginning of this essay when I listed, as one possible answer to the problem of psychoanalysis's metaphysical status, the possibility that it might be something *sui generis* which could not be fitted into any of the traditional categories.

1966

2

The Present State of Freudian Psychoanalysis

It is now over seventy years since Freud published *The Interpretation of Dreams*, the work in which, in his own view, he laid the foundation stone of his new science, psychoanalysis, by demonstrating the ubiquitous presence of unconscious mental processes. And it is over fifty years since he published *The Ego and the Id*, in which he reformulated definitively his views on the relationship between these unconscious mental processes and the 'I', the personality of which we are conscious, by imagining the mind to be analogous to a physical organ or apparatus, one part of which, the id or 'It', contains unconscious instinctual impulses striving for discharge, while the other, the ego, controls and organizes these instinctual impulses, admitting some into consciousness, repressing some, and sublimating others – using techniques called defence mechanisms to do so.

Since these two seminal works of Freud were written, vast social and political changes have taken place; the sciences with which Freud was familiar have changed almost beyond recognition, and new sciences of which Freud can never have heard have arisen, notably perhaps cybernetics and ethology. It is therefore legitimate to ask to what extent and in what ways psychoanalysis itself has changed in the last fifty to seventy years.

The first and most obvious answer to this question is a purely quantitative one: the amount of it has increased enormously. Fifty years ago the number of analysts practising analysis could be counted in scores, the great majority of analysts lived and worked in Europe, and most analyses were conducted in

German. Now analysts can be counted in their hundreds if not thousands, most of them live and work in America, and more analyses are conducted in English – and in Spanish – than in German. And psychoanalytical training institutes exist in every continent apart from Africa. Whereas fifty years ago the psycho-analytical movement was small, was centred in Vienna with colonies and outposts in Berlin, London and the United States, it is now large and predominantly American – though British and French psychoanalysts seem to be resisting Americanization quite vigorously.

In line with this expansion of psychoanalysis and the multi-plication of the number of analysts practising it – and in the number of patients being analysed – has been a change in the social position of psychoanalysis. In the 1920s there was something subversive, avant-garde, suspect and even cranky about it, and people who became psychoanalysts had to possess moral and intellectual courage and a measure of indifference to money and conventional professional advancement. Now, particularly in the United States but also to a lesser extent here, training as an analyst has become a recognized rung in the professional ladder and a way of acquiring respectability and at least moderate affluence. And whereas in the 1920s analysts were liable to be accused of corrupting moral standards and, sometimes correctly, of being socialists and revolutionaries, nowadays they are more likely to be accused of being squares and of brainwashing their patients into conformity with bour-geois standards of normality. In the 1920s there were psycho-analysts in the Soviet Union, but now there are none – though it is, apparently, just possible to practise psychoanalysis in some countries on the other side of the Iron Curtain.

But all this, it can be argued, is not a change in psychoanalysis itself, but in the attitude of society towards psychoanalysis. In the West there has been a shift, for which Freud himself may perhaps be partly responsible, away from Victorian morality, with its prudery and furtiveness about sexual matters and its unbounded faith in the value of will-power, towards greater tolerance, outspokenness and self-expressiveness – and, as a result, away from passing moral judgements on those who are anxious, depressed and unable to cope towards regarding such people as ill and in need of treatment. And in this more liberal climate those who claim to be able to explain and treat neuroses have acquired the respect and social status they deserve. In the East, on the other hand, it has been decided by fiat that psychoanalysis is anti-Marxist and not, as was originally thought, anti-bourgeois, and anathema has been pronounced upon it.

But has psychoanalysis itself changed in the last fifty years? Is the theory taught in psychoanalytical training institutes today much the same as the theory that was being formulated and expounded in Vienna in the 1920s? Do patients lying on contemporary couches receive the same interpretations as Freud's own patients received?

Now, although these questions are easy to ask, they are harder to answer – for the simple reason that analysts do not agree among themselves, and their differences of opinion are of sufficient seriousness to be reflected in the structure of psychoanalytical institutions. It is, as a result, impossible to point to any one body of theory and practice as being the contemporary representative of Freudian psychoanalysis. In this country, for instance, theoretical differences between sub-schools have necessitated the establishment of conventions to ensure that the British Psycho-Analytical Society is never taken over by any one of the three groups into which it is divided, and parts of its training scheme are run in duplicate. In a number of other countries the absence of a native genius for compromise has led to complete fission with, typically, one of the resulting fragments resigning or being expelled from the International Psycho-Analytical Association.

The contemporary fragmentation of psychoanalysis into various sub-schools, all of which claim with considerable justice that their theories are to a large extent elaborations of ideas to be found somewhere in Freud's writings, suggests that the psychoanalytical movement is at present going through some sort of crisis, through something which, if it occurred within a single person, would be called a 'spiritual crisis' or a 'mid-life crisis' or an 'agonizing reappraisal'. André Green, the French analyst, calls it a 'malaise'. It arises, he believes, from confusions 'at the very heart of psychoanalysis' which make it impossible to reconcile analytical theory and practice and will only be cured by a radical revision of classical Freudian concepts. If Green is right, and personally I think he is, the present divisions within Freudian psychoanalysis must be the reflection of some deep-seated but as yet unresolved contradiction within Freud's thinking, which makes it impossible for his followers to reconcile what they do with how they conceptualize what they do.

I should, of course, be being wise before the event if I could locate this contradiction precisely, but in the meantime it may perhaps be possible to get some idea of the general area in which it must lie by considering two of the issues about which contemporary analysts disagree and around which they tend to form sub-schools.

First, is a man a solitary or a social animal? According to Freud's instinct theory man is essentially pleasure-seeking; he has instincts which crave discharge, and until he has learnt how to adapt to his environment and to relate to others, he discharges these instincts autistically by hallucinatory wish-fulfilment. In other words, the quest for pleasure and relief from tension comes first, and only as a result of education and the pressures of civilization does he learn to relate to and share pleasure with others. This piece of Freudian theory certainly suggests that Freud thought that man is a solitary animal who has to learn how to be social. But Freud also thought that human beings remain profoundly attached to their parents all their lives, that they, that is we, can perceive one another's unconsciouses directly, and that transference, the patient's relationship to his analyst, is the effective agent in treatment; all of which suggests he also thought man to be a social animal. This contradiction in Freud's thinking is reflected in the fact that the two major sub-schools in contemporary psychoanalysis – ego-psychology and object relations theory – are divided on precisely this issue. Ego-psychologists subscribe to instinct theory and emphasize how we learn to master our impulses and adapt to our environment and how we acquire a sense of our own separate identity.

Object relations theorists maintain that we are inherently object-seeking rather than pleasure-seeking, and that our basic fear is not fear of losing our capacity for pleasure but fear of losing those to whom we are attached, and they emphasize the elemental, primary attachment of human beings to their mothers. According to the ego-psychologists, then, man's basic concern is with his identity and his capacity for pleasure, while according to the object theorists his basic concern is for his ties to others.

Secondly, do analysts observe and study their patients with objective, scientific detachment, or do they form human re-lationships with them? In other words, did Freud invent a new method for observing mental phenomena, or did he invent a new kind of human relationship in which one party, the patient, is enabled to find and understand himself? Now, in theory Freud certainly took the view that he observed his patients and that he studied mental phenomena. He claimed, indeed, that psycho-analysis was a scientific psychology strictly analogous to physics or chemistry and that the same principles of causality apply to mental phenomena as to physical phenomena. He likened the mind to an apparatus in which circulate forces and quanta of energy that are in principle measurable – though he admitted candidly that in fact they are not. On this view, analysts, while working, are scientists who observe the movements of various forces, impulses, drives, etc., in their patients' minds and then explain them by referring them to their appropriate causes. But there are many indications that in practice Freud did not subscribe to his own theory. If he had, he would surely have called what he himself said to his patients 'explanations'. In-stead, he called them 'interpretations', and he would have called his *magnum opus The Explanation of Dreams* not *The Interpretation of Dreams*. He would have advised his students to bear their knowledge of theory in mind while working with patients, but in fact he advised them to maintain an attitude of 'free-floating attention' and to forget about theory until treatment was finished. So it seems that although Freud theoreti-cally conceived of himself as a scientist observing and explaining mental phenomena, in practice and indeed in certain parts of his theory he conceived of himself as a person, a healer, who took up an intuitive, receptive attitude towards patients which enabled him to understand what their symptoms, their dreams and their free associations meant – to themselves. Here again, contemporary analysts are divided on precisely this issue. Some see their task as that of elucidating the causes and origins of their patients' illnesses; others see it as decoding their meaning.

What I am suggesting is that one of the unresolved contradictions in Freud's thinking is between psychoanalysis conceived of as a natural science – objective, detached and intellectual – and psychoanalysis conceived of as an intuitive, receptive mode of relating to others; and that awareness of this contradiction combined with failure to resolve it is part of the contemporary 'malaise' of psychoanalysis. If an analyst conceives of himself as only a scientist, he will apply theory to his patients and risk seeing only what he already knows. If, on the other hand, he conceives of himself as only a 'free-floating attention', existing 'in a state without memory or desire', as André Green recommends he should – or displaying Keatsian Negative Capability, 'being in uncertainties, mysteries, doubts', as another analyst, Bion, has recently advocated – he risks not being able to express what he discovers in terms comprehensible to others. Faced with this dilemma, it is hardly surprising that some analysts cling defensively to the theoretical model Freud constructed when wearing his 'natural scientist' hat, while others form coteries and sub-schools in which they pursue the implications of Freud's more muted, less publicized subjectivism.

1977

3

What Analysts Say to
Their Patients

According to dictionaries, interpretation is the process of elucidating and expounding the meaning of something obscure and
abstruse. Psychoanalysts use the word to describe a particular
kind of communication they make to their patients, namely
statements in which they assert that what their patient has
been telling them has wider implications than the patient has
appreciated.

The paradigm of psychoanalytic interpretation is dream interpretation, that activity by which the analyst tells his patient
that the dream he has recounted means such-and-such. This
procedure, which seems so arrogant and arbitrary to non-
analysts, is based on three assumptions.

First, that dreams have meaning: this assumption is itself
based on the wider assumption that mental activity is not
random but patterned, and that apparent trivia and absurdities
such as dreams, neurotic symptoms and parapraxes have causes
and/or meaning.

Secondly, that the meaning of dreams can be elucidated by
assuming that they are, as it were, written in a different language
from that used in waking thought – this different language
being what Freud called the primary process (or processes).
According to Freud, there are two types or modes of mental
functioning: the primary processes, being characteristic of unconscious mental activity, and the secondary processes, being
characteristic of conscious mental activity. Primary process
thinking displays condensation and displacement, so that images tend to become fused and can readily replace and symbolize

one another, and ignores the categories of space and time, whereas secondary process thinking conforms to the laws of grammar and formal logic. According to Freud, primary process thinking is exemplified by dreaming and neurotic symptom formation. It is unconscious and, as it were, subterraneous during waking as well as sleeping life. So, if dreams are texts written in the language of the primary processes, their meaning can be elucidated by unscrambling the various displacements, condensations and symbolizations contained within them and then restating the meaning in secondary process language, i.e. ordinary speech; this process of translating the non-verbal, mostly visual, imagery of dreams into verbal, discursive language being dream interpretation.

Thirdly, that the patient, the dreamer who has recounted his dream, can confirm the accuracy of the interpretation by his response to it – in the simplest instance by recollecting some event, feeling or thought that corresponds tellingly to the interpretation that the analyst has made. It is this third assumption that prevents dream interpretation from becoming an arbitrary, dogmatic and fanciful procedure.

Now, in the early days of psychoanalysis, the majority of interpretations made by analysts were probably dream interpretations, the imagery occurring in dreams being interpreted typically as either disguised representations of repressed infantile sexual wishes or as indications of some forgotten infantile sexual trauma; the interpretations were deemed to be 'correct' if and when the patient remembered some confirmatory wish or event. Hence Freud's dictum about dreams being the royal road to the unconscious.

However, as psychoanalysis developed, two implications emerged which widened the concept of interpretation. These are defence and transference.

Defence. Analysts came to see that it was not enough to tell patients what infantile wishes or traumata they had had, but that they also had to explain to patients what particular defence they used to prevent themselves becoming aware of their unconscious wishes, memories, etc. As a result, interpretations became duplex or double-barrelled; instead of 'You wanted to do such-

and-such' or 'Such-and-such happened to you', interpretations
began to take the form 'You are using such-and-such a defence
to prevent yourself remembering such-and-such a wish, feeling
or memory.' Interpretations became a matter not only of translating primary process thinking into secondary process thinking,
but also of defining which of the nine defences listed by Anna
Freud the patient was using.

Transference. When analysts began to appreciate that their
patients regularly transferred on to their analyst feelings or
ideas derived from their relationships with previous, usually
parental figures, and that this transference was an essential part
of analysis and not just a tiresome distraction, a further kind
of interpretation was introduced – the transference interpretation – by which the analyst explained to his patient that he,
the patient, was reacting as though his analyst were his father,
mother, brother, sister or whatever, and was attributing to him,
the analyst, benign or malignant paternal, maternal, fraternal
or sororal feelings towards him, the patient. Such interpretations
are triplex or treble-barrelled and take the schematic form: 'You
are using such-and-such a defence to prevent yourself becoming
aware of such-and-such a feeling towards myself, to whom you
are reacting as though I were your father or your mother.' At
this point the idea of interpretation as a process of linguistic
translation has been subsumed into the wider idea of it as an
explanatory comment on the nature of the relationship existing
between the analyst and the patient, the explanation being in
terms of the repetitive nature of the patient's contribution to
the relationship. Nowadays many analysts take the view that
only transference interpretations have any dynamic effect on
the course of treatment – that only they are mutative – and that
interpretations of unconscious content and defence play only
an ancillary role. Personally I am by no means convinced that
this is true.

The conceptual basis of psychoanalytical interpretations consists, therefore, of three premises.

First, that there are unconscious mental processes which
obey different grammatical rules from those of conscious thinking, and that anyone knowing these rules can translate primary

process statements into the language of waking thought, such translations being content-interpretations of dreams, symptoms, parapraxes.

Secondly, that the ego uses defences to prevent itself becoming aware of certain unconscious mental processes, and that anyone familiar with such defences can elucidate the precise way in which, at any particular moment, the patient is defending himself against becoming aware of some particular unconscious process, such elucidation being a combined interpretation of content and defence.

Thirdly, that patients transfer on to their analysts feelings derived from their childhood relationships, and that anyone familiar with the concept of transference can interpret what defence the patient, at any particular moment, is using to defend himself against becoming aware of what feeling towards which parent.

It should be noted that this, the classical view of interpretation, assumes that the analyst is an external, objective observer of the patient's intrapsychic processes, that interpretations are interventions from outside the system, and that even transference interpretations which mention the analyst are not really about him at all but about some parental image that preexisted in the patient's mind. It is, however, possible to look at psychoanalysis – and indeed all forms of psychotherapy – in another way, one which assumes that there actually is a relationship between therapist and patient, that interpretations constitute a special class of communication between patient and therapist, and that they are one of the several kinds of things that therapists say to their patients while relating to them.

According to this view, psychotherapy is a therapeutic relationship between two people, one of whom, the patient, is in distress of some kind, and the other of whom, the therapist, is offering him help. It is assumed by both parties to the relationship that the patient has appreciated that he cannot relieve his distress himself, and that the therapist is making some claim to possess some skills or expertise which will enable him to be helpful. As the help the therapist offers is psychotherapy, not physiotherapy or pharmacotherapy or surgery, the help offered is the opportunity for discourse and a setting in which the patient can talk about himself, his problems, hopes, fears and dreams without censorship or censure, can expect to be listened to and to receive from time to time helpful and illuminating comments. These comments, the things said by the therapist, are of various kinds, and only some of them are interpretations in the sense of expounding the meaning of something obscure or abstruse.

Some of the therapist's utterances fulfil the function of maintaining the continuity of the relationship and its setting over a period of time. This class of communication includes greetings, good-byes, arrangements for future meetings, advance notice of holidays, apologies for unavoidable cancellations.

Others are designed to make and retain rapport between patient and therapist. These are acknowledging remarks by which the therapist shows that he has followed, understood and empathized (not necessarily sympathized) with what the patient has been talking about; also questions by which the therapist seeks to clarify for himself things that he fears he has not understood or heard correctly.

Others draw attention to recurrent themes, inconsistencies or surprising omissions in what the patient has been talking about. Since the therapist is not directly involved in the patient's life, he is often in a position to notice that, for instance, the patient is preoccupied with some problem or relationship other than the one he thinks he is, or that he fails to report anger, envy or jealousy when describing situations in which most people do feel such emotions. The therapist's ability to notice such things depends not on his knowledge of theory but on his experience of living, his common sense, his intuition, his ability to discern when people are talking out of tune with themselves.

Yet another kind of communication made by therapists are expositions of general explanatory ideas. At some point during treatment patients need to become acquainted with such ideas as ambivalence (the idea that it is possible to love and hate the same person, to desire and fear the same object), transference, the formative effect of childhood relationships and experiences.

Such expositions are not themselves interpretations, but they prepare the ground for interpretation.

Finally, there are interpretations by which the therapist presents to the patient such ideas as that he may be harbouring wishes, thoughts or fears of which he is unconscious, or that he is defending himself against something in some particular way, or that he is relating to his therapist as if he were some significant childhood figure. Such content, defence and transference interpretations do indeed indicate that the therapist possesses some theoretical ideas that enable him to elucidate matters that would otherwise be obscure; but, once it is appreciated that interpretations are part of the total discourse that takes place between therapist and patient, it becomes apparent that they have a significance over and above that of elucidating obscure or abstruse mental processes taking place in the depths of the patient's psyche. They also indicate that the therapist has been listening attentively, has remembered what the patient said during previous sessions, and has been sufficiently interested to listen and remember and understand. And by indicating the therapist's sustained interest in the patient, they play an important part in maintaining a relationship which is not entirely transference, and which is surely an essential part of the healing process.

Interpretations, therefore, are not merely ideas generated by a conceptual framework possessed by the therapist and fed by him into the patient's psychic apparatus, but also sentences uttered by a real, live person who is devoting time and attention to another real, live person.

1983

4

Is Freudian Symbolism
a Myth?

It has become a commonplace among the general public, and perhaps among journalists in particular, that some things are Freudian symbols. In the popular usage of this phrase, the word Freudian is synonymous with 'sexual', the word 'sexual' is synonymous with 'genital', while the question 'What does the word "symbol" mean?' is answered by saying that it is something that stands for something else. A pipe, a sword, a gun are held to be Freudian symbols on the ground that Freud reputedly said that they stand for penises. In view of this widespread assumption, I thought it might be appropriate to start this paper by investigating whether the general public has in fact correctly divined and understood an essential part of Freud's thinking or whether some distortion of his ideas has taken place during their passage from the learned literature into the colour supplements.

Now, in one very simple sense, a distortion certainly has occurred. Freud himself was not the psychoanalyst who first attached central importance to sexual symbolism. As he himself said, he arrived late at a full realization of the importance of symbolism of any kind. The first edition of *The Interpretation of Dreams* (1900) contains only a few pages devoted to the subject of symbolism in general and only one dream exemplifying sexual symbolism. These few pages came at the end of a section entitled 'Considerations of Representability', and the matter under discussion was not primarily 'How are sexual

ideas symbolized in dreams?' but two more general ones: 'How
are thoughts, which are not necessarily visual, converted into
the visual imagery characteristic of dreams?' and 'How can
forbidden, taboo ideas be expressed in dreams in such a way
that the dreamer, when he awakens, will not understand them?';
sexual ideas being only one of several classes of forbidden ideas
which the 'dream work' has to translate into imagery that will
get past the censor.

Freud did, however, eventually get around to attaching great
importance to symbolism in general and to sexual symbolism in
particular, successive editions of *The Interpretation of Dreams*
containing additions referring to sexual symbolism. But it was
not until the fourth edition (1914) that Freud included a section
concerned exclusively with symbolism. However, even in the
present definitive Standard Edition, this section consists of only
55 pages in a work running to 623 pages.

Freud's reasons for taking fourteen years to attach central
importance to the idea with which his name has become most
widely associated are expressed clearly in the opening paragraphs of this section, and I should like now to quote extensively
from them.

The analysis of this last, biographical, dream [i.e. the one discussed
at the end of the previous section] is clear evidence that I recognised
the presence of symbolism in dreams from the very beginning. But it
was only by degrees and as my experience increased that I arrived at
a full appreciation of its extent and significance, and I did so under
the influence of the contributions of Wilhelm Stekel [*Die Sprache des
Traumes*, published in 1911], about whom a few words will not be
out of place here.

That writer, who has perhaps damaged psychoanalysis as much as
he has benefited it, brought forward a large number of unsuspected
translations of symbols; to begin with they were met with scepticism,
but later they were for the most part confirmed and had to be accepted.
I shall not be belittling the value of Stekel's services if I add that the
sceptical reserve with which his proposals were received was not
without justification. For the examples by which he supported his
interpretations were often unconvincing, and he made use of a method
which must be rejected as scientifically untrustworthy.

Stekel arrived at his interpretations of symbols by way of intuition,
thanks to a peculiar gift for the direct understanding of them. But

the existence of such a gift cannot be counted upon generally, its effectiveness is exempt from all criticism and consequently its findings have no claim to credibility . . .

Advances in psychoanalytic experience have brought to our notice patients who have shown a direct understanding of dream symbolism of this kind to a surprising extent. They were often sufferers from dementia praecox [i.e. what we nowadays call schizophrenia], so that for a time there was an inclination to suspect every dreamer who had this grasp of symbols of being a victim of that disease. But such is not the case. It is a question of a personal gift or peculiarity which has no visible pathological significance.

I should like now to make two glosses on this quotation.

1. It is apparent that in symbolism Freud encountered a phenomenon which was resistive to, and indeed incompatible with, his ideal of founding a psychology based on natural-scientific principles. Freud's original and indeed lifelong grand design was to construct a science of mind which would be analogous to the physical sciences, which used concepts such as force and energy, which was strictly determinist and in which all explanations were in terms of causation. But here in symbolism he encountered phenomena which required explanations in terms of meaning rather than cause, and in which convincing explanations could be arrived at by 'a method which must be rejected as scientifically untrustworthy' and by persons who possessed not a training in the rigours of the scientific method but a 'peculiar gift for the direct understanding' of symbolic equations. It must all have been very embarrassing for Freud, and one has to sympathize with his resistance against recognizing the importance of symbolism.

It must, however, be remembered that Freud displayed similar resistance towards two other ideas which have become generally associated with his name: the idea that human beings are as affected by their phantasies as by their actual experiences (cf. his distress at realizing that his female patients could not all have been literally seduced by their fathers); and the idea that psychoanalytical treatment is essentially a matter of transference – 'finally every conflict has to be fought out in the sphere of transference,' he says in *The Dynamics of Transference*.

2. It is evident that Freud must himself have had patients

who possessed the 'peculiar gift' of being able to translate symbols intuitively, that it would have suited his theoretical book if they had all turned out to be mad, but that in fact they often were not – but note his phrase 'no *visible* pathological significance'. It followed from *this* embarrassing observation that symbolism in the Freudian sense could not be either a pathological phenomenon capable of a causative explanation, or one of the so-called 'primary processes' which Freud postulated were characteristic of unconscious mental activity. As is well known, Freud held that there are two types or principles of mental functioning, one discursive, verbal, conforming to the laws of grammar and formal logic and characteristic of conscious thinking; the other non-discursive, condensive, iconic, ignorant of the categories of space and time and characteristic of unconscious thinking. It would have been methodologically convenient and economical if Freudian symbolism could have been included in the latter, and most analysts other than Freud have in fact done so, but the existence of 'peculiar' people like Stekel – and also, as Freud himself pointed out, of artists and jokers – makes it impossible to do so.

II

Having described Freud's rather reluctant acceptance of the fact that there is such a thing as what has come to be called Freudian symbolism, I must turn to the question as to whether this symbolism is exclusively sexual, as popularizations of psychoanalysis would have one believe. The answer to this question is equivocal. According to Freud's tenth Introductory Lecture, 'The range of things which are given symbolic representation in dreams is not wide; the human body as a whole, parents, children, brothers and sisters, birth, death, nakedness – and something else besides.' This 'something else besides' turns out to be 'the field of sexual life – the genitals, sexual processes, sexual intercourse. The great majority of symbols in dreams are sexual symbols. And here a strange disproportion is revealed. The topics I have mentioned are few, but the symbols for them are extremely numerous.' Freud then goes on to list over thirty symbols for the male genitals and over twenty for the female.

Reading this lecture one is indeed left with the overwhelming impression that, in Freud's view, Freudian symbolism is predominantly sexual, but I must confess that I think that Freud reached the conclusion that 'the great majority of symbols in dreams are sexual' by a mixture of logical error and intellectual sleight-of-hand.

The logical error consists in failing to appreciate that the topics which he designates 'few' and the 'symbols' which he designates as 'numerous' are not of the same logical type, and cannot therefore be compared numerically with one another. The topics mentioned – birth, death, sex, etc. – are general ideas arrived at by abstraction, the symbols mentioned – umbrellas, revolvers, Zeppelins, cupboards, apples, etc., etc. – are specific objects, or, to be pedantic, concepts of a lower level of abstraction. It is therefore hardly surprising that there are more symbols than topics symbolized. The entities classified must of necessity be more numerous than the classes into which they are classified.

The intellectual sleight-of-hand consists of (a) asserting that the range of things which are given symbolic representation is not wide, when in fact the list of things which he says are symbolizable embraces almost the whole range of human experience, apart perhaps from work, intellectual activity and some kinds of play, and (b) detaching the sexual life from the other members of the list of things deemed symbolizable and treating it as though it had no intrinsic connection with them. But this is, of course, not so. To go through his list: we only have a body because our parents once had sexual intercourse; we only have children because we have had intercourse; we only have brothers and sisters because our parents had intercourse more than once; birth and death are the first and last members of the series birth, copulation and death; nakedness has obvious connections with both the sexual life and with the interfaces between the self as private and public being, as biological and social being.

What, it seems to me, Freud should have said was that the range of things which are given symbolic representation embraces all aspects of man's biological life-cycle, and that scrutiny of dreams reveals that human beings are much more preoccupied with their biological destiny and with their intimate personal relationships than most of them realize. Freud, strangely, seems always to have assumed that it is normal for human beings to be oblivious and obtuse about the importance of this emotional, poetic, mythopoeic, imaginative aspect of human experience, and that people who are aware of it are 'special cases', with gifts that are 'peculiar' in both senses of the word. As I have said elsewhere ('Beyond the Reality Principle', in *Imagination and Reality*), Freud's conception of the normal person was 'cast in the mould of the scientist at work'. Hence, incidentally, his ambivalence towards artists, whom he both admired, for their natural understanding of things that he had had to learn the hard way, and disparaged, by trying to demonstrate that they were all neurotic. To be fair to Freud, I must add that late in his life he abandoned this attempt: 'Before the problem of the creative artist analysis must, alas, lay down its arms,' he remarked in *Dostoyevsky and Parricide*, published in 1928.

In parenthesis I must mention that I believe that Freud's insistence in 1917 that the great majority of symbols are sexual was polemical, and was an attempt to preserve the scientific purity of psychoanalysis from contamination by Jungian ideas about archetypes, which he regarded as mystical and irrational. He wanted psychoanalysis to remain grounded in biology, and genitals are more down-to-earth than mandalas.

The same concealed polemical motive can also be discerned in Ernest Jones's paper of 1916, 'The Theory of Symbolism', which remains to this day the classic statement of the psychoanalytical position, and which only a few analysts – in this country Marion Milner, Hanna Segal and myself – have challenged. In this paper Jones makes two points which I should like to discuss in some detail, one because it has been largely responsible for the difficulties in communication which have notoriously always existed between psychoanalysts on the one hand and anthropologists and linguists on the other, and the other because it is highly germane to the general theme of symbols and sentiments.

The first is Jones's argument, or rather assertion, that there is such a thing as 'true symbolism', which is psychoanalytical and predominantly sexual and can be differentiated from what he calls 'symbolism in its widest sense'. According to Jones's distinction words, emblems, tokens, badges, charms, conventionalized gestures, etc., are not true symbols, even though they 'represent some other idea from which they derive a significance not inherent in themselves', and are only loosely and vaguely called symbols by those ignorant of psychoanalysis. 'The thesis will here be maintained that true symbolism, in the strict sense, is to be distinguished from other forms of indirect representation.'

On the face of it, the claim that only Freudian symbols are true symbols is both arrogant and parochial. One would, after all, not allow a mathematician to get away with the assertion that the only true symbols are algebraic, or a linguist with the assertion that the only true symbols are words. But in Jones's defence it must be mentioned that in 1916 it was generally believed that the concept of evolution could be applied to human societies, and that it was, therefore, legitimate to equate phylogenetically the 'infantile phantasies of civilised neurotics and the dreams of healthy civilised adults with the rites, folklores, myths, religions, etc., of primitives'. As a result of this evolutionary assumption, Jones could without personal arrogance make remarks in 1916 which ring false in 1974: for example, 'Much more significant for the genesis of symbolism is the phylogenetic fact that in primitive civilisations an importance was attached to sexual organs and functions that to us appears absolutely monstrous', and 'The tendency of the primitive mind – as observed in children, in savages, in wit, dreams, insanity, and other products of unconscious functioning – to identify different objects and to fuse together different ideas, to note the resemblances and not the differences, is a universal and most characteristic feature . . .'

Now, given this assumption that civilized Western Europeans are more evolved than lesser breeds, Jones was, of course, justified in postulating that symbols encountered in dreams and neurotic symptoms had some sort of evolutionary priority over other more sophisticated kinds of symbols such as words, emblems or crests, the use of which demands a considerable degree of ontogenetic and phylogenetic development. Jones's position assumes, incidentally, that civilized children dream and phantasize before they learn how to talk – which may well be true – and that primitives think while awake in a way that resembles the way in which civilized people think while asleep – which I presume is not.

According to Jones, 'only what is repressed is symbolised; only what is repressed needs to be symbolised' and true psycho-analytical symbols 'represent ideas of the self and the immediate blood relatives or of the phenomena of birth, love and death. In other words, they represent the most primitive ideas and interests imaginable.' Note again the curious use of the word 'primitive' in a context which seems to demand 'basic' or 'fundamental'. 'The two cardinal characteristics of symbolism in this strict sense are (1) that the process is completely uncon-scious . . . and (2) that the affect investing the symbolised idea has not, in so far as the symbolism is concerned, proved capable of that modification in quality denoted by the term "subli-mation".'

III

I shall now consider these two cardinal characteristics separ-ately. First, the idea that the process underlying symbolism is completely unconscious. This statement is, I think, capable of two interpretations. It could mean either (a) that an innate and unconscious sense of similarities determines whether particular objects are utilizable as symbols for other particular objects, or (b) that the person using a true symbol is unconscious of its true meaning. Both interpretations can be found in the psychoanalytical literature, the first to explain the apparent universal or constant meaning of certain symbols, the second to explain the difference between 'true' symbols and metaphors. To clarify, here are four illustrative examples, all of which depend on the fact that the human mind is capable of conceiving a similarity between genitals and a violin or other stringed instrument. The two clinical examples are not my own; I have taken them from Hanna Segal's paper 'Notes on Symbol Forma-tion' (*International Journal of Psycho-Analysis*, 38).

1. A male violinist was asked, while having a psychotic

breakdown, why he no longer played the violin. He answered, quite seriously, 'Why? Do you expect me to masturbate in public?', thereby implying that for him at that moment his violin *was* his genitals. The symbolism was fully conscious, but in a curious way, since he had temporarily lost sight of the fact that a symbol only *represents* something other than itself. He equated the symbol with its referent and could, therefore, no longer perform in public. I would remind you here of my earlier quotation from Freud in which he expressed his original suspicion that people with a direct understanding of symbolism were insane.

2. Another male violinist was having psychoanalytical treatment on account of, *inter alia*, inhibitions about performing in public. During the course of his treatment he reported material, including a dream in which he and a woman were playing duets together, which suggested that he unconsciously equated genitals and violins; after this had been interpreted to him, he resumed playing in public. In this case the symbolism was initially completely unconscious; only in dreams did he equate violins and genitals, and his analyst had to draw his attention to the fact that he did so. But after he had recognized his unconscious tendency to fuse, or rather confuse, violins and genitals – and after, presumably, his sense of guilt about sexual matters had been reduced – he could again perform in public.

3. The French novelist Honoré de Balzac, who died in 1850 and cannot, therefore, have read any Freud, is reputed once to have remarked that the love-making of many men resembled a gorilla trying to play a violin. In order to have been able to make this remark, Balzac must have been able to conceive of a similarity between men of a certain type and gorillas and of another similarity between women as sexual beings and violins. Since he was awake when he said it, he must have been fully conscious of these similarities and have assumed confidently that his audience could also become conscious of them. He was in fact talking metaphorically, in perfect confidence that his audience would neither assume that he thought that clumsy men are in fact gorillas or that amorous women are in fact violins, nor that they would fail to appreciate that clumsy men

can be likened to gorillas and that women can be likened to violins. According to Jones's formulations, such metaphorical statements are not truly symbolic, since the process is not completely unconscious. Yet it is difficult to see in what way the process of symbolization differs when it occurs consciously and emerges as a metaphor, and when it occurs unconsciously and emerges as a dream image. It seems to me more economical and logical to say that the process is identical in both cases and that symbolism, or rather the capacity to symbolize, is a general mental capacity, which can be used consciously or unconsciously, while awake or asleep, neurotically or creatively, with or without insight into its implications.

4. The sculptor Ossip Zadkine, who was born in 1890 and who may well, therefore, have read Freud, and whose work is characterized by a 'flair for metaphor and transformation' and 'a vocabulary in which voids replace solids, concavities replace convexities', as Jean Cassou remarks in his Introduction to the Arts Council Exhibition, 1961, has produced a number of works in which human bodies and string instruments, mostly violins and cellos, are fused. In some of these the strings of the instrument pass through the genital area, leaving the viewer in no doubt that Zadkine is equating string instruments and genitals – and string instruments as sources of music with human bodies as sources of erotic sensations. Here again the symbolism is patently conscious; sculptors are not asleep while they sculpt and must be presumed to reflect upon what they are doing. But since Zadkine could have read Freud, one would have to possess biographical information about him before deciding whether he spontaneously equated string instruments with genitals, or whether he was self-consciously exploiting the concept of Freudian symbolism. Personally, I suspect the former, but it is, I understand, a fact that artists who work for advertising agencies do consciously exploit the idea of Freudian symbolism, knowingly introducing Freudian symbols into advertisements and hoping thereby to add unconscious sex-appeal to the wares they are trying to sell. Whether such gambits are effective remains dubious and there is, I understand, some evidence that they may on occasion backfire. The slogan 'There's a Tiger in My Tank'

is said to have frightened some motorists off buying the petrol
it advertised. Surrealist painters also used Freudian symbolism
self-consciously.

Jones's second cardinal characteristic of 'true' symbolism is
'that the affect investing the symbolized idea has not . . . proved
capable of that modification in quality denoted by the term
"sublimation"'. In other words, true symbols retain the
emotional tone that is appropriate to the referent symbolized,
while other classes of 'symbolism in its widest sense' possess an
emotional tone of some other quality, this other quality being
only definable by reference to a concept of sublimation. The
implication here is that images and actions are only true symbols
if they are accompanied by, or evoke, the feelings naturally
aroused by the phenomena of birth, love and death, but are not
true symbols if they arouse some other more 'sublime' effect.
According to this view, violins were 'true' symbols for the
psychotic violinist I mentioned earlier since he conceived himself
to be masturbating if he played one. They were also true symbols
for the inhibited, neurotic violinist when he was dreaming that
he was playing duets with a woman violinist, but ceased to be
when, after recovery, he could again play in public. They were
not true symbols for Balzac when he made his remark about
gorillas playing them, since he and his audience were, presumably, amused not sexually aroused by it. And Zadkine must be
presumed to have been having aesthetic not sexual emotions
while sculpting his torsos.

It seems to me that this second cardinal distinction between
true and other symbols is open to four objections. First, Jones
has really made a distinction between two different kinds of
affect, unmodified and modified, not between two different
kinds of symbol. Secondly, there are too many intermediate
phenomena which resist classification on the basis of Jones's
distinction; for instance, obscene language, pornography, erotic
art, intentional and unintentional *double entendres*. Thirdly,
the propriety of using vivid sexual imagery in speech varies
from generation to generation in a way that cannot possibly
be explained by reference to the prevailing extent of sexual
repression. The virgin Queen Elizabeth I could say without

losing dignity: 'If I had been born crested not cloven, your Lordships would not treat me so', but one cannot imagine either Queen Victoria or our present Queen speaking in such a way. And yet it is hard to believe that Elizabeth I was the least repressed of these three Royal Ladies. Nor, I think, could one safely assert that there is greater sexual repression in those parts of the English-speaking world where male gallinaceous birds have to be called roosters than in those parts where they are still cocks.

Fourthly, the essential nature of the distinction between un-modified, erotic and modified, sublimated affects remains ob-scure and mysterious. Indeed much of the obscurity and esoteri-cism of contemporary psychoanalytical theory seems to derive precisely from the difficulties it has encountered in trying to formulate and explain the differences between instinctual and sublimated activities, and in establishing what kinds of child-hood experience facilitate or compel the transformation of instinctual drives into sublimations. According to Heinz Hart-mann, who until his recent death was the doyen of American psychoanalysis and the psychoanalytical theorist whose think-ing was most akin to that of Freud, sublimations are 'auton-omous', i.e. immune from interference by changes in instinctual tension, occupy 'a conflict-free area of the ego', and use 'de-eroticized', 'de-aggressified', 'neutralized' energy, and their development is facilitated not, as early analytical theory main-tained, by frustration, but by experience of 'delays in gratification'. Now, although I have no doubt that Hartmann knew what he meant by such formulations – and, in fact, I do too, though I do not subscribe to them, since they seem to me to be the result of a heroic attempt to reconcile loyalty towards outmoded theory with respect for facts – they are hardly formu-lations likely to assist communication between psychoanalysis and the other humane sciences.

IV

It might be anticipated that abandonment by psychoanalytical theory of the idea that there exists only one 'true' kind of symbolism, which is characterized by unmodified affects and is concerned only with representation of 'the most primitive ideas and interests imaginable', would have important effects on clinical practice. But this seems in fact not to be so. Indeed, it would seem that the effect of the revision of theory suggested in this essay would merely be to legitimize changes in practice that have already occurred. Jones's classic paper was written nearly sixty years ago, and since 1916 psychoanalytical theories of all varieties have increased enormously in sophistication; and I doubt whether many, if any, analysts are deterred from making interpretations that occur to them by the thought or theoretical scruple that what they want to say would be only a metaphorical statement and not a truly symbolic interpretation. In any case the practical exigencies of clinical work make it inconceivable that any analyst would monitor all his utterances in order to ascertain what sort of metaphor or symbolism he was using at any particular moment. Furthermore, advances in ego-psychology since 1916 have made analysts much more aware of the interconnections between different levels or parts of the mind and less inclined to envisage their role solely as pointing out the 'primitive', unconscious, infantile sources and meanings of what their patients tell them.

I suspect, indeed, that the original formulations by Freud and Jones have survived basically unchallenged for two, basically adventitious reasons; because their emphasis on the specifically sexual appeals to the popular imagination, and because piety prevents psychoanalysts from criticizing their Founding Fathers. The paper in which I first presented the view of symbolism proposed here ('Symbolism and Its Relationship to the Primary and Secondary Processes', in my book *Imagination and Reality*) was written before Jones's death, and he wrote to me expressing his general agreement and drawing my attention to the extent to which his earlier ideas had been presented as a reaction against Jung's flight into mysticism.

To summarize:

1. The concept of Freudian symbolism has passed into general circulation and refers to the idea that many, perhaps most objects are sexual symbols.

2. Although the idea is popularly believed to have originated

in Freud's book *The Interpretation of Dreams*, published in 1900, Freud did not in fact attach paramount importance to symbolism, whether sexual or otherwise, until it was forced upon his attention by Stekel and by a number of peculiarly gifted patients.

3. Freudian symbols are not in fact exclusively sexual; they represent, to quote Jones again, 'ideas of the self and the immediate blood relatives or of the phenomena of birth, love and death', in fact everything that comprises man's biological destiny.

4. Psychoanalytical theory has attempted to pre-empt the concept of symbolism by asserting that the only true symbols are those which analysts encounter when interpreting dreams and neurotic symptoms.

5. By doing so psychoanalytical theory has offended against common usage and has created well-nigh insuperable barriers between itself and other humane disciplines.

6. According to the view expressed here, these barriers could be lowered by recognizing that symbolization is a general capacity of the mind, which can be used both by the discursive, syntactical, rational form of thinking characteristic of waking, intellectual activity ('secondary process thinking' in psychoanalytical terminology) and by the non-discursive, condensive, affective form of thinking characteristic of dreaming, imagining, joking and creating ('primary process thinking' in psychoanalytical terminology); and by recognizing that these two types of thinking are not necessarily opposed to one another, as most formulations of psychoanalytical theory imply, but can work in harness.

7. Since Freudian ideas have, after a fashion, passed into general currency, self-conscious, contrived and fanciful manipulations of the idea of Freudian symbolism have become possible. The artefacts produced by such self-conscious manipulations are meretricious, since they can be passed off as products of the creative imagination.

8. The revision of the psychoanalytical theory of symbolism suggested in the second half of this paper has less relevance to clinical practice than might be expected. It would probably do

little more than legitimize changes that have already occurred in interpretative modes as a result of the increase in sophistication of theory that has taken place since Freud and Jones wrote their classic statements of the theory of symbolism sixty years ago.

1974

FREUDIANA

5

The Freudian Slip

In writing *The Freudian Slip*[1] Sebastiano Timpanaro has, if I understand him rightly, had two aims, one specific and one general. The first is to demonstrate that Freud's theory that slips of the tongue and pen, failures in remembering, bungled actions and 'parapraxes' generally are due to interference by repressed, unconscious thoughts does not stand up to textual criticism of the work *The Psychopathology of Everyday Life* in which Freud originally formulated it. The second is to discuss whether Freudian psychoanalysis is a science and whether it can be reconciled with Marxism; in particular, with his own specific brand of Leopardian Marxism, which is optimistic in so far as it believes that there could and indeed one day will be a society in which repression and oppression no longer occur, and pessimistic in so far as it believes that anxiety arising from 'biological frailty' will always be part of the human condition.

Freud's *The Psychopathology of Everyday Life* first appeared in two instalments in 1901 as articles in a learned journal. It was published as a book in 1904 and then went through ten editions in the next twenty years, during the course of which it grew from 92 to 310 pages. This expansion was almost entirely due to the addition of further illustrations, most of which were provided by Freud's friends and disciples and many of which are patently autobiographical. As a result, the version we now have consists largely of anecdotes about slips of the tongue, mistakes and failures of memory committed by Freud and his

[1] Sebastiano Timpanaro, *The Freudian Slip: Psychoanalysis and Textual Criticism* (London: New Left Books, 1976).

circle, embedded in which are a few pages of psychological theorizing.

Although it has been one of the best selling and most translated of Freud's works, it has also been one of the least criticized. Timpanaro attributes this to the 'conspiracy of silence' with which, allegedly, the academic world originally greeted Freud's writings. I suspect, however, that the explanation really lies in something elusive and ambiguous about the book itself. The general idea that slips and stupid mistakes may on occasion be psychologically motivated is so plausible as hardly to seem worth questioning, while it is hard to put one's finger on why most of the examples Freud gives are so unconvincing. The field has, as a result, been left open to Timparano to use his professional critical tools to demonstrate, first, that Freud was really arguing that all slips are motivated, and, secondly, exactly why the examples are not as convincing as Freud himself seems to have thought they were.

Timpanaro's argument is fourfold. First, as he demonstrates at length, the majority of the slips cited by Freud can be explained in the same way as can the errors made by compositors, proof readers and transcribers of manuscripts. Most are the result of what he calls 'banalization', that process by which a familiar word is spoken, read or transcribed in preference to an unfamiliar one; that process by which, for instance, my own surname tends to be re-endowed with the 'e' after 'Ry' that it no doubt once had, even by people who know me quite well – though one old man who habitually does so wishes, I am sure, to remind me that his father knew Gissing, the author of *The Private Papers of Henry Ryecroft*. Others are due to lapses of attention which may cause one either to repeat a word, phrase or syllable which one has already uttered or written or to leap ahead of oneself, omitting the intervening words. Writers, particularly transcribers, make these errors continually, and in Timparano's view it is absurd to assume that they always have psychological causes; it is sufficient to assume an ultimately neurophysiological tendency to subsume the unfamiliar under the familiar, to perseverate, and to anticipate oneself, particularly when engaged in boring activities.

Secondly, Freud fails to reveal or inquire into the wider social context in which a slip takes place. For instance, when Freud describes how a chance acquaintance, 'a young man of academic background', left out a word from a line of Virgil he was quoting, he omits to mention – and perhaps did not even know – that the line in question is grammatically most peculiar and the version the young man gave conforms better with Latin grammar as taught in schools than does the correct original, and also makes the point he was making as well as the line actually written by Virgil does. Nor does Freud inquire as to whether the young man would have made the same mistake if he had had occasion to quote the line a month, a year, five years earlier. However, undeterred by such scholarly niceties, Freud asks the young man to associate to the missing word and soon establishes that he is worried about his mistress's missed period, an anxiety which Freud then asserts is the cause of the young man's lapse of memory. The reader will appreciate that Timpanaro is dauntingly erudite, but the point he is making is that Freud does not provide the kind of background information which would enable one to decide whether the slips he quotes are interferences by repressed thoughts or merely banalizations. The young man's misquotation of Virgil could well have been analogous to that which makes even quite well-educated Englishmen think that Coleridge wrote 'Water, water, every where, but not (or never) a drop to drink', when in fact he wrote 'Nor any drop to drink'.

Thirdly, many of Freud's examples of slips are not slips at all but gaffes, *faux pas*, occasions on which the writer or speaker said something that he was in fact thinking but wished, for reasons of tact, decorum or moral cowardice, *not* to utter. In such cases the mistake is due not to interference by an unconscious idea but to a conflict between two fully conscious wishes, one to be discreetly hypocritical, the other to be truthful. An example is that of the baptized Jew who, while in the company of a gentile lady who was expressing anti-semitic opinions, called his sons 'Juden' (jews) when he 'meant' to say 'Jungen' (youngsters). As the reporter and in all probability perpetrator of this 'slip', the analyst Viktor Tausk, says: 'I ought to have made a bold declaration of the facts in order to set my sons the example of "having the courage of one's convictions", but I was afraid of the unpleasant exchanges that usually follow an avowal of this sort.'

Fourthly, even in those examples given by Freud in which he does show convincingly that the slip is due to interference by some repressed idea, the idea repressed is often not, as according to Freudian theory it should be, a sexual idea, but one about money, racial prejudice, careers, professional rivalry and, though Timpanaro himself does not use the word, snobbery.[2] The frequency with which the original Freudian slips were about social issues is, understandably, interpreted by Timpanaro as a reflection of the strange fact that Freud and his circle all han-kered after recognition by the very society their new science was covertly criticizing. Psychoanalysis, he says, 'reveals the imprint of that "singular synthesis of implacable critical spirit and implacable bourgeois correctness" which Claudo Magris argues was characteristic of Central European civilization'. A synthesis of such incompatibles can hardly have made life easy, and it is not surprising that it seems to have induced an epidemic of parapraxes. In a passage not quoted by Timpanaro, Freud says:

> In healthy people egoistic, jealous and hostile feelings and impul-sions, on which the pressure of moral education weighs heavily, make frequent use of the pathway provided by parapraxes in order to find some expression of their strength, which undeniably exists but is not recognized by the higher mental agencies.

This is, incidentally, a most curious passage. It implies that health is not a matter of integration or wholeness but the possession of harmless safety valves for those impulses that moral education represses. Given this peculiar view of health it is hardly surprising that Timparano comes to the conclusion

---

[2] In Freud's first and major example of faulty remembering he claims to have been disconcerted by his failure to remember the name Signorelli despite being as familiar with it as with the name Botticelli, and his chain of associations leads through Signor and Herr to Bosnia-Herzovina, where the peasantry have great confidence in their doctors and attach high importance to sexual enjoyment. One wishes Freud could have reported forgetting the name of a tree or cooking utensil or losing a shopping list.

that psychoanalysis is 'a self-confession by the bourgeoisie of its own perfidy', or that Reich should have sought a kind of health that does not rely on having harmless leaks in one's character's armour.

Despite his marshalling of so many cogent objections to Freud's theory of slips, he does not mention what is to my mind the most cogent of all, and one which Freud did mention after a fashion in a footnote added in 1920. This is that it is as easy (or difficult) to obtain associative chains leading to significant unconscious or concealed preoccupations by presenting words, pictures or numbers to someone as by asking him to associate to a slip he has himself made or to a number he has himself chosen. It follows from this that, given a hidden preoccupation and a coexisting wish to reveal or confess it, an associative track will eventually reach that preoccupation regardless of where or with what it started, and the eventual arrival at 'significant material' is not therefore evidence that the starting-point was in any sense caused by it. The young man of academic background would eventually have told Freud about his mistress's missed period whatever word in whatever language Freud had asked him to associate to. Freud's insistence that there is a causal relationship between slips and underlying repressed ideas derives from his desire to prove that mental phenomena are causally determined, and he seems to have believed that there was no difference between a motive and a cause. If one could demonstrate motives behind apparently random items of behaviour such as slips, bungled actions, etc., one would, in his view, have proved that they have a determining cause; thereby striking a blow for science in its battle against superstition. This is one of the few aspects of Freud's book not dealt with thoroughly by Timpanaro, presumably because he too believes in determinism and that all mental and social events have causes. One senses that he has little time for latter-day analysts like myself who are more concerned with the meaning of actions than with the causes of 'mental phenomena'.

In addition to being impressed by the frequency with which Freud interpreted slips as being the result of repressed thoughts about money, professional status, etc., Timpanaro is surprised by the absence of any reference to two other sources of anxiety which must have impinged upon Freud and his circle. He finds it remarkable that none of Freud's interpretations of slips in *The Psychopathology of Everyday Life* – or of dreams and symptoms elsewhere – refers either to anxiety arising from the bourgeoisie's awareness of its inherent insecurity as a privileged minority living among and on the numerically much larger proletariat, or to anxiety arising from man's 'biological frailty', from his awareness that he and his nearest and dearest may and indeed eventually will fall ill and die.

Now, although it is indeed remarkable that Freud's writings as a whole reveal an astonishing obliviousness and ignorance of social factors, it is not, I think, remarkable that a specific 'bourgeois anxiety' and dread of the threatening proletariat does not show up in his interpretations of slips, dreams and symptoms. All children and indeed most grown-ups fail to distinguish between social reality and the reality of the natural world, and the possibility of radical changes in the structure of society seems as unreal to them as does the possibility of an earthquake in a country in which they do not occur. As a result, evidence of the possibility of violent social change tends to evoke incredulity rather than anxiety. Hence we find that refugees and exiles usually flee long after the writing has been clearly written on the wall, and that those who have enjoyed high social status in their country of origin often seem not really to believe that they have lost it. Or, to put the matter another way, no individual or group of people can dread an entity that does not enter into their scheme of things, and if it does impinge upon them they are more likely to deny the fact than to make slips or dreams about it. If they do develop a neurosis about it, it will be a traumatic neurosis rather than a psychoneurosis. In any case, the text in which Timpanaro has sought in vain for references to a dread of the emergent proletariat was written thirteen years before the First World War, before Western society had revealed its capacity to create and survive cat-astrophes. And, it is tempting to think, the synthesis of 'implac-able critical spirit' and 'implacable bourgeois correctness' which Timpanaro attributes to Freud's generation of Central European intellectuals could well generate an equally implacable refusal to face facts: Freud's refusal to leave Vienna until after the Nazis had arrived there certainly suggests this.

Timpanaro's surprise that anxiety arising from man's 'biological frailty' plays no part in Freud's interpretations of slips, dreams and symptoms strikes me, on the other hand, as entirely justified. I too find it hard to believe that thoughts about the health and survival of oneself and one's loved ones do not preoccupy us unconsciously and contribute to slips and dreams. In my book *The Innocence of Dreams* I suggest that dreams are not, as Freud maintained, disguised hallucinatory wish-fulfilments, but meditations upon, and reassessments of, one's 'biological destiny'; that, in particular, dreams of travelling dreamt by the elderly are preparations for their last journey. I also suggest that Little Hans's famous dream that his mother 'was gone and I had no Mummy to cuddle with' may not have been an incestuous sexual dream, as Freud interpreted it, but a self-confrontation with a true fact of his biological destiny — that one day, of necessity, his mother would be gone.

If Timpanaro and I are right about this, Freud's exclusion of biological frailty from his scheme of things must have been a defence, perhaps against the very admission of frailty itself. I find it tempting to surmise that the Freudian 'system', in which everything is referred back to one's own wishes and one's own personal biography, contains an elaborate but concealed defence of an illusion of the total autonomy of the self — a typically bourgeois illusion, Timpanaro might say — and a denial of the extent to which we are the creatures of biological and historical destiny. When Freud, in the aftermath of the First World War, also had to recognize that he was growing old, he produced his theory of the death instinct; according to which destructiveness, decay and death are still our own wishes, not the effect of social and biological processes we are powerless to resist. But I can think of passages in Freud that do not fit this surmise and, in any case, he was, like the rest of us, of contradiction all compact.

Although I have in the main been convinced by Timpanaro's demonstration that Freud's theory of slips does not hold water and reveals more about his social milieu than it does about psychological verities, I am, I must confess, less happy about his discussion of the reconcilability (or otherwise) of psycho-analysis to Marxism. This is due not only to my ignorance of the controversial issues which are, all too obviously, preoccupying contemporary Marxists, but also to his ignorance of the contem-porary psychoanalytical scene. My ignorance of the work of Legrand, Althusser, Geymonat, Jervis, Lukács, Musatti and others and of the precise differences between materialist, prag-matic, voluntarist and Leopardian Marxism,[3] is matched by his of the work of Klein, Winnicott, Fairbairn, Szasz, Bateson and others, and of the differences between ego-psychology, object theory, instinct theory, transactional analysis and action language.

All I can do, therefore, is to report that in my opinion Timpanaro has got contemporary psychoanalysis all wrong, that his conception of it bears little resemblance to the realities of its practice today in this country and the United States, and to mention some of the ways in which his preoccupation with the early history of psychoanalysis has led him astray about its present state.

Firstly, Timpanaro is deeply impressed by the authoritarian-ism of psychoanalysis, and he is right in thinking that this heritage from its early days continues to be the bane of psycho-analytical organizations, which still display a tendency to spon-taneous fission similar to that displayed by left-wing political and nonconformist religious organizations. But he is wrong, I think, in supposing that the relationship between analyst and patient is necessarily authoritarian. Although it is, in some of its facets, a power game, not all the cards are held by the analyst. Timpanaro has evidently not encountered Gregory Bateson's

---

[3] Of all these the Leopardian version sounds to me by far the most attractive, since it sees man as part of nature, not inherently alienated from it, and casts nature as both the bountiful source of all pleasure and as the tragic source of all unavoidable pain and suffering. But I suppose that, like the best Italian wines, Leopardian Marxism would not travel well. Perhaps in England we should cultivate a Blakean or a Coleridgean Marxism, but the dovetailing of the two components would require the cutting away of a lot of dead wood — as has, I imagine, Timpanaro's grafting of Leopardi on to Marx.

double-bind hypothesis or Eric Berne's *Games People Play*, and is unaware of the intricacy of what goes on between modern analysts and their patients.

Secondly, Timpanaro seems not to have heard of transference and to be unaware of the enormous role it plays in analytical practice. As a result, he has no conception of psychoanalysis as a relationship between two people, as a therapeutic alliance, and tends to see it as a situation in which the patient submits himself to an analyst who utters dogmatic and arbitrary statements which the patient has to accept.

Thirdly, Timpanaro seems to think that symbolic interpretations are arbitrary; and, indeed, in the analytical literature they often seem to be so. But, as I have tried to show elsewhere, they are really based on the interpreter's understanding of metaphor, and it was only Freud's distrust of intuition and his obsession with causation that led him to present symbolism as an arbitrary discovery of psychoanalysis.

Fourthly, Timpanaro seems not to have discovered that psychoanalysis has become mother-orientated. Whereas in early Freudian days psychoanalysis was all about rivalry with the father, jealousy of the father, defiance of the father, submission to the father, nowadays the talk is all about the pre-oedipal relationship to the mother, the Primary Maternal Preoccupation displayed by the Good Enough Mother when she is adapting her infant to its Average Expectable Environment, even the infant's innate envy of its mother. Although this may perhaps be due to some social change – a shift towards matriarchy or matrism is discernible in other areas, too – it does mean that some of Timpanaro's remarks about Freudian theory 'eternalizing' the bourgeois family as Freud knew it fall wide of their mark and sound dated.

This is perhaps the place for me to mention that I was at times struck by some resemblance between Freud's and Timpanaro's habits of thought. They both seek to impress by a display of erudition; they both continue to drive home points long after they have made them; and they both seem to believe that 'correct' total interpretations or formulations are achievable. But this appearance of resemblance between them is perhaps a reflection of my insularity. As Timpanaro points out, English culture was never affected by continental romanticism, so Hegel and Nietzsche are not in my bones, while logical empiricism, to which Timpanaro is, he says, 'a stranger by intellectual background', is.

However, despite his anachronistic view of contemporary analytical practice, Timpanaro has, I think, put his finger on something amiss at the very centre of psychoanalytical theory. There is a peculiarity about the concept of the unconscious, though I do not think it helps much to call it collective or to discuss whether or to what extent it is a biological, romantic, materialist, idealist or vitalist concept. The point is rather that it is a concept owing its existence to the fallacy of reifying a quality. There never could be such a thing as an unconscious, since consciousness and unconsciousness can only be qualities or attributes of something else, in this case of the actions (including the thinking activity) of an agent, and as a result to speak of someone having an unconscious is loose thinking, analogous to speaking of someone having an anger when what we really mean is that they can at times be angry or act angrily. Dangerous and confusing things start happening if we forget that distinctions of quality require adverbs and adjectives rather than nouns for their formulation. It is one thing to say that people are sometimes unconscious of what they do or think, another thing to say that they have an unconscious.

Timpanaro is also right to mention that he is not entirely convinced that Freud was always honest. I too have often felt that there was something less than straightforward, something disingenuous, about his selection of which details about himself or his patients he should disclose or withhold on grounds of discretion, about his capacity to pass over obvious weaknesses in his arguments as though he had himself not noticed them, and about his tendency to have it both ways by offering incompatible interpretations simultaneously: as he does, for instance, in his analysis of the Wolf Man's infantile neurosis.

And, lastly, it must be true that psychoanalysis arose and took the form it did in response to specific social tensions and that it would cease to be of anything other than historical interest if ever those tensions were eliminated; a psychology that assumes the universality of neurosis would cease to make any sense in a world in which the only source of anxiety was man's mortality and biological frailty. But as, due to unforeseen circumstances, the revolution seems to have been postponed indefinitely, contemporary analysts and psychotherapists can, I think, work on without being unduly disturbed by the thought that their theory is 'neither a natural nor human science, but a self-confession by the bourgeoisie of its own misery and perfidy, which blends the bitter insight and ideological blindness of a class in decline'.

PS The slips occurring in a book on slips are possibly of some slight interest. One is a classic example of banalization. Dr Sachs's idiosyncratic and indeed affected spelling of his first name, Hanns, has reverted to the more familiar Hans, under the influence, no doubt, of the better-known Meistersinger of that name. Another is numerical, 1833 for 1883, and has Freud writing letters to his fiancée twenty-three years before he was born.

1976

6

Not So Much a Treatment,
More a Way of Life

'In lapidary inscriptions a man is not upon oath,' observed Dr
Johnson, and neither is he, I suppose, when writing blurbs,
introductions and forewords; particularly when, as in the present case, the book has been composed in a spirit of piety and
reverence. Anyone cursorily inspecting *The Wolf-Man by the
Wolf-Man*[1] would assume that it consisted of an autobiography
by an ex-patient of Freud's accompanied by a complementary
case history written by Freud; and, furthermore, that the autobiographical part would be illuminated by the insights which
its author had gained while being analysed. The blurb refers to
Freud's contribution as a 'complete case history' and, quoting
the editor's Introduction and Anna Freud's Foreword, asserts
that 'there is no other book which gives us the human story of
a struggling, passionate individual, seen from his own point of
view and from that of the founder of psychoanalysis', and that
it affords 'a unique opportunity to witness a human being's
inner and outer life unfold before our eyes from childhood to
old age'. Readers of the book will, however, discover that none
of these statements is strictly true. The book is, none the less,
of considerable interest.

In fact *The Wolf-man by the Wolf-Man* is a compilation of
eight discrete items, written at various dates between 1914 and
1968, involving not two but four authors (the Wolf-Man himself
and three analysts, Freud, Ruth Mack Brunswick and the 'editor', Muriel Gardiner); and, although it is indeed true that the

[1] Muriel Gardiner, ed., *The Wolf-Man by the Wolf-Man* (New York: Basic
Books, 1971).

Wolf-Man is seen from two different points of view – his own and that of the three analysts who have written about him – there is a curious disharmony between the points of view which makes it impossible to understand the connection between the Wolf-Man's life as he sees it and the 'inner life' attributed to him by the analysts. In addition to his analyses by Freud and Ruth Mack Brunswick and his friendship with Muriel Gardiner, the Wolf-Man has had psychotherapy from three other analysts during the course of his life.

But who is this mysterious Wolf-Man? He is an emigré Russian aristocrat, the son of a prominent liberal politician, who is now a widower aged 83 living in Vienna. In 1910, when 23 years old, he consulted Freud, who analysed him until 1914, when he returned to Russia apparently cured of a severe and complex neurosis after what in those days was a very long analysis. In 1919 he reappeared in Vienna, an impoverished emigré from the Soviet Union, and had a further few months' analysis from Freud, who treated him for nothing and in addition made an annual collection on his behalf from within psychoanalytical circles – and continued to do so for six years, after his analysis was over and after he had got a job in an insurance company. Between 1926 and 1927 he had a further five months' analysis from Ruth Mack Brunswick, again free, and was analysed by her again 'somewhat irregularly over a period of several years', starting in 1929. He was widowed in 1938, survived the Second World War, and in the last twenty-five years has been treated by three other unnamed analysts, one of whom is 'an analyst from abroad who has spent several weeks in Vienna almost every summer in order to see the Wolf-Man daily'.

The reason for the remarkable interest and concern in the Wolf-Man shown by the psychoanalytical movement – and for his peculiar pseudonym – is that in 1918 Freud published a paper entitled 'From the History of an Infantile Neurosis', in which he discussed in detail the theoretical implications of a nightmare the Wolf-Man had had just before his fifth birthday. In this nightmare he saw six or seven white wolves perched in a walnut tree outside his bedroom window.

It is this paper which is reprinted in the present volume as 'The Case of the Wolf-Man'. However, it is not, and was not intended to be, a case history of the Wolf-Man or even an account of his analysis. 'In spite of the patient's direct request,' writes Freud, 'I have abstained from writing a complete history of his illness, of his treatment, and of his recovery, because I recognized that such a task was technically impracticable and socially impermissible.' Nor does it concern the illness which brought the Wolf-Man into analysis in 1910, but an earlier neurosis from which he had suffered as a child.

Furthermore, the paper's avowed intention is not expository but polemical. It was, so Freud says in a footnote, written as a response to 'the twisted reinterpretations which C. G. Jung and Alfred Adler were endeavouring to give to the findings of psychoanalysis', and its main purpose was to demonstrate that the accounts given by analytical patients of having as children observed their parents' intercourse were not, as Jung apparently maintained, fantasies made up during their adult illness, but true recollections.

To this end Freud set out in this paper to analyse not his patient's adult neurosis but his infantile one, the formation of which could not, or so Freud thought, have been the result of the patient's attempt to retreat from facing his real-life problems, and the details of which could not have been distorted by any analyst's interpretative interventions, and to demonstrate that the infant Wolf-Man's nightmare was a symbolic representation of an act of parental intercourse which he had witnessed when he was aged one and a half. To be more specific, Freud sought in this paper to prove that it was a historical fact, demonstrable by psychoanalytical techniques, that on a summer afternoon in 1889 the Wolf-Man's parents had, at approximately five o'clock, interrupted their siesta to perform *coitus a tergo, more ferendo* – his mother crouched on all fours, his father standing behind her – and that this activity had woken up their son, who was sleeping in their bedroom during a bout of malaria.

In view of the ingenuity which Freud displays and the number of pages which he devotes to hammering home his point, it is disconcerting and indeed annoying to discover later in the paper that he is not altogether convinced by his own arguments. It is, he says, equally possible that the Wolf-Man had watched animals copulating on his father's country estate and had transposed his observations on to his parents. Nor, we discover even later, does Freud think that the matter is of any great importance, since 'phylogenetically inherited schemata' of the Oedipus complex make it inevitable that children should construct fantasies about their parents' sexual activities. If this is the case, then Freud's polemics with Adler and Jung must have been a storm in a tea-cup, and this paper should have been entitled 'Much Ado about Nothing'.

Although this paper's polemical intentions and theoretical obsessions make it valueless as biography, it is, of course, of considerable historical interest, particularly perhaps in showing the extent to which Freud was personally not wholly at ease with two of the concepts with which his name has become most closely associated: sexual symbolism and transference. We know from other sources that Freud, as a scientist, was embarrassed by the apparent arbitrariness of sexual symbolism (see his attitude towards Stekel) and that it took him years to accept the fact that transference was an essential part of psychoanalysis and not a regrettable distraction from it. His need to refer the Wolf-Man's dream back to putative real occurrences can be seen as an attempt to legitimize its sexual interpretation, while the fact that he spent hours of the Wolf-Man's analysis interpreting a childhood dream and reconstructing his infantile neurosis can itself be interpreted as a technique for distancing it (and himself) from the transference here and now.

A similar diffidence about making transference interpretations can also be discerned in Ruth Mack Brunswick's account of the Wolf-Man's second analysis. Throughout she refers everything back either to his childhood or to his transference on Freud, and asserts, despite obvious indications to the contrary, that the Wolf-Man's feelings about *her* were of little importance. 'It will be seen throughout the present analysis that my own role was almost negligible; I acted purely as mediator between the patient and Freud.' However, nearly twenty years after his last contact with her (and after her early death) he was speaking 'glowingly of how young, active and energetic she had been'. In fact, though neither Ruth Mack Brunswick herself nor the editor mentions it, she was ten years younger than the Wolf-Man, and, since by all accounts he was very attracted to women and by his own admission was pursued by younger women until he was well into his sixties, I find it impossible not to surmise that his wish as a man to impress her as a woman did not contribute to her outstanding therapeutic success with him.

At the risk of appearing facetious, I must make one further point before leaving the analysts' contribution to this book. Both the Wolf-Man's proper analyses centred round his sado-masochism, and one of the theoretical issues raised by his case is whether sadism is primary and masochism one of its vicissitudes, or vice versa; in ordinary language, whether sadists are sheep in wolf's clothing or masochists are wolves in sheep's clothing. Freud certainly thought that the Wolf-Man was a sheep in wolf's clothing, since he maintained that he had a primary feminine wish to be, as Strachey infelicitously translates it, 'copulated with by' his father, and interprets the wolf-dream as representing his wish to take his mother's place in the parental intercourse he had observed. But the Wolf-Man, I suspect, sees it the other way round. Why else should he be proud of his analytical nickname and prefer to be known by it long after all conceivable practical reasons for concealing his real name (patronymic) have vanished? Incidentally, sheep do figure in the material presented by Freud, who also insists that the animals which the Wolf-Man may have seen copulating were sheep-dogs.

Of the two items in this book written by the Wolf-Man himself, one is his 'Memoirs', which takes his life up to 1938, and the other is 'My Recollections of Sigmund Freud'. (His life from 1938 to the present is covered by four pieces written by the editor.)

'My Recollections of Sigmund Freud' leaves the reader with the impression that he and Freud spent much of his analysis chatting about art and literature, but this need not be taken too seriously, since it is quite patently tendentious. It is designed to impress on the reader that the Wolf-Man was no ordinary patient but a privileged intimate of the founder of psychoanalysis, though in fact there is little here that could not have been concocted by an enterprising journalist familiar with Freud's writings. (According to Ruth Mack Brunswick the Wolf-Man talked to her as though he was much more intimate with Freud and the Freud family than in fact he was.) Personally I received the impression from these recollections that the Jewish analyst and the gentile nobleman must have simultaneously deferred to and patronized one another, Freud expressing his admiration for his patient's high intelligence, as exemplified by his ready understanding of Freudian theory – 'he even once said it would be good if all his pupils could grasp the nature of analysis as soundly as I' – the patient complimenting Freud on his exceptional understanding of himself, which was in such striking contrast to that of the previous psychiatrists he had employed. In this context a remark in a letter of the Wolf-Man's, written in 1970, is revealing: 'Professor Freud also had a great deal of personal understanding for me, as he often told me during the treatment.' I find it impossible to resist the conclusion that intellectual and social snobbery played a larger part in the extended relationship between the Wolf-Man and the analysts than any of them would care to admit.

And money too. According to Ruth Mack Brunswick the fees the Wolf-Man paid Freud during his first, pre-war analysis were of a size which absolved him from any realistic need to feel guilty about receiving free treatment after he had become a penniless emigré, while it is clear that throughout the 1920s and 1930s, and again after the Second World War, money flowed, albeit in driblets, in the opposite direction, i.e. from analysts to the Wolf-Man. Although the editor refrains with old-fashioned delicacy from discussing the matter openly, there is enough evidence scattered throughout the book to make it clear that there were (and perhaps still are) financial advantages attached to being the psychoanalytical movement's prize patient – Russian lessons could be given, paintings (including ones of the famous dream) could be sold.

I would not touch on the still taboo subjects of snobbery and money, were it not for the fact that there is something suspiciously extravagant and excessive about this book's frequent references to the Wolf-Man's exceptional intelligence and sensibility, and to the fortitude with which he has faced adversity. There is also, I feel, a note of special pleading in the reasons given for his remaining in Vienna, where as a result of the collapse of the Austro-Hungarian Empire employment, particularly perhaps for educated people, was peculiarly hard to get, instead of moving elsewhere or perhaps even returning to Russia. Muriel Gardiner states categorically that as the son of a well-known liberal politician he would have been shot on his return to Russia, but his mother, the politician's widow, stayed there until 1923 and returned there again, apparently of her own free will, in 1924 for an unspecified number of years, after which she moved first to Prague and later to Vienna, where she lived with her widowed son until her death in 1953. (For psychoanalytical *cognoscenti*: the role of money in the Wolf-Man's attachment to the psychoanalytical movement was 'over-determined'. Both Freud and Mack Brunswick state that he unconsciously equated money and faeces, while the latter states that the symptom which necessitated his second analysis with Freud was constipation. This was interpreted as a manifestation of unresolved transference. Mack Brunswick also states that the Wolf-Man blamed Freud for having dissuaded him from returning to Russia in 1920 'to save the family fortune' by insisting that his desire to do so was merely a resistance against further analysis.)

The remarkable thing about 'The Memoirs of the Wolf-Man' is that, with one dramatic exception, it is so unremarkable. Although the Wolf-Man does sometimes tell us that Freud attached significance to some event he is describing, and even occasionally tells us how Freud interpreted it, his memoirs are conspicuously not replete with analytical insights, and the reader is given no clue as to whether or not he acquired any deeper understanding of himself or others during his years with Freud. For the most part the Memoirs keep to the surface of things and long passages convey exactly the flavour one would expect from the reminiscences of a reasonably intelligent aristo-crat who has survived a revolution and fallen on hard times. Places visited, persons met are mentioned and commented upon in conventional terms – 'I noticed that in Tiflis there already existed streetcars, something which did not yet exist in Odessa', 'Captain L.'s hobby was mathematics, and one could say that he knew Einstein's theory of relativity inside out' – and parts of it are quite amusing, notably his accounts of the various private sanatoria he stayed in before his analysis with Freud. These must have been the most extraordinary places, more like luxury hotels than hospitals, and it is difficult to see what useful function they fulfilled – apart, of course, from providing the very rich with excuses for making trips abroad and transferring their money into more deserving pockets. At one near Frankfurt it was compulsory to dress for dinner and 'every male patient was assigned to a young lady – all supposedly girls from good families'. While staying in one at Munich, where his physician, the great Professor Kraepelin, visited him once a fortnight, the Wolf-Man took rooms in the town where he spent nights with the nurse whom he eventually married.

In one respect, the picture evoked by these memoirs does not tally with that presented by Freud and Ruth Mack Brunswick. They both assert that prior to his first analysis the Wolf-Man was totally incapacitated and incapable even of dressing himself. The memoirs show that a doctor often formed part of his travelling entourage and that he had a valet, but they also show that his trips abroad were both planned and conducted in an almost leisurely manner, and there is no hint that he was ever incapable of engaging in all the usual activities of rich young men travelling abroad: sight-seeing, meeting friends and womanizing. On one occasion the Wolf-Man had to cut short a trip to Spain, where he did not visit any sanatoria or consult any specialists – indeed this was after he had started his analysis – on account of his physician's neurotic dislike of the country. I suspect that accompanying rich aristocrats on their trips abroad was a recognized way by which Russian doctors ob-tained a free holiday, and the aristocrats obtained educated male travelling companions.

The one dramatic theme in this otherwise pedestrian story is the Wolf-Man's account of his courtship and marriage. This is so extraordinary, and indeed so horrifying, that I am loath to take the edge off any reader's surprise by saying much about it. But, briefly, he fell in love with his wife at first sight on his first night at Professor Kraepelin's sanatorium, married her six years later against his mother's wishes but with Freud's approval, and apparently adored her until her carefully planned but apparently motiveless suicide fourteen years later. Purely by chance, he discovered after her death that her account of her ancestry, which he had accepted without question and which had always formed an important ingredient of his romantic conception of her, was untrue and presumably a delusion. There is no evidence anywhere in this book that Freud or Ruth Mack Brunswick, or indeed anyone else, was ever at all curious about what kind of woman the Wolf-Man had married.

1971

7

Soul Murder

Of recent years the English reading public has become familiar, largely through the writings of R. D. Laing, with the idea that schizophrenia is not a disease with as yet unidentified biochemical or genetic causes, but is a disturbance in communicative functions engendered by a specific and peculiar type of family. This idea is attractive, not only because there may be some truth in it, but also for two other reasons. It provides a social explanation of schizophrenia which is comprehensible to people who lack any training in medicine or the biological sciences, and it can be formulated in terms of villains and victims. In a popular version of the theory, the patient whom psychiatrists label 'schizophrenic' is presented as being the victim and scapegoat of a vicious family constellation, at the centre of which stands a villainous 'schizophrenogenic' mother who bludgeons, bewitches and bewilders her offspring and drives some of them crazy.

In fact, this theory of schizophrenogenesis derives from a highly abstract paper by Gregory Bateson published in 1956, in which the mother, whose propensity to issue contradictory and confusing injunctions is adduced as the proximate cause of her child's schizophrenia, is presented as being as much a victim of the morbid family process as her children. It remains, however, a peculiarity of the theory that it is extraordinarily difficult to illustrate without evoking partisan sympathy for the schizophrenic patient, who is usually presented as young and sensitive, and hostility for her mother, who is usually presented as middle-aged and obtuse.

In *Soul Murder*[1] Dr Morton Schatzman, an American counter-culture psychiatrist working in London, offers a variation on this theme which is remarkable in a number of respects. Firstly, the victim–patient is a deceased middle-aged German judge, Daniel Paul Schreber (1842–1911). Secondly, the schizophrenogenic parent is his father, a distinguished nineteenth-century German physician and pedagogue, Daniel Gottlieb Moritz Schreber (1808–61). Thirdly, the evidence or clinical data consists of books written by both father and son. And fourthly, the son's illness was analysed by Freud in 1911 in a paper in which he interpreted the son's paranoid delusions of being persecuted by God as the reversal of repressed homosexual longings for his father. This paper is still regarded as one of Freud's major works and his explanation of the origin of delusions of being persecuted is still widely accepted among psychoanalysts.

As Schatzman points out, one of the most extraordinary features of Freud's paper is that it is based solely on Senatspräsident Schreber's *Memoirs of My Nervous Illness* without any reference to the works of his father, many if not all of which were still in print in 1911. Freud seems to have accepted without question the received opinion that Schreber père was an admirable person, 'by no means unsuitable for transfiguration into a God in the affectionate memory of the son', and the idea of correlating the son's account of his illness with the hygienic and character-training techniques advocated in the father's books did not occur to him.

Schatzman, however, does not appreciate – or perhaps he thought it irrelevant to his theme – that there is something strange about Freud having written the paper at all. Freud had only limited clinical experience of schizophrenic and paranoid patients, he never met Schreber in any capacity, and, according to Jones, he said that he had learned 'the secret of paranoia' from his friend and father-figure Fliess, the ENT specialist who played a catalytic role in his self-analysis. Furthermore, two months before writing the paper, Freud had written to Ferenczi:

[1] Morton Schatzman, *Soul Murder: Persecution in the Family* (London: Allen Lane, 1973).

'Since Fliess's case, with the overcoming of which you recently saw me involved, that need (to uncover my personality completely) has been extinguished. A part of homosexual cathexis has been withdrawn and made use of to enlarge my own ego. I have succeeded where the paranoiac fails.' Freud must, then, have had his personal reasons for writing about paranoia and for wanting to believe that it originated in love for a father who deserved to be held in 'affectionate memory'.

However, whatever may be the truth about Freud's father, Schatzman demonstrates convincingly that Schreber's father was a man who may perhaps have been revered by his children, but who could hardly have been held in affectionate memory. He belonged to that class of persons who assume that a father is God's representative within the family, who demand blind obedience of their children, and who believe that the first duty of parents is to break their children's spirit and ensure that they identify completely with the moral standards that they, the parents, incarnate. He was, however, unusual in insisting that the task of breaking a child's spirit should begin at birth and in having been able to use his prestige as a physician to invade the nursery and enforce disciplinary regimens, including the use of mechanical restraints, designed to nip all signs of self-will and degeneracy ('innate barbarity') in the bud. By collating the father's account of how he brought up his children with the son's account of his mental illness, Schatzman has no difficulty in showing that many of the son's hallucinations and delusions were replicas and transformations of physical assaults he must have suffered as a child, and that his ideas about God, by whom he believed he was both persecuted and loved, applied all too aptly to his father. He also argues convincingly that the son was unable to react to his father's persecution with resentment and hatred, since it was represented to him as evidence of his father's devotion.

Dr Schatzman does not, however, address himself to the other side of paranoia, the delusions of grandeur which invariably accompany those of persecution; according to Schreber fils, in a passage which Schatzman does not quote, 'he who entered into a special relationship with divine rays as I have is to a

certain extent entitled to shit on all the world'. The reason for
this omission is that Schatzman, despite his overt claim to be
making a contribution to the psychopathology of paranoia, is
in fact basically concerned with politics. He is interested in
the Schrebers not as an example of a schizophrenogenic or
paranogenic family but as a paradigm of the Reichian authoritarian family. As a result he is concerned primarily to prove
that Schreber père was a tyrant and his son a victim of oppression, and only secondarily is the tragedy of the family considered as a whole. And, in this context, an investigation of the
connections between arrogance and feelings of being persecuted
might well have proved embarrassing. In fact, Schatzman is
confused about the relation between tragedy and politics. On
the one hand, he makes no attempt whatsoever to understand
sympathetically the religious position that compelled Schreber
père to persecute his children in this world in the hope of
protecting them from eternal damnation in the next; but, on
the other, he does discuss briefly the possibility that the father
might have become melancholic, had he not persecuted children.

1973

8

Freud: Living and Dying

In 1915, while a medical student, Dr Max Schur, the author of *Freud: Living and Dying*,[1] attended the course of lectures which were later published as the *Introductory Lectures on Psycho-Analysis*. After qualification, he practised internal medicine and in 1928 became Freud's physician, as such responsible for the management of the after-effects of the cancer of the maxilla which Freud had developed in 1923 – and of the surgery with which it had been treated. With one short interval he remained Freud's physician until the latter's death in 1939, becoming in the meantime a psychoanalyst himself. After Freud's death he settled in New York, publishing numerous papers, of which at least two can be regarded as biographical essays on Freud. He himself died in 1969 after having devoted many years to the preparation of the present volume.

Schur was therefore uniquely placed to write a monograph on Freud's last illness. Even though he only came on the scene five years after the diagnosis of cancer had been made and the crucial surgery performed, he had, of course, access to the earlier medical reports and knowledge of the standing and professional reputations of the various physicians and surgeons who had already treated Freud. However, Schur decided not to confine himself to matters which came within his own personal experience and professional competence as a physician, but to embark on a much more ambitious project – a psychoanalytical study of Freud's attitude to death and his relationships with men

[1] Max Schur, *Freud: Living and Dying* (New York: International Universities Press, 1972).

(Freud's 'latent homosexuality', in both his own and Schur's terminology).

To my mind this decision of Schur's was unfortunate, even though – in view of his intimate knowledge of Freud as a friend and patient and his interest in psychoanalytical theory – one can easily understand and sympathize with his reasons for making it.

My reason for regretting that Schur did not resist the temptation to venture on a full-scale psychoanalytical study of Freud is twofold. First, Schur lacked the literary skill which might have enabled him successfully to marry a clinical account of Freud's illness and a human one of Freud's courage and endurance in the face of suffering. The sheer accumulation of clinical detail given in Schur's last ten chapters does indeed leave the reader, especially if he himself happens to be medically qualified, in no doubt that Freud both suffered appallingly and bore suffering with fortitude, but Schur's shifts from writing a case report to writing a human document, and from biography to autobiography, also leave him exhausted and confused.

Nor, incidentally, is Schur altogether successful in handling two embarrassing facts which emerge from his account of Freud's illness. Freud behaved unwisely, and arguably even irresponsibly, when he first noticed that he had a growth in his mouth; and he was himself responsible for much of his suffering, since many of his later operations were the result of his refusal to give up smoking. 'Refusal' rather than 'inability' is unfortunately the right word; although Schur talks about Freud's 'nicotine addiction', he also states unequivocally that he was capable of giving up smoking for weeks on end, but that the condition of his mouth was never his reason for doing so.

Secondly, Schur brought to his project a quality which I can only call intellectual innocence. He seems to have written *Freud: Living and Dying* without realizing the necessity of constructing any clear image in his mind of whom he was writing it for, and oblivious of the ironies and paradoxes involved in applying psychoanalytical concepts to the very person who first conceived them – and indeed of the methodological pitfalls that surround psychoanalytical biographies in general.

According to the introduction 'this book addresses itself not only to students of the behavioral sciences' but also to everyone interested in the application of psychoanalytical ideas to 'education, anthropology, literature and sociology'. None the less Schur uses not only psychoanalytical but also medical technical terms without explanation, so that in fact whole sections of the book will only be comprehensible to psychoanalytically trained doctors. He is also entirely haphazard in his selection of which characters mentioned in the text require introducing to the reader and what terms, social conventions, etc., require explanation. In general he assumes that his readers will be familiar with the names and careers of all the early analysts, even to the extent of knowing why Marie Bonaparte's analysis had frequently to be interrupted on account of her 'manifold private and social responsibilities', but at the same time finds it necessary to enlighten them as to the meaning of 'goy' and 'in partibus infidelium'. His definition of the latter is, incidentally, incorrect.

Schur's obliviousness of the fact that there is something ironical and paradoxical about using Freudian ideas to analyse Freud himself shows itself in at least two different ways.

Firstly, one of Schur's aims in writing this book was undoubtedly to affirm that Freud displayed exceptional courage and endurance in the face of illness and death, and that he achieved, after his self-analysis, an unshakeable serenity, which enabled him, despite residual neurotic symptoms, despite occasional depressive moods, despite freedom from illusions, and despite years of continual physical pain, to remain creative and capable of enjoying life until the end. But it does not seem to have occurred to Schur that courage, endurance and serenity are virtues which belong to a system of moral values which Freud himself unwittingly did much to undermine by his advocacy of psychic determinism. It is, after all, illogical to admire moral attributes if one believes that will is an illusion and that all behaviour is causally determined, and paradoxical to admire them in the very person who converted the world to a determinist view of human nature.

Schur's book is indeed a pretty example of the point made by Geoffrey Gorer in his essay in *Psychoanalysis Observed*, that, in practice, Freudian concepts are only invoked to explain what used to be called vices and never to explain virtues. 'I know of no studies to show people are not *really* responsible for their heroism or piety, their diligence or their integrity.'

Schur does, however, have interesting things to say about *how* Freud retained his serenity throughout his illness and pain. He argues convincingly that Freud's formulation of the death instinct concept (to which Schur himself does not subscribe) 'enabled him to deal better with his own fear of death', and that his refusal to give up smoking derived from his conviction that it enabled him to remain creative – presumably, though Schur does not quite say so, by helping him to 'bind' anxiety.

Secondly, Schur seems not to appreciate that there is something tautological about analysing Freud in terms of his own ideas. If one grants, as one obviously must, that Freud was an honest and creative person, then the ideas which he formulated during his self-analysis must of necessity correspond in some way to his personality. To reapply these ideas to Freud, as Schur does, is therefore to do no more than reassert the existence of the correspondence which can be originally assumed. This tautology can, of course, be obviated in three different ways: by demonstrating that Freud's genius resided precisely in a degree of detachment which enabled him to observe himself as though he were someone else; by showing that many of the concepts used by Freud in his self-analysis in fact arose during his contact with his patients, in which case he would have been analysed as much by them as by himself; and, thirdly, by showing that the concepts Freud arrived at during his self-analysis are as applicable to others as to himself. This last course was that adopted by Freud himself, and it would be possible to describe the development of psychoanalysis as a process by which Freud's private, introspective hunches have been sifted clinically, by himself and his followers, some becoming public, scientific concepts and others being discarded.

Unfortunately, however, Freud's authority has been such that ideas which should perhaps have remained part of his own private myth have become accepted as universally valid. This is, I suspect, true of two concepts used by Schur in analysing

Freud's attitude to death; as a result, Schur's interpretation of Freud's personality is in all essentials identical with Freud's own conception of himself.

The two concepts I have in mind are, first, that relationships with men can be explained in terms of 'latent homosexuality', and, secondly, that the ego has a 'narcissistic libidinal cathexis' derived from its identification with (introjection of) *past* lost and abandoned objects – in other words, that homosexuality is an instinct, against which defences have to be erected before 'aim-inhibited', 'sublimated' friendships with men can develop (rather than, as some contemporary analysts including myself would hold, a defensive strategy used by people with conflicts about power and doubts about their sexual identity) and that the core of the ego is self-love and not a sense of community or identity with *present* objects.

These two ideas, 'latent homosexuality' and the narcissism of the ego, play an essential part in both Freud's general theory of the origin of the fear of death (which Freud assumed to be universal) and in Schur's specific interpretation of Freud's personal attitude to death. The intimate connection between them can be demonstrated by juxtaposing two apparently unconnected quotations from Freud, but before doing so it is necessary to summarize briefly the thread of Freud's biography with which Schur is particularly concerned.

Freud's father died in 1896 at the advanced age of eighty-one, when Freud himself was aged forty. Freud reacted to his father's death by something other and more than normal grief. Why this was so does not emerge from either Schur's or Jones's account, but Freud's later writings on religion suggest that he must have deified (or idealized) him. In any case, he developed anxiety, depression and other neurotic symptoms, and embarked on his self-analysis. Although much of this self-analysis consisted of writing *The Interpretation of Dreams*, another component of it was his relationship with Wilhelm Fliess, a nose and throat specialist in Berlin who was addicted to what now seem merely fanciful numerological speculations about biological periodicity. Fliess and Freud corresponded regularly and met for 'congresses'. Their conversations were not recorded and Fliess's letters to Freud do not survive, but Freud's to Fliess do, and form the basis of our knowledge of what Jones called 'the only really extraordinary experience in Freud's life'.

According to Schur, Freud's letters to Fliess display 'transference-like manifestations with their effusive admiration and hidden, denied ambivalence', while Jones refers to the relationship as a 'passionate friendship'. Both agree that Freud identified Fliess with his father, though in other respects their interpretations of the 'Fliess episode' do not always tally.

However, like so many passionate friendships between men, that between Freud and Fliess ended bitterly. Freud eventually found it impossible to conceal from either himself or Fliess his disbelief in Fliess's numerological theories, and was also deeply mortified by Fliess's dismissal of his psychological theories with 'the thought-reader merely reads his own thoughts into other people'; while Fliess, in 1906, some years after intimacy between the two had ceased, publicly charged Freud with leaking his (Fliess's) ideas about bisexuality to one of his patients.

However, in 1910 Freud was still preoccupied with Fliess, as a letter to Ferenczi shows (Schur, p. 256):

> You not only noticed, but also understood, that I no longer have any need to uncover my personality completely, and you correctly traced this back to the traumatic reason for it. Since Fliess's case, with the overcoming of which you recently saw me occupied, that need has been extinguished. A part of homosexual cathexis has been withdrawn and made use of to enlarge my own ego. I have succeeded where the paranoiac fails.

In other words, Freud, in his own view, recovered from the loss of his friendship with Fliess at the cost of losing his need and capacity for intimacy and by becoming more than averagely self-sufficient and narcissistic.

This is the first of the two quotations I wish to juxtapose. The other is from *The Ego and the Id* (Schur, p. 367):

> It would seem that the mechanism of the fear of death can only be that the ego relinquishes its narcissistic libidinal cathexis in a very large measure – that is, that it gives up itself, just as it gives up some *external* object in other cases in which it feels anxiety. I believe that the fear of death is something that occurs between the ego and the super-ego.

Now, although this second quotation purports to be an objective and generally applicable explanation of the fear of death, comparison with the first, admittedly subjective letter entitles one to question its universal validity. It is, in fact, by no means self-evident that Freud's relationship with his father and then Fliess has its counterpart in everyone's biography, nor that everyone becomes so preoccupied with their *past* objects that their attitude to death can be explained without reference to their *present* ones. Freud's idea that 'the fear of death is something that occurs between the ego and the super-ego' assumes, it seems to me, a greater degree of internalization, introversion and self-sufficiency than is usual, and ignores completely the role played by fear of separation from those who are loved now and concern for the future of those who will be left behind.

There is, however, no need to believe that Freud's explanation of the fear of death was true even for himself, since to do so would be to take it for granted that the surviving, written evidence, whether personal or theoretical, left by Freud is an accurate and complete reflection of his attitude towards living and dying. Inhibitions, personal reserve, social conventions, the fact that people have no need to write long letters to those they live with and see daily, and the further fact that many people adopt a specific stance when they put pen to paper or only do so in particular moods, may all contribute to a biased weighting of the available written evidence. Although Freud wrote more about his (and other people's) relationships with his father and other men, he also had largely unrecorded relationships with his mother, his wife, his sisters and his daughters.

Schur, I think, fails to appreciate this methodological pitfall to psychoanalytical biography. He also falls into the rather similar trap of interpreting single threads in Freud's life in isolation from its total pattern. For instance, he discusses Freud's 'latent homosexuality' in relation to his father, to Fliess and to his disciples, but not in relation to his brothers and sons, and does so as though it were possible to interpret a man's attitude to other men without considering his attitude towards women. Although Schur may perhaps have had good discretionary reasons for restricting himself in this way, he gives no indication of appreciating the extent to which he diminished the psycho-analytical value of his book by doing so.

He seems also to have been oblivious of one further catch about writing psychoanalytical biographies. This is that what is sauce for the goose is sauce for the gander. Schur assumes that his knowledge of psychoanalytical theory enables him to make valid interpretations about Freud's unconscious motives, and to use slips of the pen and even turns of phrase as evidence of, for instance, Freud's unconscious ambivalence towards father-figures. But since Freud was patently a father-figure to Schur, the same assumption would enable and entitle any reader of Schur to recognize and draw attention to evidence of Schur's unconscious hostility towards Freud. I shall, however, refrain from doing so.

1972

9

Carl Jung and Analytical Psychology

Carl Jung's *Analytical Psychology*[1] makes generally available the text of five lectures he gave, in English, to the Institute of Medical Psychology (the Tavistock Clinic) in London in 1935. Jung seems to have delivered the lectures without reference to a prepared script and to have answered questions as fluently as he lectured, and one is immediately impressed by his mastery of colloquial English and by his artistry in putting across in a foreign language not only his theory of psychology but also his own conception of himself.

This is, I think, the right way to put it. These lectures do not reveal Jung's personality; rather, they portray the persona he wished to present. C. G. Jung, Jung clearly wished his English audience to believe, was a direct man, down-to-earth even when scaling the heights or plumbing the depths, a countryman more at home with peasants and aristocrats than with urban middle-class intellectuals, too virile and familiar with the facts of nature to have much time for those sex cases which so interested Freud, but none the less, as befits a pastor's son, heir to the Christian spiritual tradition. At times it is clear that he is contrasting himself with Freud but wishes his audience to appreciate that he is too much of a gentleman to do so explicitly.

Of course, Jung may really have been like his persona. But his *Memories, Dreams, Reflections*, which led some reviewers to label him psychotic, reads to me like the account of a life-long identity crisis, and it is hard not to suspect him of attitudinizing.

[1] C. G. Jung, *Analytical Psychology: Its Theory and Practice* (New York: Pantheon, 1968).

One of the unexpected and confusing consequences of the rise
of dynamic psychology has been the fact that its practitioners,
if sufficiently distinguished, are able to foist on to their suc-
cessors their own idea of themselves, using their professional
prestige and skills to get it accepted. Both Freud and Jung seem
to have built into their theories and writings a conception and
an interpretation of their own personalities, and to have done
so so successfully that it seems almost impertinent to wonder
whether they may after all *not* have been exceptions to the rule
that it is not given to man to be objective about himself, that
we are not in a position 'to see ourselves as others see us'.

In view of the history of Jung's personal relationship with
Freud and of the fact that Freud's ideas have achieved wider
acceptance than Jung's, it is impossible to read these lectures
without speculating how far the divergences between Freudian
and Jungian theories are really substantial and to what extent
they merely reflect incompatible temperaments. Certainly there
are real theoretical differences. For instance, Jung held that the
ego has its own sources of energy, and therefore asserted the
reality of will, whereas Freud held that the ego borrowed
energy from the id, and therefore asserted the inevitability of
unconscious causation. But some of the divergences between
them seem to be artefacts of their dissimilar uses of metaphor
and of their having chosen different bridges by which to establish connections between the psychology of the unconscious
and existing aspects of culture.

Both Freud and Jung seem to have felt it necessary to make
a crucial, though to my mind unnecessary, step from fact to
metaphor by writing as though unconscious mental processes
were entities, things occupying a space: the unconscious. They
both drew diagrams of the mind and located different sorts of
mental activity at different points on the diagram. Inevitably,
however, the decision as to where to locate any particular
process or function on the diagram has effects on its theoretical
relation with other processes which derive as much from the
facts of geometry as from those of psychology. The best example
of this metaphorical artefact is provided by those functions
which are traditionally described as higher, finer and spiritual

and which from an evolutionary standpoint must be regarded as late developments of human nature. Freud discussed these in terms of sublimations and ego-functions and located them in the ego, but Jung discussed them in terms of symbols of transformation and, using imagery derived from one of his own dreams, located them below Freud's unconscious, in a lower storey, which he called the collective unconscious. As a result, the fact that human beings, at a certain level of evolutionary development, produce myths, religions, arts and sciences is explained in contradictory ways by the two systems of thought. But both explanations can be seen to be erroneous and indeed otiose once one remembers that the unconscious is only a metaphor and that mental processes do not really take place inside anything and do not have spatial relations to one another.

One cannot, incidentally, help regretting that none of the pioneers of the unconscious thought naturally in auditory, musical terms. If they had, we would perhaps have a psychology in which thoughts are conceived of as themes, which can occur in different modes and keys, which can vary in their audibility, which can be harmonious or discordant, and which can undergo development and variation.

Jung's location of the symbols of transformation in the collective unconscious is only one of several formulations which seem topsy-turvy to anyone who has become acclimatized to the Freudian view that psychology should be based on the physical and biological sciences. While reading these lectures I several times found myself feeling that it might be possible to find some single conversion factor which could be used to transform Jung into Freud, or vice versa. However, although their diagrams of the mind tally, more or less, if one is rotated through ninety degrees, the relationship between them is really more complex. If one is the right way up, the other is not only upside-down but also inside out. Perhaps a suitable subject for a Ph.D. thesis by someone interested in both linguistics and geometry would be: 'Some unexpected and unintended consequences of the use of spatial metaphors in psychology, as exemplified by the theories of Freud and Jung'.

Some of the divergences between Freud and Jung are, however, better attributed to the fact that they chose opposed solutions to the problem of how to imbed the idea of the unconscious into existing traditions of Western thought. Freud opted for the scientific solution, attempting to show that psychoanalysis was a logical development of rationalism, an extension of the methods of the physical and biological sciences into psychology, and as such deserving the respect and prestige which contemporary culture accords scientific endeavour. Hence his likening of his discoveries to those of Galileo and Darwin. Jung, on the other hand, proceeded in a more dialectical manner, claiming that the psychology of the unconscious constituted a rediscovery of insights which had been overlaid and forgotten by the scientific revolution of the seventeenth to the nineteenth centuries. Hence his interest in alchemy and medieval cosmology. He writes in this volume:

We take up the torch that was abandoned by our old colleagues of the seventeenth century when they put it down in order to become chemists. In so far as we psychologists are emerging from chemical and material conceptions of the psyche, we are taking up that torch again, continuing a process which began in the West in the twelfth century – for alchemy was the work of the doctors who were busy with the mind.

To Freud and Jung these two solutions must have seemed irreconcilable. But now, a generation later, it seems less certain that allegiance to the scientific tradition involves a reductionist approach to the religious quest, or that a concern with transcendence involves a dismissive attitude towards the material, biological origins of the psyche.

1969

PSYCHOANALYSTS
AND OTHERS

10

Psychoanalysis and Beyond

Readers of Peter Fuller's Introduction and of my various articles in this book will appreciate that I trained and began practice as an analyst in an intellectual climate that was both controversial and confusing. On the one hand there was a group of analysts centred around Anna Freud who claimed, with historical justice, to be Sigmund Freud's legitimate intellectual heirs and believed that intensive study of Freud's writings was the royal road to learning the theory and practice of psychoanalysis. On the other was another group centred round Melanie Klein who similarly claimed, with, I think, less justice, to be true followers of Freud, but who none the less believed that immersion in Melanie Klein's writings and a Kleinian analysis was the only true path to the depths of the unconscious.

And in between these two largely, but not quite exclusively, foreign and German-speaking groups was a third, largely English-speaking, group which was at first only definable in rather negative terms. It did not, to begin with at any rate, have a generally accepted leader, and when Winnicott became its main spokesman and figurehead, he consistently denied that he was its leader and even that there was any group for him to lead. But in so far as one can attribute qualities to a group that denied that it was one and would only use the neutral terms 'middle' and, later, 'independent' to describe itself, it can be said that it repudiated the idea of any royal road to becoming an analyst – even to the extent of encouraging its trainee analysts to have part of their training under the supervision of a member of one of the other two groups – and that it attempted to steer a middle course between what it felt to be the rigidity of the

Anna Freud group and the intensity and exclusiveness of the Kleinians. It was, in fact, all very English, very liberal, very eclectic, and at times, perhaps, wishy-washy.

Both my two training analysts, Ella Sharpe and Sylvia Payne, were members of the Middle Group. The latter was, indeed, the main architect of the arrangement by which these three groups or schools of psychoanalysis, all claiming legitimate descent from Freud but in fact divergent in their interpretations of his message, contrived to remain (as they still do) within the same organization: the British Psycho-Analytical Society. However, although my own analyst was the main architect of this arrangement, and although, too, its formal structure came into being while I was a student, it was only some years after I had qualified as an analyst and set up in practice that I realized what intense loyalties and enmities were imperfectly concealed behind a façade of tolerance and broad-mindedness. And only then did I appreciate that the divergences of opinion about theory between the three groups really were differences of substance; that Anna Freud, Melanie Klein and D. W. Winnicott really did have different conceptions of human nature, of health, of how an analysis should be conducted and what constituted a successful one. Anna Freud and her circle seemed to believe that the aim of analysis was understanding and mastery of man's inheritance of uncivilized and unruly impulses; Melanie Klein and her circle that it was reconciliation to man's original and innate propensity to destructiveness, greed and envy; while Winnicott was a meliorist, believing in the efficacy of maternal love in leading man towards faith, hope and charity.

It was, indeed, all most confusing, and several of my own early writings, those collected in *Imagination and Reality*, were attempts to sort myself out, to discover how much value I could attach to the libido theory and the mechanism of defence as taught by Anna Freud, to Melanie Klein's views on symbol formation, to Winnicott's and Marion Milner's on illusion and disillusion. Most of them were in fact first read to Scientific Meetings of the British Psycho-Analytical Society, at which Anna Freud, Melanie Klein and Winnicott were present – or were conspicuous by their absence – and their contributions to the discussions afterwards had to be scanned as much for their often condescending tones of disapproval or approval as for any substantial contribution they might be making to the topic of the paper.

In the early 1960s, however, it occurred to me that there was really no reason why I should continue to feel constricted by such an inbred, politicizing atmosphere, in which attempts to be broad-minded were all too liable to be interpreted as trimming, and that it should be possible to take up a stance external to both psychoanalysis as a theoretical system and the psychoanalytical movement as a socio-historical phenomenon; one which would, hopefully, enable me to be objective about both. To this end I read, and on occasion reviewed, books about such disciplines as ethology, linguistics and communications theory, which clearly had a direct relevance to analytical theory and practice, and also read widely but in a rather haphazard fashion books on the sociology and history of political and religious movements, to which the psychoanalytical movement seemed to bear a disconcerting resemblance. In taking up such a wider viewpoint I was, of course, much assisted by the fact that I had read history at Cambridge before training in medicine and psychoanalysis – and by the happy chance that James Mitchell, then a director at Nelson, invited me to compose a dictionary of psychoanalytical terms. Writing this book, which was published in 1968 under the title *A Critical Dictionary of Psychoanalysis*, enabled, compelled me to take all current psychoanalytical theories and systems to pieces so that they could be subsumed into sets of cross-referring dictionary entries. And it also helped me, I like to think, to convert a retreat and withdrawal that could have been entirely negative into a positive, constructive contribution to knowledge. I was enabled to compose a conspectus or panorama that embraced the ideas of Freud and all the British analysts who had been writing, teaching and propagandizing while I was a student and a junior analyst – Anna Freud, Melanie Klein, Winnicott, Fairbairn, Michael Balint, Marion Milner – and to include in addition entries referring to Jung and to the earlier writings of Laing and Gregory Bateson.

Slightly earlier I had also written a paper, which I did not read to a Scientific Meeting of the British Psycho-Analytical Society but which was included in *Imagination and Reality*, enumerating what were to my mind the essential theoretical differences between Middle Group thinking and classical Freudian theory. I entitled this paper 'Beyond the Reality Principle', partly in the hope of being provocative – in 1920 Freud called one of his papers 'Beyond the Pleasure Principle' – and partly to emphasize that its main contention was that Freud's conceptions of the ego and its adaptation to reality were restrictive and impoverishing and failed to take proper account of the role played by imagination and emotion in healthy and creative living.

By assuming, as Freud did in his theoretical writings but not always in his clinical papers, that the unconscious, the id, was 'a chaos, a cauldron of seething excitement . . . which was a slave to the pleasure principle and neglected the reality of the external world' and had therefore to be repressed, modified and organized before an integrated, rational and realistic ego could develop, Freud was, it seemed – and still seems – to me, taking an intellectualist, anti-emotional stance. By describing unconscious mental processes as primitive, archaic, irrational and unrealistic and attributing to the healthy ego a rational, objective state of mind which is in fact that of a scientist or professional man while at work and not that of an ordinary, healthy human being at home, at play or in love, he ensnared his theory in a paradox, to which most of his followers have loyally accommodated themselves: the effect of psychoanalytical treatment is to create personalities which embrace just those emotional, imaginative elements that its theoretical conception of a rational ego excludes.

The snarl-up created by Freud's assumption that there is an intrinsic opposition between a chaotic, primitive, emotional, pleasure-seeking id and a rational, realistic, integrated ego is exemplified by the following quotation from a book written by one of Freud's most devoted and loyal disciples, *The Ego and the Problem of Adaptation* (1937: English translation, 1958) by Heinz Hartmann:

From the point of view of the psychology of the neuroses, affective action – in contrast to the theoretical ideal of rational action – often appears as a deplorable residue of primitive mental conditions and as a deviation from the normal. We see much more clearly that affective action gives rise to therapeutic difficulties than that it also gives an impetus for mastering reality. Yet we do know the crucial role of affectivity in organizing and facilitating many ego-functions. Freud implied this when he said that analysis is not expected to free man from all passions.

This quotation shows clearly that the theoretical ideal of a rational ego gives rise to conceptual confusions if one has to use it when trying to assign positive value to emotions. Small wonder that it was an analyst, David Eder, who produced the chilling aphorism: 'We are born mad, acquire morality, and become stupid and unhappy. Then we die.'

It is, I believe, the major achievement of the British Middle Group of analysts that it has extricated itself from the impasse created by Freud's antithesis between emotional, unorganized id and rational, organized ego by assuming that we are born, not mad and unintegrated, but innately whole ('The pristine personality of the child consists of a unitary dynamic ego,' in Fairbairn's view) and already adapted to the environment we are likely to encounter, namely a mother who is herself adapted to receive and respond to us; and that the various splits in the personality with which psychopathology has made us familiar only occur in so far as we have experienced frustration (Fairbairn), separation and/or loss of the mother or later significant figures (Bowlby), or failure of the mother and later figures to provide a setting which facilitates growth (Winnicott). According to this view the various clinical categories with which analysts are familiar arise from differences in the intensity of the childhood frustrations, separations and environmental failures and in the age at which they have occurred; psychoanalytical treatment is not so much a matter of making the unconscious conscious, or of widening and strengthening the ego, as of providing a setting in which healing can occur and connections with previously repressed, split-off and lost aspects of the self can be re-established. And the ability of the analyst to provide such a setting depends not only on his skill in making 'correct' interpretations but also on his capacity to maintain a sustained interest in, and relationship with, his patients. The way in which even the apparently detached intellectual activity of making interpretations can also fulfil the functions of communicating sustained interest and concern was the theme of a paper I read at the Freud Centenary celebrations in 1956.

Since composing my dictionary and writing 'Beyond the Reality Principle', of which the last five paragraphs have been a paraphrase, I have been influenced by two sets of ideas, which have in combination taken me beyond psychoanalysis, at least as Freud conceived it.

The first is the idea that psychoanalysis is concerned not so much with the causes of human behaviour as with its meaning, and is not, as Freud thought, one of the natural sciences but one of the humanities. According to this idea, which I first encountered in Thomas Szasz's *The Myth of Mental Illness* (1962) and in H. J. Home's paper *The Concept of Mind* when it was read to the British Psycho-Analytical Society some years before its publication in 1966, analysts, when they are told about a dream or a symptom, are concerned not with the causes of the imagery or gestures involved but with what they mean to the patient, or, rather, what the patient means by them, even though on occasion some historical or biographical research may be needed to discover why such-and-such an image or gesture has acquired the particular, individual meaning that it has for this particular patient.

As the essay in which I formulated my own version of this idea is included in this volume, there is no need for me to restate it here. But I must mention that it is closely linked in my mind with another idea, one which I had encountered several years earlier in Susanne Langer's *Philosophy in a New Key* (1951). This is that human behaviour is actuated not only by the need to satisfy instinctual impulses but also by the need to maintain meaningful contact with others – that, as Susanne Langer herself put it, 'human behaviour is not only a food-getting strategy, but is also a language ... every move is at the same time a gesture'. Another way of putting this is to say that man is innately a symbolizing animal who generates meanings whenever he acts.

According to Susanne Langer there are two types of symbolism available for expressing and communicating meanings: discursive symbolism, which is language as the term is ordinarily understood, i.e. words with fixed meanings arranged in series according to agreed rules, and non-discursive symbolism, in which images are presented simultaneously and derive their meaning from their context in the total pattern. In *The Innocence of Dreams* I have argued that dreaming is an intra-psychic communicative activity using non-discursive symbolism and that the 'primary' processes – condensation, displacement and symbolization – which Freud discovered to be characteristic of dreaming, are the figures of speech of a non-discursive language which uses images, particularly bodily images, as its vocabulary and sources of metaphor. Such a view of the matter implies, of course, an agent, a self who is more than our usual waking state, who generates meanings, sends messages and constructs dreams and symptoms, and it regards dreams not as 'mental phenomena' that we sometimes observe but as expressive activities to which we sometimes listen.

The second set of ideas by which I have been influenced relates to the politics and power relationships of small groups, and concerns the ways in which spouses can manoeuvre one another into false positions, parents can put their children into 'impossible situations', from which illness is the only escape, and therapists can unwittingly misuse their authority to do much the same to their patients.

My appreciation of the importance of power relationships in marriages, in families, and in therapeutic relationships began, I think, in 1957 or 1958 when Peter Lomas, later the author of *True and False Experience* (1973), drew my attention to an article in *Behavioral Science*, Vol. I (1956), by Gregory Bateson, entitled 'Toward a Theory of Schizophrenia'. In this paper, which has since become famous, Bateson and his co-authors drew attention to a peculiar kind of impossible Catch-22 situation in which children can be caught, and suggested that it might play an important part in the genesis of schizophrenia.

This situation they called a 'double bind'; it is an experience in which the victim is the object of incompatible emotional demands made by the binder in a context from which there is no avenue of escape; as may occur, for instance, if a mother demands physical demonstrativeness from her child but in fact always flinches and winces when he or she gives it to her. In such a situation, which can occur between spouses as well as between parents and children, the victim is in an impossible position; he or she can be neither affectionate nor reserved without incurring rejection.

Bateson's original hypothesis was that the childhood of future schizophrenics was characterized by recurrent experiences of being put into a double bind, usually by their mothers, and that schizophrenia was an effect of the resulting confusion. But over the years it has become apparent that future schizophrenics are not the only victims of double binds, that mothers are not the only double binders, and that many of the impasses, confusions, crossed purposes and misunderstandings into which couples and families get themselves can be elucidated by using the double-bind hypothesis. As a result, many of the things said to patients by contemporary therapists – I am, I suppose, really talking about myself here – are not psychoanalytical interpretations in the sense of referring back to infantile stages of libidinal development or early object relations, but are elucidations of how the patient was in the past put into double binds, is in the present still being put into double binds, and how he or she used to and still does put others into double binds.

Double binds can only occur if the victim is, or imagines himself to be, weaker than his binder, if he feels he has no avenue of escape from the binder, and if he lacks the ability to enlighten the binder about his double-binding propensities. Now, these conditions do in fact apply to small children, who are physically weaker than their parents, are dependent on them, cannot usually seriously entertain the idea of running away from home, and lack the vocabulary to enlighten their parents about their ambivalences and duplicities. As a result, people who seek psychotherapy and become someone's patient may imagine that they are again in the weaker position, that their therapist is more powerful and authoritative than themselves, that they are not entitled to break off treatment or find another therapist, and that it would be impossible to enlighten their therapist as to *his* failings. And, given the professional status of therapists and the prestige that attaches to the possession of expertise – and the fact that the patient has only one therapist, while the therapist usually has several patients – it may indeed be true that patients are at risk of being put into a double bind. But whether they actually are will depend on two things: the therapist's personality, and the extent to which he adheres to the standard rules of psychoanalytical techniques, some of which are, I believe, authoritarian. If the therapist is self-important and stands on his dignity while working, and if he assumes without question that *all* criticisms of himself are projections and manifestations of negative transference, the patient will indeed be in a fix from which he may find it hard to extricate himself. And if the therapist decides unilaterally how often his patient will come to see him, insists on his lying on a couch and tells him to associate freely – and does all these things without explaining why in language that enables the patient to see the sense of the analytical rules, the stage is set for another kind of fix: one in which the patient either becomes defiant, and breaks the rules for the sake of doing so, or submissive, in which case he will secretly harbour and accumulate resentment against his therapist. A surprising amount of the hostility and negative transference about which analysts write so much is, I believe, a response to authoritarian tendencies in either the therapist's personality or in the way in which he enforces as rules arrangements which should be for the mutual convenience of both parties. Here again, in believing that the practical arrangements about treatment should be arrived at by mutual agreement and not enforced by the therapist for reasons that the patient cannot initially appreciate, I – and, indeed, many other therapists – have gone beyond psychoanalysis as Freud conceived it.

1984

11

Melanie Klein

Melanie Klein, who died in 1960 at the age of seventy-eight, was the most controversial figure that has yet appeared on the British psychoanalytical scene. Viennese by birth, she trained as an analyst in Budapest and Berlin and then, at the suggestion of Ernest Jones, settled in London in 1926. From the very beginning of her career she showed an original and independent vision of the nature and scope of psychoanalysis, one which led her and a considerable section of the British Psycho-Analytical Society along a path which diverged widely from that taken by psychoanalysis on the continent and in America.

In the early 1920s psychoanalysis, particularly in Vienna, underwent a significant change of approach. Previously the centre of interest had been the unconscious itself, and research was focused on the nature of unconscious drives, on their infantile origins, and on the way in which they manifested themselves symbolically in dreams and symptoms. Then, follow-ing the publication in 1921 of Freud's *Group Psychology and the Analysis of the Ego*, attention shifted to the ego and research concentrated on the way in which the individual strives to master, control and contain his unconscious drives. The findings of this research were conceptualized in terms of the notion of 'defence' and human personality came to be described as an ego which uses mechanisms to defend itself against impulses deriving from the unconscious, or, as it was now called, the id. This view of human nature which, particularly in its more naive formulations, represents the individual – and civilization – as perpetually on the defensive against the inroads of dangerous impulses, reached its clearest expression in Anna Freud's *The*

Ego and the Mechanisms of Defence, which appeared in 1936. This work remains the foundation stone of that school of psychoanalysis – ego-psychology – which claims the most direct descent from Freud and the Vienna Psycho-Analytical Society, which has become the predominant psychoanalytical influence in the United States, and which writers such as Helen Merell Lynd, Allen Wheelis and Richard Lapiere have in mind when they express misgivings that it is being used or misused to justify a social philosophy of adjustment which values conformity higher than creativity.

Melanie Klein took a very different path. For her, psycho-analysis remained the study of the unconscious, and she pinned her faith on the idea that those problems of character and personality which her Viennese colleagues were explaining in terms of defence could be solved by analysis of ever deeper levels of the unconscious and by applying psychoanalytical technique to small children. In contrast to the Viennese school, whose approach to children was markedly pedagogic, Klein believed that they could be analysed as fully as adults by means of a new technique which she introduced. She provided her child patients with toys, and then interpreted their play as being expressions of unconscious phantasies in exactly the same way as she interpreted the dreams and free associations provided by adult patients lying on the couch.

Her work with very young children led her to believe that the origins of guilt and anxiety lay much earlier in childhood than Freud had believed, and that the phantasies which she uncovered, which referred in the main to the infant's relation to its mother's breast, were responsible both for distortions of character in adults and for susceptibility to schizophrenia and manic-depressive psychosis, illnesses which were generally believed to be inaccessible to psychotherapy. In all her work she laid great emphasis on destructive aggression, which she held to be innate and a manifestation of the death instinct. She and her followers are indeed almost the only psycho-analysts who have applied clinically this speculative notion of Freud's.

At this point, which was reached in the mid 1930s, Melanie

Klein's ideas, like those of many other explorers into the un-known, came into conflict with common sense. Not only was she maintaining that mental illness originated in phantasies occurring at a time in an infant's life when most authorities held that it was as yet scarcely a psychological entity, but she was also advocating, for both children and adults, very long analysis in the hope of reaching these early phantasies. These conclusions aroused widespread scepticism and hostility, to which Klein reacted, understandably but regrettably, by idealiz-ing her own work and using it as the basis for a new 'Kleinian' system of psychoanalysis in which Freud's concept of the Oedipus complex occurring in childhood was replaced by her own concepts of the schizoid and depressive positions occurring in infancy. This development in her thinking, which isolated her from the mainstream of psychoanalytical thought, was accelerated by the arrival in London, as refugees from Nazi persecution, of a considerable section of the Viennese Society. It was exacerbated by her lack of any formal scientific training, which made her incapable of subordinating her own private way of thinking to the discipline of scientific discourse.

All this had several unfortunate effects. It compelled her pupils and associates to become disciples, and put those who wished to assimilate her findings into a wider framework into the position of appearing to be doubting Thomases who lacked the courage to accept her revelation. It also created severe problems of communication; the new theory became esoteric in that within the new system the familiar psychoanalytical concepts underwent subtle and confusing shifts of meaning. As a result, analysts who are anxious not to be tarred with the Kleinian brush have been known not to say what they think for fear of it being taken in a Kleinian sense, while those who have tried to re-establish contact have become involved in problems of exegesis that would baffle a theologian. Last but not least, it has put emotional obstacles in the way of objective sifting and appraisal of the work of one of the most intuitive and creative minds that have been dedicated to psychoanalysis.

It is unlikely that anyone who is not already familiar with Melanie Klein's way of thinking will make much of her *Narra-*

tive of a Child Analysis,[1] which was already in press at the time of her death. This describes in detail her treatment of a ten-year-old boy, and apart from five pages of introduction and 'Final Remarks' the whole text consists of a report of the ninety-three sessions that comprised the treatment. Although the report is annotated with comments on particular points of technique and theory, it contains no general statement of principles nor any comparison with the work of other child analysts. As a result, the reader with no professional interest in the matter will become confused by detail and will at times feel that there is something Pinteresque about this strange encounter between an inhibited, very English little boy and a high-powered Continental woman. The more analytically sophisticated reader will wonder why Melanie Klein missed, in the second session, clear indications that Richard was determined not to be intimidated by her. 'He pointed out Switzerland on the map saying it was a small neutral country that was encircled by the huge Germany . . . Brave little Switzerland had dared to shoot down planes, German or British, which flew over her territory.'

1961

---

[1] Melanie Klein, *Narrative of a Child Analysis* (London: The Hogarth Press and The Institute of Psycho-Analysis, 1961).

12

Fairbairn and Guntrip

Despite his isolation in Edinburgh, where for many years he was the only practising psychoanalyst, W. R. D. Fairbairn has had a considerable influence on psychoanalytical thinking in Great Britain. This is in part attributable to his elegant and pellucid literary style, which perhaps belongs more to the eighteenth century than to the twentieth, but has also been earned by his capacity to see clearly what the fundamental theoretical problems of psychoanalysis are and to suggest simple and comprehensible solutions to them. His solution to the controversies regarding early ego development and the relation between libidinal energies and object relationships constitutes a serious challenge both to ego-psychology and to Kleinian psychoanalysis.

This he has done by postulating what he has himself called a revised psychopathology, the basic assumptions of which are:

1. The infant begins life in a state of primary integration. 'The pristine personality of the child consists of a unitary dynamic ego.'

2. The ego is from the beginning object-seeking.

3. In so far as the environment provides good object relationships, the ego remains outwardly directed and good ego development results.

4. In so far, however, as the search for good objects is frustrated, the frustrating object is internalized, the pristine, unitary ego becoming split into two parts, one remaining attached to the good external object, the other becoming attached to the exciting but frustrating internal object.

5. The internalized object itself becomes split into exciting

and rejecting parts, this being accompanied by a split in the internally directed fragment of the original ego. As a result, the unitary ego of the infant responds to frustration by internalization and splitting and is eventually replaced by three part-egos, each attached to a corresponding type of object.

6. These processes of internalization and splitting are not only responsible for, but are themselves what constitute, differentiation and structural development of the psyche.

7. Libido attaches inherently to structure and is the energy with which the ego seeks objects. Libido is not pleasure-seeking but object-seeking.

8. Psychoanalysis is a science of mind and its basic concepts should be psychological and not biological.

On the basis of these assumptions Fairbairn has developed an internally consistent and, to use Harry Guntrip's word, 'complete' general theory, from which he has derived both criteria for diagnostic classification and phases of psychical development.

This complete 'object relations' theory of the personality is described and its wider implications elaborated in Harry Guntrip's book, *Personality Structure and Human Interaction* (ch. 13 onwards),[1] which constitutes an impressive contribution to psychoanalytical thinking. Dr Guntrip demonstrates convincingly that Fairbairn has made an important contribution to our understanding of schizoid and hysterical disorders and of the types of object and ego fragmentation which underlie them. He has also provided a clear picture of the development of Fairbairn's thought and of the way in which his complete rejection, on methodological grounds, of Freud's mechanical notion of a psychic apparatus in favour of a description of psychic structure exclusively in terms of the relationship between the ego and the internal object leads to a remarkable simplification of object theory, since it renders non-existent the problem of the relationship of phantasy to structure. Whereas Kleinian theory conceives of phantasy as being the 'content of unconscious mental processes' (as Susan Isaacs has it in her

[1] Harry Guntrip, *Personality Structures and Human Interaction* (London: The Hogarth Press and The Institute of Psycho-Analysis, 1961).

1948 paper, 'The Nature and Function of Phantasy'), thereby hypothesizing imageless structures (i.e. id, ego and super-ego) which contain phantasies and internal objects, Fairbairn and Guntrip make the economical and clarifying assumption that phantasy and structure are identical; that internal objects are structures, and that 'phantasy is primarily a revelation of endo-psychic structure'. This is perhaps the most valuable contribution made by Guntrip, though I think, as I shall explain later, that he is wrong in objecting to apparatus concepts on the ground that they are 'impersonal'; the point is that they are imageless (non-imaginative) and therefore non-psychological.

Despite being impressed and convinced by this step in Fairbairn's and Guntrip's thinking, I remain sceptical about Guntrip's further claim that Fairbairn has evolved a general theory which has solved all basic psychopathological problems and which should replace all previous theories. Not only are such claims inherently suspect, since they appear to derive from the systematizing tendency which belongs more properly to philosophy than to a clinical science, but Fairbairn's theory has at least three characteristics which make it particularly difficult to accept.

Firstly, Fairbairn attributes 'good ego' development to the child's experience of 'good object' relationships, but explains all differentiation and structural development to 'bad object' relationships and to the resulting internalization of the bad object, the possibility of good objects being internalized being explicitly rejected. This position involves Fairbairn in what is, to my mind, a contradiction, namely that of attributing ego development entirely to satisfaction and ego differentiation solely to frustration. This not only belies the observations which led both Freud and Klein to postulate the existence of benevolent internal entities, but also leaves out of account those differentiations which make possible the development of reflective self-awareness.

Secondly, Fairbairn's view that good objects are not internalized compels him to maintain that the personality is inherently dependent and that even the adult's need for objects is basically an attenuated form of infantile dependence. His notion corresponding to the classical idea of genitality is indeed 'mature dependence'. Although Fairbairn may be right in dismissing the idea of independence as an illusion, his view that there are no good internal objects would seem to make nonsense of the distinction, which even non-analysts in general accept, between inner and outer security and between clinging dependence and self-reliance.

Thirdly, Fairbairn's 'complete' theory leaves no place open for psychological secondary sexual characteristics to play any important part in human psychic development. This aspect of his thinking is presumably linked with his rejection of biological concepts and his adoption of a conception of libido which makes it intrinsically subordinate to the object-seeking tendencies of the infant.

Dr Guntrip is a devoted and uncritical admirer of Fairbairn and argues, to my mind unconvincingly, that his object relations theory is a full and, one gathers, final synthesis of dynamic psychobiology, as represented by classical psychoanalysis, and dynamic psychosociology, as represented by Adler, Horney and Fromm. He also discusses with scholastic thoroughness the precise relationship of Fairbairn's theories to those of Klein, Winnicott and Balint, being in every case more concerned to convict these workers of error than to emphasize what they and Fairbairn have in common.

With respect to Klein, he emphasizes particularly the unnecessary complications introduced into her system by her attempt to use the death instinct as a clinical and etiological concept and adduces as a major argument in favour of Fairbairn that, in contrast to Klein, he allows for the possibility of dynamic interaction between the environment and endopsychic structure. He also argues that Melanie Klein's theories contain an internal contradiction deriving from her failure to appreciate that her emphasis on object relationships should have led her to abandon Freudian libido theory.

However, Guntrip's preoccupation with the precise relationship of Fairbairn's theories to those of Klein and other analysts derives, I believe, not only from a wish to establish clarity in an obscure and controversial field but also from an emotionally determined need to establish a respectable psychoanalytical pedigree for Dr Fairbairn – and, derivatively, for himself. To do this he has, for instance, to prove that Melanie Klein is in the true psychoanalytical tradition, and then demonstrate that Fairbairn's theories represent the truth that emerges from Klein's when one discards her errors. A similar motive lies behind his argument, mentioned above, that object relations theory is a synthesis of two opposed tendencies in the history of psychodynamic theory, the biological and the socially orientated, an argument which receives no support whatsoever from the declared sources of either Klein's or Fairbairn's thinking.

One has, indeed, the impression that Guntrip, whose background is theological, is not really at home with the scientific method, and that his passionate attachment to Fairbairn's theories derives not, for instance, from his realization that the hypothesis of a unitary dynamic ego is more plausible and workable than Freud's assumption of primary chaotic id, but from the fact that Fairbairn has evolved a non-biological version of psychoanalysis. Guntrip, it seems to me, belongs to the class of person who, two generations ago, would have rejected psychoanalysis as being an offence against human dignity but who, in this age and generation, has been compelled to come to terms with it; and a version of psychoanalysis which plays down erotism and virtually ignores the soma suits him very well.

That this charge is not an idle one will, I hope, become clear when I turn to Guntrip's philosophy of psychotherapy, but first I must justify my use of the term 'scholastic' when describing his method of argument and presentation. There is hardly a page in this book without a quotation, and Guntrip's usual technique is to cite the theoretical conclusion reached by those he quotes without either giving their reasons for reaching it or referring to the particular range of clinical facts they had in mind. He then follows with a note of approval or stricture, according to whether it agrees with or deviates from the Fairbairn–Guntrip line; the whole procedure is at times, indeed, reminiscent of the way in which the Counsellors of the Inquisition annotated writings suspected of heresy. Having said this,

I must hasten to add that Guntrip approaches theory with nonconformist earnestness and not with papist guile, and that Guntrip's and Fairbairn's points of view are not in fact identical. For instance, Guntrip finds the whole notion of libido unacceptable, whereas Fairbairn is only opposed to the idea of an unorganized reservoir of undifferentiated libido.

Guntrip's method of argument by covert appeals to authority or to the arcane sources of insight possessed by his hero – methods which can incidentally be encountered elsewhere in the psychoanalytical literature – clearly derives from his philosophy of psychotherapy, which is so curious and unexpected in a psychoanalyst that fairness demands that it should, so far as possible, be stated in his own words.

According to Guntrip, who is here following John Macmurray, 'science is primarily intellectual investigation of impersonal phenomena, and religion is primarily emotional experience of personal relationships, from which the schizoid person is detached and which he often consciously dislikes and has little capacity to understand'. Science has been the creation of the schizoid individual, and Freud, by reason of his physiological and neurological training, and also by reason of his own temperament, failed in his 'struggle . . . to transcend physiology and neurology and arrive at a true psychology' which would be 'truly personal' and which could take account of the 'unique individual', we will dare say 'the spiritual self'.

Fairbairn has observed that a schizoid trend can confer marked intellectual insight into psychological realities . . . only a man of an introspective intellectual type could have developed psychoanalytical theory out of a self-analysis, and probably for this reason Freud's theory and technique bore the 'impersonal' stamp of the 'pure science' point of view. Freud must have had some personal reasons for overvaluing the impersonal scientific method, as also for his hostility to religion.

Fairbairn, however, because of his 'difference from Freud in type of mind and basic approach', has succeeded where Freud failed and arrived at a psychology which is fully personal and which recognizes the true significance of religion.

Religion is concerned with the basic fact of personal relationships and man's quest for a radical solution to the problems that arise out of his dependent nature ... The fundamental therapeutic factor in psychotherapy is more akin to religion than to science, since it is a matter of personal relationship ... religion has always stood for the good object relationship. [NB these quotations are all from Guntrip, not Fairbairn.]

The view of religion, of science and of psychoanalysis implied in these quotations is so confused that I can only voice my relief that I am under no obligation to analyse it in detail. Three points are, however, perhaps worth making about it. First, all Freud's arguably hostile remarks about religion refer to cosmology, ritual and, as in *The Future of an Illusion*, to religion when used as a defence against the sense of futility; one can only surmise what he would have made of the idea that 'religion is primarily emotional experience of personal relationships'. Secondly, the contention that lack of appreciation of religion is a schizoid trait demands both supporting clinical evidence and some analysis of the various classes of religious feeling; I suspect many religious people would fail to recognize their own experience in Dr Guntrip's formulations. Thirdly, Freud cannot be criticized for failing to produce a 'personal' psychology, when it was precisely his achievement to recognize the extent to which human behaviour is determined by impersonal forces and to initiate a technique by which these impersonal tendencies could be personalized. Although there are, I believe, good reasons for dissatisfaction with Freud's terminology of the id, the ego and the super-ego, Guntrip's dismissal of the concept 'id' on the grounds that it is impersonal reveals his failure to understand a whole area of Freud's work, since Freud chose this term (*das Es*, the It) precisely because repressed, unconscious mental processes operate impersonally and only acquire humanity and individuality after they have become conscious and egotized.

At this point it becomes clear that the ideal of a 'truly personal' psychology, owing nothing to the biological sciences, is a chimera, and that Guntrip's claim that object relations theory constitutes a complete theory of personality is based on a restriction of the field of psychological inquiry which excludes just those phenomena which are most difficult to fit into it. Nowhere does Guntrip discuss symptom-formation, dream-work, symbolism, working-through, psychosomatic diseases or affects, and yet these are the areas of analytical inquiry which most strongly suggest that mental processes obey laws which have some relation to biological ones, and in which some of the 'impersonal' concepts rejected by Guntrip have proved most useful. The fallacy behind Guntrip's idea that psychology should transcend physiology is his assumption that psychological and biological concepts are antithetical and mutually exclusive, and his obliviousness of the possibility that they can be related hierarchically. The demand that psychology should transcend biology is, in the last resort, as ridiculous as the demand that biology should transcend physics and chemistry. In each case the problem is to state the nature of the relationship existing between the concepts appropriate to each, not to deny that the relationship exists. Guntrip's rejection of the connection between biology and psychology compels him to formulate a theory of personality which is incapable of even raising the problem of the ontogenesis of mental activity and which is only applicable to the psychopathology of people in whom psychic processes have fully evolved. The objection to Freud's apparatus and topographical concepts is not that they are physiological or impersonal but that, being based on mechanical and geo-graphical metaphors, they lack both the dynamic quality of physiological concepts and the imaginative quality of pheno-menological concepts and, as a result, encourage the formu-lation of psychoanalytical ideas in terms that are static, reifying and non-psychological. Although one regrets the confusion created by Guntrip's preoccupation with the ideal of the 'truly personal', one must also express one's gratitude for his demon-stration that many of Freud's metapsychological concepts con-stitute an unnecessary and obstructive complication of psycho-analytical theory.

1961

13

D. W. Winnicott

Although his ideas have as yet made little impact in the United States, D. W. Winnicott, who died in 1971, was for the last fifteen to twenty years of his life by far the best known psychoanalyst in the British Isles. This was partly due to the mere fact of his being very English – to date most British analysts have been either *émigré* (Melanie Klein) or refugee (Anna Freud) Central Europeans, Scotsmen (Edward Glover and W. R. D. Fairbairn), or Welshmen (Ernest Jones). But the reason for his reputation also and more particularly was that he possessed to a remarkable degree the capacity for describing even highly sophisticated psychoanalytical ideas in simple, vivid and homely language. As a result he was widely appreciated not only as a writer but also as a broadcaster and public speaker.

His gift for popular exposition was combined with another quality which must have derived from his own genius and not from his clinical experience or his knowledge of psychoanalytical theory. This was an extraordinary intuitive understanding of both mothers and babies, which enabled him to describe what mothers feel about their babies and what babies feel about their mothers with an intimacy and immediacy that was uncanny. When reading his *The Child and the Family*,[1] particularly its first section, 'The Ordinary Devoted Mother and Her Baby', it comes as a repeated shock to remember that as a man Winnicott can never himself have been a mother, and that he could presumably no more remember his own babyhood than the rest of us can.

Although, when speaking professionally, Winnicott attri-

[1] D. W. Winnicott, *The Child and the Family: First Relationships* (London: Tavistock Publications, 1957).

buted his insight into mothers and babies to his analytical familiarity with transference and counter-transference phenomena encountered during the treatment of regressed patients and to his experience as a paediatrician – his *Collected Papers*[2] are correctly subtitled 'Through Paediatrics to Psychoanalysis' – he also openly admitted to a strong maternal identification in his own personality, even allowing Katherine Whitehorn to describe him as a Madonna in an article she wrote about him in the London *Observer*.

Not surprisingly, his unusual gifts and personality turned him into a cult figure with a 'following' largely but not entirely consisting of adoring women. In both books under review, his descriptions of patients make it clear that a high proportion of his adult patients came to him already familiar with his ideas, and with faith in him personally, and that many of the children he treated were those of former and grateful patients. He was, indeed, one of those rare creatures who are correctly designated charismatic, a fact which creates difficulties in assessing the scientific value of his work.

There were, however, disadvantages in being an intuitive English Madonna. First, it made him somewhat of an outsider, a loner within the psychoanalytical movement, with its predominantly intellectual, rationalist, and Central European style of thinking. He had no time for impersonal, mechanical abstractions such as the mental apparatus or cathexes and counter-cathexes, and in spite of his preoccupation with infancy he was unable to accept Melanie Klein's view that all psychopathology originates in the infant's innate ambivalence towards the breast. As a result, he achieved full recognition within the British Psycho-Analytical Society only during the last years of his life.

Secondly, his intuitive understanding of the maternal–feminine in human nature was not matched by a corresponding feeling for the paternal–masculine. The index of *Playing and Reality*[3] contains fifty-five entries for 'mother' but only three

[2] D. W. Winnicott, *Collected Papers: Through Paediatrics to Psycho-Analysis* (London: Tavistock Publications, 1958).

[3] D. W. Winnicott, *Playing and Reality* (London: Tavistock Publications, 1971).

for 'father', a disparity which is made all the more remarkable by the fact that in Winnicott's view both culture and religion are derivatives of play. Even if one accepts Winnicott's idea that the capacity to play originates in the infant's initial interactions with its mother, the extension and imaginative elaboration of play into culture and religion must, it seems to me, involve the father as a person who performs some function other than that of an auxiliary mother – which is how Winnicott all too often conceives of fathers. Not only do fathers play with children (as opposed to infants) as much as if not more than mothers do, but our culture, in spite of the emancipation of women during this century, still shows obvious traces of being predominantly created and transmitted by men. And God, in spite of some of the new theologians still the central religious concept, remains persistently masculine.

Winnicott's blindness to things masculine and sexual is responsible for the one disastrous passage in *Playing and Reality*. In a section entitled 'Pure Male and Pure Female Elements' he asserts that 'the male element *does* while the female element (in males and females) *is*' and correlates femininity with quiet identification with objects and masculinity with instinctual drives towards objects recognized as separate from the self. 'This pure female element has nothing to do with drive (or instinct),' he writes. And even more curiously: 'Exciting implies: liable to make someone's male element *do* something. In this way a man's penis may be an exciting female element generating male element activity in the girl.' This idea that being is feminine and doing is masculine, that calm is feminine and desire, even female desire, is masculine, reads strangely when one remembers that nowadays even ladies move, even if one assumes, as Winnicott does, that everyone is psychologically bisexual.

Such verbal confusion is, however, exceptional in Winnicott's writings. In this passage he has, it seems, tried to extricate himself from the classical psychoanalytical assumption that all need for others is based on instinctual impulses and to find a theoretical explanation of the fact that human beings need quiet communion with others as much as they crave relief from instinctual tension. But he has chosen a peculiarly unfortunate way of doing so.

Thirdly, Winnicott's reliance on intuition and identification rather than on intellect and observation proves a handicap when it comes to formulating theory. *Playing and Reality* is an attempt to construct a theoretical basis for Winnicott's clinical insights, to legitimize his intuitive understanding by formulating it in terms acceptable to other psychoanalysts. Unfortunately, from this point of view it must be adjudged at least a partial failure. His main thesis, which I shall describe later, comes across clearly enough, but in many other respects the book is disappointing.

Although laid out as though it were a proper book with a developing argument, it is in fact a compilation of articles written independently of one another but strung together by linking passages to give it some semblance of unity. As a result it is tediously repetitive and in one important respect confusing and misleading. Since Winnicott does not expound those aspects of classical or Kleinian theory that he is either rejecting or attempting to reformulate, readers who are unfamiliar with the theoretical controversies and intellectual climate of the British psychoanalytical scene will often fail to appreciate what Winnicott is fighting against even though they may understand what he is fighting for.

For instance, chapter 6, 'The Use of an Object', seems to me to be an attempt to formulate an alternative statement of Melanie Klein's 'depressive position' without accepting her ideas about the death instinct and innate envy. But Melanie Klein is not mentioned once in the chapter, though sentences like 'It is not possible for me to take for granted an acceptance of the fact that the first impulse in the subject's relation to the object is destructive' and 'It is no good saying that a baby a few days old envies the breast' are pointless unless read as intended rejections of Kleinian theory.

Rather similarly, or perhaps conversely, Winnicott also offends against the conventions of scientific writing by failing to acknowledge to what extent his ideas resemble those of others. As a result he often writes as though he were being more original than in fact he is – or even than, if challenged, he would have claimed to be. For instance, according to Winnicott, 'Psychoanalysis always likes to be able to eliminate all factors that are environmental, except in so far as the environment can be thought of in terms of projective mechanisms,' whereas *he* believes that whether 'individuals live creatively and feel that life is worth living . . . is directly related to the quality and quantity of environmental provision at the beginning or in the early phases of each baby's living experience'. But in fact only Kleinian analysts have sought to eliminate the environment, and Winnicott's general position is and has been shared by numerous other analysts, notably by Erikson,[4] Balint, Bowlby and Spitz, to cite only workers whose ideas have developed independently of his.

But Winnicott makes no attempt to correlate his own ideas with those of others or to work towards a consensus of terminology. His theorizing remains, in spite of the occasional use of abstract nouns, a personal statement, too idiosyncratic to be readily assimilated into the general body of any scientific theory. He often sounds like a voice crying in a wilderness that is in fact inhabited, or like a visionary who is disguising himself as a thinker.

The essential thesis of *Playing and Reality* is none the less capable of abstract formulation. Psychoanalytical theory has alway postulated the existence of two realms of experience: one psychical, subjective, located inside the self, and manifesting itself most nakedly in dreams; the other environmental, objective, and located outside the self. According to most formulations, the former, internal or psychical reality, is in inherent opposition to the latter (external reality), so that the developing infant has to learn to renounce its tendency to hallucinatory wish-fulfilment in favour of adaptation to the environment.

In Winnicott's view, however, health and creative living depend on the establishment of a third 'transitional' or 'intermedi-

---

[4] See E. H. Erikson, *Childhood and Society* (New York: W. W. Norton, 1950), ch. 8: 'Mothers, I think, create a sense of trust in their children by that kind of administration which in its quality combines sensitive care of the baby's individual needs and a firm sense of personal trustworthiness within the trusted framework of their culture's style.'

ate' realm, in which the subjective and objective are fused (or remain undifferentiated). In this transitional area, objects are felt to be parts of both internal and external reality, to possess both selfhood and otherness, and activities are both wish-fulfilling and adaptive. All playing, all culture, and all religion belong in this transitional realm, which only develops in so far as the mother responds sufficiently sensitively and promptly to the infant's tendency to hallucinate the objects of its desire, to create for itself the illusion that it has subjectively created objects that objectively exist independently of it. To the extent that this illusion is successfully created, and premature disillusionment is avoided, the individual will feel at home in the world and have a creative relationship with it.

Although this concept of a transitional reality, which mediates between the private world of dreams and the public, shared world of the environment, is perhaps the most important contribution made to psychoanalytical theory in the last thirty years, it must be admitted that from a general, cultural point of view it is not entirely original. It is, after all, what the poets call Imagination, that 'intermediate faculty' (Coleridge) which enables its possessors to inhabit a world of 'both what they half-create and what perceive' (Wordsworth), to 'half-create the wondrous world they see' (Young's *Night Thoughts*, vi, 424).

Winnicott is truly at his best in *Therapeutic Consultations in Child Psychiatry*.[5] In it he describes simply and vividly, and with a minimum of theoretical comment, twenty-one therapeutic consultations with children, in which he makes contact with the patient by playing the 'squiggle game'. In this game therapist and patient doodle together and produce a series of drawings, which the therapist uses to understand and at times interpret the patient's current anxieties and conflicts. Winnicott is consistently successful in getting across the atmosphere of each consultation, and it is a revelation to watch how rapidly he makes contact with each patient and how illuminating this technique of imaginative participation in child's play can be. I cannot

[5] D. W. Winnicott, *Therapeutic Consultations in Child Psychiatry* (London: The Hogarth Press and The Institute of Psycho-Analysis, 1971).

conceive of anyone reading these descriptions without being enriched in his understanding of his children, his patients, and indeed of himself.

1972

14

Bowlby: Attachment and Loss

One of the most important developments in psychoanalysis since the war has been the emergence of 'object theory' as a rival and probable successor to the instinct theory of classical Freudian psychoanalysis. Whereas instinct theory seeks to explain both normal emotional development and the pathology of the neuroses in terms of instincts and their vicissitudes, to use a phrase of Freud's, and postulates that the growing individual passes through a number of libidinal stages of psychosexual development, notably the oral, anal and phallic phases, each centred on a specific organ or 'erotogenic zone' in which he experiences instinctual tension and from which he seeks pleasure, object theory conceives him to be seeking a 'good' relationship with an object, originally 'the breast' and later 'the mother', the erotogenic zones of classical theory being regarded as vehicles of communication with the object rather than as sources of pleasure. According to this latter-day psychoanalytical view, man is an object-seeking, not a pleasure-seeking creature, using pleasure to cement relationships with objects, not objects as things from which to extract pleasure.

To the great confusion of both psychoanalytical students and the interested lay public, three different versions of object theory are in circulation, propounded by Melanie Klein, D. W. Winnicott and W. R. D. Fairbairn. These agree in locating the origins of all psychopathology in disturbances in the relationship of the infant to its mother and in deriving their sense of conviction from their own clinical experience as psychoanalysts, but disagree in the importance they attach to innate aggression (Klein) and environmental frustration (Winnicott, Fairbairn) and in the extent to which they are traditionalists, seeking to superimpose object theory on to classical psychoanalysis (Klein, Winnicott), or radicals, seeking to eliminate all traces of instinct theory and eager to start afresh (Fairbairn).

Although trained by Kleinian psychoanalysts, Bowlby has never accepted the basic Kleinian concept of innate destructiveness (the death instinct), and in a series of studies dating from 1951, when the World Health Organization published his *Maternal Care and Mental Health*, he has propounded a fourth version of object theory which differs from those of Klein, Winnicott and Fairbairn in two fundamental respects. Firstly, it derives from direct observation of infants who are separated from their mothers and from follow-up studies of children with a history of separation and *not* from psychoanalytical experiences with patients. Secondly, its theoretical basis consists of concepts derived from the new science of ethology and *not* from psychoanalysis. In Bowlby's view psychoanalysis has been hamstrung by its failure to discard Freud's assumptions about the nature of instinct when these became outdated by later developments in biology, ethology and neurophysiology. In particular, he holds that modern analytical biology and control theory have rendered Freud's concept of mental energy otiose, and that instinctual behaviour is better explained in terms of innate behaviour patterns, activated by eliciting stimuli and maintained and controlled by feedback mechanisms, than by postulating hidden internal forces such as 'libido' and 'aggression' which are held under tension and crave discharge. Although he does not explicitly mention the fact, he has aligned himself with both the learning theorists and the existentialists in rejecting the essentialist philosophical assumptions of Freudian psychoanalysis.

Attachment is the first of the three volumes which together provide a definitive statement of Bowlby's position.[1] It contains, firstly, a general theoretical discussion of his reasons for discarding Freud's instinct theory and replacing it by control systems

[1] John Bowlby, *Attachment and Loss*, 3 vols.: *Attachment*; *Separation: Anxiety and Anger*; *Loss: Sadness and Depression* (London: The Hogarth Press and The Institute of Psycho-Analysis, 1969, 1973, 1980).

theory, and, secondly, an account of the processes by which the human infant becomes attached to objects. In it Bowlby presents overwhelmingly convincing evidence that the study of animal and particularly primate behaviour is of supreme relevance to human psychology – a fact which the psychoanalysts, with their interest in symbolic communication, have been inclined to doubt – and makes it abundantly clear that most current ideas about the nature of the infant's tie to its mother are hopelessly naive and oversimplified. I doubt whether anyone who reads this book will ever again be able to maintain that the human infant's dependence on its mother derives solely from its need for her breast as a source of milk and 'oral satisfaction', or that infantile anxiety and ambivalence are simply responses to 'oral frustration'. From now on he will have to recognize that the mother–infant relationship is an enormously subtle interaction, in which the infant's smiling, crying, clinging, grasping, babbling, looking and listening – and the mother's responsiveness to these messages – play as important a part in attaching infants to their mothers – and mothers to their infants – as do sucking and suckling.

What happens when attachments are broken is the theme of the third volume, *Loss*; in the second volume, *Separation*, he considers the effects of temporary and threatened disruptions of the bonds established between children and their mothers. Here again he marshals his material so clearly and thoroughly that, with one perhaps unimportant reservation, his conclusions are entirely convincing.

Dr Bowlby is almost unique among psychoanalysts in believing in the principle of economy of hypothesis and in preferring simple, commonsensical explanations to ones which are complex and obscure. As a result, his findings are refreshingly straightforward and tend, perhaps rather boringly, to be precisely what warm-hearted but naive non-intellectuals have always thought. These are, briefly:

  1. The distress experienced by infants and children when separated from their mothers and other familiar figures is an elemental fact of the human condition, which does not require complex, psychopathological explanations and has precise ana-

logues in the behaviour of the young of other species. It is, therefore, normal and not neurotic.

2. Individuals, who have reason to be confident that 'attachment figures' will be available to them when they need them, are less prone to anxiety than those who lack reasons for such confidence.

3. Confidence, or the lack of it, in the availability of 'attachment figures' is established during the years of immaturity and tends to persist relatively unchanged throughout life. Good mothering and a secure, happy home life form, therefore, the basis for an inner sense of security in later life.

4. Any individual's expectations regarding the accessibility or inaccessibility of attachment figures are an accurate reflection of his actual experience, and are not the result of innate or self-created fantasies, as many psychoanalysts have maintained.

5. Anxiety is not explicable solely in terms of the anxious individual's attitude towards whatever he appears or claims to be frightened of; it is also, and indeed predominantly, due to his lack of a sense of secure attachment to the figures who should provide him with a safe base. Animals and children do not only run away from objects which frighten them, they also run towards those that provide security. Children who suffer from 'school phobias' are not primarily frightened of school, but feel, with good reason, insecure at home. Dr Bowlby provides convincing and often horrifying evidence that children who refuse to go to school have powerful reasons for remaining at home; they believe, understandably and sometimes indeed correctly, that their parents may abandon them if they let them out of sight, or may drop dead, or may be unbearably lonely while their child is away at school. Parents who enforce discipline by threatening to leave home are far from uncommon, and many children sense that their insecure mothers are pathetically dependent on them.

6. The unconscious hostility of children towards their parents, which is often adduced as an irrational, neurotic *cause* of disturbed behaviour in children, is in fact an understandable *effect* of the actual emotional atmosphere existing within the child's family. Child psychiatrists too often side with parents

and accept their view of themselves too readily; they often fail to discover, or even look for, shameful family secrets which would explain the child's 'symptoms'.

7. In our culture too many children experience too many separations from their mothers too young, at grave cost to their present and future happiness.

My only reservation about all this is that Bowlby at times writes about 'separation anxiety' as though he were propounding a general theory of anxiety. As a result, the unwary reader might well conclude that there is less to the problem of anxiety than there actually is. He does not mention Freud's concept of anxiety as a signal, nor does he give any inkling of the considerations which led Liddell, a physiologist working on the related problem of vigilance, to observe that 'anxiety accompanies intellectual activity as its shadow', or led Mary Douglas, the anthropologist, to argue that anxiety lurks in the margins between accepted categories.

Loss, the third and final volume of Bowlby's trilogy, appeared seven years after *Separation* in 1980. In it he describes how human beings react when their attachments are severed by permanent loss, and in addition sums up his work of the preceding thirty years. Its opening words are: 'This is the third and final volume of a work that explores the implications for the psychology and psychopathology of personality of the ways in which young children respond to a temporary or permanent loss of mother-figure,' and near the end of it he explicitly draws attention to how little his views have changed over the years. Anxiety, phobia, depression, suicide and 'disturbances of parenting and marriage' have, he believes, already been proved to be the results of actual or threatened disruption of 'affectional bonds', and he leaves his readers in little doubt that he believes further research will merely confirm, refine and extend his hypothesis.

In view, then, of the fact that this third volume is the conclusion and culmination of nearly thirty years' work, it is only fitting that comment and criticism of it should be preceded by praise and congratulations. Few people, it seems to me, are today as persistent and consistent, as single-minded, as Dr

Bowlby has shown himself to be; his attitude towards his life's work and achievement has a Victorian monumentality about it which is enviable and all too rare.

But, having said this, I must confess that I have reacted somewhat less enthusiastically to *Loss* than I did to *Attachment* and *Separation*. This is partly due to the fact that his previous books have made his position so familiar that this last volume contains few surprises; it largely consists of documentation and explication of what careful readers of Volumes I and II must already have realized Dr Bowlby thought. But there is also something else amiss with it, something which arises from his preoccupations with psychoanalytical theory and scientific methodology and interferes with his otherwise admirably lucid exposition of the facts about attachment, separation and loss.

In his preface to this volume Dr Bowlby states that 'my initial frame of reference was, and has in many respects remained, that of psychoanalysis', but that 'the theory advanced here has come to differ from the classical theories advanced by Freud and elaborated by his followers' and draws

on recent work in cognitive psychology and human information processing in an attempt to clarify problems of defence. As a result the frame of reference now offered for understanding personality development and psychopathology amounts to a new paradigm and is therefore alien to clinicians long used to thinking in other ways.

But in fact Dr Bowlby does not confine himself to using his new paradigm to clarify problems of defence; he also applies it to, for instance, phantasy, which is surely not a defence, and to Winnicott's distinction between true and false selves. As a result he tends to distract his readers by leaving them in doubt as to whether he appreciates the importance of those aspects of human nature which are referred to by those psychoanalytical concepts he ignores. Dr Bowlby has nothing to say about the Oedipus complex in any of his three volumes; and in this present volume he fails to discuss whether the capacity to mourn is affected by the presence or absence of sublimations and 'autonomous ego functions', i.e. by the capacity to maintain interests that are *not* directly connected with instinctual needs or present attachments. One surmises that it is, and that Dr

Bowlby has made things too easy for himself by assuming *tout court* that 'intimate attachments to other human beings are the hub around which a person's life revolves', without considering in any detail those qualities that may make it possible to experience bereavement without feeling totally bereft.

Although Dr Bowlby's frame of reference is, after his own fashion, psychoanalytical, his views on scientific methodology are such as to make most psychoanalytical clinical data inadmissible evidence. He seems to think that reminiscences and retrospective studies are inherently contaminated and biased sources of information, but that accounts of interviews with persons when actually bereaved and/or depressed are inherently reliable. He tends to be dismissive of psychoanalytical accounts of losses and their effects experienced by patients in their childhoods, but to be trusting of the accounts of 'semi-structured interviews' conducted by psychiatrists, psychologists and sociologists with persons presently bereaved. Although the former is an understandable reaction to the speculative excesses of, particularly, Kleinian analysts, the latter shows a touching faith in the ability of interviewers to avoid unconsciously influencing their subjects and in the value of the statistics with which they adorn their findings.

It is, for instance, disconcerting to discover that the Harvard Bereavement Study, on which Bowlby leans heavily, confined itself to people under the age of forty-five 'because it was believed' (by whom and why?) 'that bereaved subjects under the age of forty-five are more likely than older subjects to have an adverse outcome to their mourning', and that 40 per cent of those approached refused to cooperate, while another 15 per cent 'refused later interviews'. As a result, the sample actually used and from which statistical conclusions were drawn consisted of a minority of the bereaved persons approached and included a high proportion of people who were mourning a death that was both unexpected and untimely, a loss that was compounded by shock and, no doubt, a sense of the injustice of fate. Bowlby's use of such figures, coupled with the thoroughness with which he expounds and conscientiously draws attention to their weaknesses, makes heavy going for the reader, who has to plough through a morass of insignificant statistics if he is not to miss the gems buried in it. Dr Bowlby would have done better to expound his theory of attachment and loss in simple, unjargonized English with the occasional telling example, relegating both the statistics and the revisions of psychoanalytical theory to appendices. As it is, his ideas and his findings are in danger of getting lost in a maze of figures and abstractions.

Since his findings are of vital importance to all who have the care of children, who are members of any of the helping professions, and indeed to all those of us who have attachments, I have dared to summarize them, though not in the order in which Bowlby himself presents them.

1. Infants attach themselves to a mother figure whom they recognize and distinguish from all other figures during the middle of the first year of life. This is later than a few but earlier than most analysts and psychologists have assumed.

2. Children have 'a germinal capacity for mourning' by the age of sixteen months, in as much as they have constructed and can retain an image of an absent mother.

3. Under favourable conditions, which include warmth, tact and truthfulness in their surviving relatives, children from the age of four onwards can mourn a lost parent in a way that does not differ essentially from the healthy mourning of adults.

4. Under unfavourable conditions, however, disordered mourning may occur, which, again, does not differ essentially from disordered mourning in adults.

5. Those who have lost a parent before the age of seventeen are at greater risk than others of developing a psychiatric disorder in adult life, and, if they do, it is more likely to be a 'psychotic' or 'endogenous' than a 'neurotic' or 'reactive' depression. But, none the less, not all children who have lost a parent are at risk of falling psychiatrically ill in adult life.

6. Healthy mourning can conveniently be divided into four stages: (a) numbing, (b) yearning and searching for the lost figure, (c) disorganization and despair, (d) reorganization. True sorrow is being resisted in stage (b) and admitted in stage (c).

7. Anger occurs so commonly during the first two stages

that it must be regarded as normal and as analogous to the protests children make before they have become reconciled to a separation.

8. A need to locate the lost person in some particular place, in heaven, a grave or a shrine, must also be regarded as normal.

9. Disordered mourning is of two main kinds: (*a*) chronic mourning, accompanied by depression, persistent anger and self-reproaches, with true sorrow notably absent, and (*b*) prolonged absence of conscious grieving, which occurs in people who are proud of their self-sufficiency and in those who have never mourned a childhood loss. Such people are prone to sudden, apparently causeless bouts of tears or depression.

10. Disordered mourning occurs most commonly in those who have lost a husband, less commonly in those who have lost a wife, a parent or a child, and only infrequently in those who have lost a sibling.

11. All societies have rituals concerning the disposal of the dead and the appropriate behaviour of the bereaved. There is a dearth of evidence as to whether, in our society, religious beliefs, affiliations and rituals affect the course of mourning, but an ample amount to show that the behaviour of relatives, friends and others plays a leading role in assisting or hindering it. This last forms the basis of Dr Bowlby's belief that it is possible to help those who suffer separation and loss and to reduce the incidence of disordered mourning and its manifold consequences.

1969
1973
1980

BEYOND SEX AND
SENSATION

15

The Psyche and the Senses

In this chapter I intend to discuss some of the implications of the fact that the sensations produced by the sense organs do not exist in a void, but are experienced by a perceiving agent; and that, in the case of human beings, this perceiving agent is a person possessing qualities which make it necessary to assume that he has a mind or psyche.

It is, fortunately, unnecessary for my purpose to define mind or even to decide whether, or in what sense, there is such a thing as mind, since all I intend to do is to draw attention to a number of mental qualities and to show, among other things, that these qualities so affect and modify sensations that it is an illusion to suppose that anyone has experiences which are sensations and nothing else. My central thesis is indeed that the psyche converts meaningless physiological sensations into significant, psychological experiences and that these experiences are unique creations of the person who has them. I am, in other words, arguing that the psyche transforms sensations, which are discrete and passively received, into experiences, which form part of a continuum and are actively created.

The most obvious mental quality possessed by human beings is the capacity to be conscious. Human beings, like animals, perceive and act, but, unlike animals, they also know that they perceive and act, and at some point in their childhood they acquire the additional capacity to be self-conscious, to know that they know, and to reflect on the sensations they receive, the actions they perform and the experiences they have. As soon as they have acquired self-consciousness, it becomes possible for them to reflect upon the sensations they have and to compare them with other sensations they have previously received; and, furthermore, to anticipate, with either pleasure or dread, the possibility that they may have further sensations and experiences in the future. Consciousness and, more particularly, self-consciousness introduce, therefore, an element of critical comparison into all experience and sensations cease to be isolated, discrete events, becoming instead experiences which derive their meaning and value from comparison with prior experiences. To an extent which varies with the age, education and sophistication of the subject, experiences contain a critical, comparative element which derives from his earlier experiences and from his reflective capacity, not from the sensations themselves. To take a simple example: a child's experience of his first meal at school does not consist simply of the taste of the food he receives. It includes also an evaluation of whether it tastes nicer or nastier than the food he receives at home and the anticipation that later meals at school will resemble it, an anticipation which will fill him with hope or foreboding, depending not only on his comparison of the taste of home and school food but also on whether he has dreaded or looked forward to going to school. What I am suggesting here is that the experience of, for instance, eating food, contains meanings which cannot be attributed to, or deduced from, the sensations of eating it, but which derive from the total psychological context in which the sensations have been perceived.

The same point can usefully be made in another way. Since consciousness is individual, and each person has a continuous sense of his own unique being, which is maintained despite the apparent discontinuities created by sleep, general anaesthetics, concussion, etc., all sensational events become experiences as they are assimilated into that continuum of being that constitutes his identity. They are construed and interpreted in the light of the individual's previous experiences, and after being assimilated and construed they become part of the person's psyche and influence the meaning he attaches to all later experiences.

There are, however, two exceptions to the generalization that all sensations can be converted into experiences by comparison with prior similar sensations. The first is the infant's first contact with the outside world immediately after birth. Although none of us can remember them, we must all have had entirely novel sensations of noise and light, of cold air on our skin, of being handled, immediately after we were born. All the evidence suggests that this sudden bombardment with novel sensations was extremely unpleasant and bewildering, and mothering the new-born seems largely to consist of providing them with conditions which simulate the peace, darkness and warmth of the womb, while at the same time converting them to the belief that sensation can be enjoyable and satisfying. But it remains true throughout life that we view sensation as a mixed blessing; although sensations can be enjoyable, exciting, stimulating, enriching, there are limits to the amount of stimulation we can tolerate, after which sensation and consciousness becomes a burden from which we seek oblivion in sleep.

The second exception is adolescence, when both body and mind acquire new potentialities, erotic, emotional, intellectual and aesthetic. At this time physiological changes produce concomitant changes in both the range and intensity of sensations and in the capacity of the psyche to convert its intake of sensations into significant experiences, these being so great as to constitute a dialectical transformation of the quality of all experience. Although, objectively speaking, pictures will have been seen before, music heard before, people loved and touched before, adolescence is often remembered as a time when pictures and music and love were encountered for the first time and as revelations. The world is perceived and experienced through new eyes, and in two respects adolescence may resemble life immediately after birth when the sensory world was encountered for the first time; it may be bewildering, and the need for intermittent relief from sensation in sleep may be enormous.

Man's conscious sense of his own continuous being compels him, therefore, to convert the physical sensations he receives into mental experiences which derive their significance from the place they occupy in his biography and from the connection he establishes between them and all his other experiences. As a result the meaning any perceptual event has depends less on the sen-

sation itself than on the age, sex, education, occupation and
health of the perceiver. This is perhaps most obviously true of
sensations produced by works of art. Looking at, say, Botticelli's
The Birth of Venus will be a very different experience for a child,
a teenager, a man, a woman, an artist, an art dealer or an old
person who knows he is near to death, even though the painting
may produce an identical image on their respective retinas.

The dependence of the meaning of experiences on the psyche
of the experiencer can, on occasion, lead to striking discrepancies between sensations and the experience constructed round
them. An Australian woman was once walking through Covent
Garden when she suddenly burst into tears; the scent of a
consignment of eucalyptus blossom in the Market had brought
back to her vivid, overwhelming recollections of the Australian
bush, which she had not seen for many years. This transformation of a pleasant, in itself trivial sensation into a distressing,
powerful emotional experience of homesickness was due, I
suspect, to a conflict between wishes to forget and to remember,
to break with the past and to preserve a sense of continuity
with it. A rather similar conflict must, one surmises, have been
present in Proust's mind when he tasted the madeleine which
started him on his *A la recherche du temps perdu*. I shall return
later to a discussion of the effects on sensation and experience
of attempts by the psyche to disown parts of its experience.

It is perhaps enlightening to liken the psyche's conversion of
physical sensations into mental experiences to the attitude of
an organism towards objects which come close enough to it to
be ingested. Some will be ignored as irrelevant, others will be
tasted but spat out in disgust, others will be ingested but later
expelled as useless and unassimilable, but some will be digested,
absorbed and assimilated into the structure of, in one case, the
body, and in the other case, the mind, the selection being made
on the basis of the physiological and psychological needs of the
organism and mind respectively.

This analogy cannot, however, be taken too far, since it is
unfortunately not true that we have full freedom of choice in
our psychological diet and can always expel sensations and
events, without assimilating them into our psyches, if they

disagree with us. If that were so, unhappy childhoods, deprivations and experiences of maltreatment and cruelty would
leave people unharmed. But the analogy does, none the less,
draw attention to the fact that what we perceive and the
interpretation we give to sensations are affected by our psychological needs. If we are hungry, we will be all eyes for food. If
we are in love, we will be quick to notice those who resemble
the loved one and may momentarily mistake them. If we are
touched by someone we love, it will be pleasant, perhaps even
thrilling, whereas an identical touch by someone we dislike or
fear will be distasteful. And occurrences which at one phase of
our life are enjoyable and significant may at another mean
nothing to us. In general, the meaning given to any sensation
depends on the perceiver's mental attitude towards the source
of the sensation, and on his expectations from that source.

There exists, however, a type of occurrence in which sensations are forced upon consciousness and the psyche which it
has no option but to perceive, but which it is equally unable to
assimilate and convert into experiences of a meaningful, let
alone enriching kind. These are the sensations produced by
traumatic events, that is by unexpected disasters such as earthquakes, car or plane accidents, or sexual or other physical
violations. The immediate effect of such experiences is a state
of shock, in which the victim is unable to comprehend what
has happened to him. Such events are experiences in the sense
that the occurrence thereafter forms part of his biography, but
are not experiences in the sense that they acquire meaning or
significance for him. He may, if he is lucky, get over it, but he
will not have been enriched by it. Memories of traumatic events
are more like foreign bodies embedded in the psyche than
essential parts of it, since they remain disconnected from the
continuum of experience.

In striking contrast to memories of traumatic events, which
are conscious but are not true parts of the psyche, are the
repressed parts of the self, which are unconscious and yet do
form parts of the psyche. These are parts of the self, containing
memories, wishes and emotions, which were once conscious
but which have been disowned and repressed at some time in

the past, usually in childhood, in order to avoid confrontations with figures in the outside world, typically parents, who, it is imagined – often rightly – would disapprove of them and withdraw security and affection if they received expression. These repressed parts of the self continue, however, to crave expression, and as a result the repressing, disowning, central psyche has to avoid becoming conscious of those features of the present which might resonate and revive them. This leads inevitably to impoverishment of both sensation and experience.

If, for instance, someone as a child repressed his sexual and aggressive potentialities, he will as an adult be an inhibited, meek person with an impaired capacity for enjoying erotic and assertive situations. Or, if someone has disowned his childhood *en bloc* and can no longer remember what it was like to be a child, his capacity to enjoy and understand children will be impoverished. Or, if someone has disowned all feeling, his capacity to love and to enjoy the arts will be reduced. In all these all-too-common instances, disowning by the psyche of parts of itself and its own past experience reduces the indi-vidual's capacity to appreciate sensations and convert them into experiences. It is as though, in the process of converting sensations into significant experiences, the psyche acts as a reso-nator which adds to all present perceptions harmonics derived from its past, and repression impoverishes experience by cutting out some of the possible harmonics. Or, to shift from a musical to a linguistic metaphor, repression reduces the number of meanings – and the overall intensity of meanings – that can be attributed to messages received from the senses.

Another mental quality involved in the conversion of sen-sations into experiences is the capacity to attach symbolic meanings to them. It is characteristic of human beings, as opposed to animals, that they are capable of accepting symbolic substitutes for the original objects of instinctual wishes, so that, for instance, listening and looking can become substitutes for eating, intellectual curiosity can become a substitute for wishes to explore one's own and other people's bodies, and nature and ideals can be loved as though they were people. Although the connection between mental 'sublimated' activities and biologi-

cal drives was originally discovered during investigation of the
meaning of dreams, neurotic symptoms and inhibitions, it is
also revealed by language, which allows one to describe music
as the food of love, to describe inquisitive people as 'nosey' and
curiosity as devouring, to personify nature as a mother, and
to attribute gender to ideals, institutions, countries and even
abstract ideas. It would seem, indeed, that built into the psyche
is a symbolic or metaphorical network of connections and
resonances which makes us react to all the objects we perceive
as though they were to a greater or lesser extent representatives,
substitutes or equivalents of people, bodies or parts of bodies,
and that this symbolic network is responsible for our imaginative, as opposed to literal, response to what we perceive.

This capacity of the mind to endow all its perceptions with
additional symbolic meanings can be exemplified by our responses to scenery and architecture. It is, for instance, what
makes us feel that bleak countrysides are unfriendly and un-
welcoming, but that lush valleys are not, that mountains, cliffs
and large buildings are majestic and awe-inspiring, that tall
buildings, particularly if they lack windows, are austere and
forbidding, and that houses with bay windows and wings coming out to meet one are inviting. In all these instances we react
to things – scenery and buildings – as though they were people
who might embrace, ignore or cold-shoulder us. And it is the
same symbolizing capacity of the mind which is responsible for
what has become known as Freudian symbolism: that is, the
tendency to endow even inanimate objects with gender on the
basis of any discernible resemblance to sexual organs.

Although there is much that remains obscure and controversial about the connections between repression and symbolization, it seems that some measure of repression of instinctual
impulses is necessary to initiate the formation of symbols, but
that excessive repression diminishes the capacity to endow the
sensory world with symbolic meanings. Although it would be
rational to be immune to the pathetic fallacy and to perceive
scenery as only geological formations, buildings as only brick
and mortar, paintings as only pigments on a canvas, something
important is lost if one cannot react to them in terms of the

symbolism and metaphor that can be read into them – and that in the case of artefacts such as paintings has in fact been written into them. Repression therefore impoverishes appreciation of the sensory world by reducing the symbolic resonances and meanings that can be read into sensations.

It would seem, too, that these symbolic resonances and meanings hark back to infancy, before the discrete objects that compose our sensory world were recognized as entities in themselves but were still regarded as extensions of ourselves or our mothers; and when all pleasurable sensations were interpreted as evidence of her love and all painful ones as evidence of her neglect or hostility.

1979

16

The Psychology of Orgasm

Orgasm is the climax of the sexual act, being that moment at which tension is followed by release, excitement is replaced by relaxation, and, in technical terms, tumescence gives way to detumescence. In the male it is accompanied by ejaculation and in the female by spasmodic contractions of pelvic and vaginal muscles. Although there is controversy about the precise physical processes involved in female orgasm, the physiology of orgasm is a straightforward matter in comparison with its psychology, about which there remains something mysterious and indescribable.

A case could, indeed, be made for maintaining that orgasm is an inherently ineffable experience, its ineffability deriving from the change in the quality of consciousness that occurs during it. Freud maintained that we are unconscious during orgasm, and although most people disagree with him about this, there is certainly such a loss of self-consciousness during orgasm that no one is ever, while having one, in the detached frame of mind necessary for acute and accurate psychological analysis of the experience. However, most attempts to describe it retrospectively are in terms of words such as release, ecstasy, joy and bliss, and include references to the melting away of self-consciousness and to feelings of merging with the partner to the act. It is noteworthy that religious mystics resort to sexual, orgastic metaphors to describe their experiences of religious ecstasy and that, contrariwise, lovers sometimes use religious terms (e.g. adoration, worship) to describe their sexual experiences and their feelings about the beloved.

In addition to the difficulties involved in describing an experience which is characterized by diminution of self-consciousness, there is also the further difficulty involved in describing and explaining pleasure – and orgasm is probably the most acute pleasure of which men and women are capable. The problem here is that although the pleasure appears to be a physiological phenomenon and to be the result of physical stimulation – and although, too, we are inclined to think of pleasure as being the opposite of pain – all the evidence is in favour of the view that pleasure is basically a psychological phenomenon, dependent on the subject's state of mind and attitude towards the physical stimulation. It is a matter of common observation that it hurts to have a pin stuck into our skin and that this is so regardless of our feelings about the person wielding the pin, but that being touched, stroked and caressed is only pleasurable if we are fond of the person who is touching us and, furthermore, that it will only be erotically exciting if we find that person attractive. In other words, the pleasure of orgasm seems to depend not so much on the physical stimulation that occurs in the preceding love-making as on our psychological feelings about our partner and on our being in the right sort of mood to welcome erotic excitement.

So far I have written as though orgasm only occurred during sexual intercourse, but this is of course not so. It can also occur as the climax of masturbation, spontaneously during sleep, and even occasionally – particularly in teenagers – involuntarily and unexpectedly while awake. However, even in these circumstances, the orgasm is not a purely physical phenomenon. Masturbation is almost invariably accompanied by vivid sexual day-dreaming, spontaneous orgasms during sleep are regularly accompanied by erotic dreams, while involuntary, unexpected orgasms while awake occur typically while reading sexually stimulating literature, watching erotic scenes in films, etc.

The point I am making here is that orgasm is a psychosomatic phenomenon, which only occurs if the imagination as well as the body is engaged in the experience – the imaginative, psychological contribution being provided by day-dreaming in masturbation, by night-dreams in spontaneous orgasms occurring in sleep, and by our feelings about our partner in orgasms occurring during sexual intercourse.

The nature of the imaginative activity is, however, extremely variable, since it depends on the temperament and personality of the subject, on his or her mood, and on the degree of physiological tension which is impelling him or her to seek orgasm. At one extreme the accompanying phantasies of a crude, unimaginative person who is at a high level of physiological tension may consist solely of images of sexual organs without any reference to the personality of the real or imagined partner; at the other, a romantic woman may, as Stendhal mentions in his *De l'Amour*, be so psychologically immersed in her sense of union with the beloved that she is entirely oblivious of what her body is doing, and incapable of saying afterwards whether she has had an orgasm or not.

Most of what I have said so far applies to the orgasms of both men and women, but in fact male and female orgasms differ profoundly from one another, both physically and psychologically, and much marital disharmony and, indeed, general misunderstanding between the sexes stems from failure to appreciate this fact – and from the related fact that, in our culture at least, many people have great difficulty in imagining what it would be like to be a member of the other sex, and therefore lack any intuitive understanding of the physical and emotional needs of their partners.

The most striking difference between the sexes in respect of orgasm is that male orgasm is a necessary part of the art of procreation, whereas female orgasm is not. Unless the male is capable of sustaining erection, penetrating and having an orgasm, conception cannot follow. Male orgasm is, therefore, a biological necessity, whereas female orgasm is a biological luxury, since copulation and conception can occur without it; all that is *necessary* – as opposed to desirable – is that the woman should respond sufficiently to love-making to allow penetration, so that male orgasm can occur *intra vaginam*.

There is something very peculiar and puzzling about this difference between the sexes, and its consequences are varied. On the one hand, it may lead to the idea, which was commonly

held among the Victorian middle classes, that women do not
have sexual feelings or needs, that 'Ladies don't move', as Lord
Curzon is reputed to have said, and that, therefore, the sexual
act was a marital duty of the wife's, which she engaged in solely
for her husband's sake – doing so willingly if she was fond of
him and resentfully if she was not. This attitude is, incidentally,
far from being dead today and is exemplified by women who
count themselves lucky that their husbands do not 'bother' them
very often.

On the other hand, the reverse state of affairs can occur. It
can be assumed that every woman 'ought' to have an orgasm
whenever her husband does, and if – as often happens – she
does not, then marital trouble is liable to ensue. Either the wife
accuses her husband of being selfish and technically incom-
petent, or the husband accuses his wife of being frigid – or
alternatively and more nobly, each spouse blames himself for
the joint failure to achieve their ideal of simultaneous mutual
orgasm. An American psychoanalyst, Leslie Farber, has written
an ironically amusing account, entitled 'I'm sorry, Darling',
about the knots many advanced American middle-class couples
tie themselves into in their self-conscious pursuit of female
orgasm.

The truth of the matter seems to be that women vary enormously in their natural capacity and aptitude to experience
orgasm. Some do so easily and frequently; others do so only
rarely, or only under very special psychological and physical
conditions – there are, for instance, women who only do so if
they believe that the intercourse is likely to lead to pregnancy,
while there are others who only do so if they are confident that
it will not. Yet other women go through life without ever having
an orgasm. According to some estimates as many as 40 per cent
of all women belong to this last group.

It should not, however, be thought that women who rarely
or never have an orgasm are frigid or that they do not enjoy
sexual intercourse. Frigidity and 'lack of orgasic capacity' are
not the same thing, despite being frequently confused. Frigidity
is complete failure to respond to sexual stimulation and renders
penetration either impossible or painful for both partners, while

'lack of orgastic capacity' is failure to achieve orgasm despite enjoying the preliminaries of making love and despite welcoming penetration. Women who lack orgastic capacity indeed frequently enjoy the sexual act very much, appreciating the sense of intimacy involved, taking vicarious pleasure in their man's orgasm, and enjoying being enjoyed. There is, however, an unfortunate group of women who feel themselves coming to an orgasm but do not in fact quite make it. As one such woman put it, they feel as though the gates of paradise had been suddenly slammed in their faces. They experience considerable distress and post-coital tension; either they or their husbands are in need of either sexual counselling or psychotherapy.

Nor are women who lack orgastic capacity necessarily as neurotic as are men who suffer from the apparently analogous complaint of impotence. There are probably two reasons for this disparity between the sexes. Firstly, in our culture at least, male self-confidence is closely linked with the sense of achievement, whereas female self-confidence is linked with the sense of being appreciated, and this difference in the basis for self-evaluation applies in the sexual field as much as elsewhere. And, secondly, women often develop a predominantly maternal character which leads them to set higher store on giving pleasure than on receiving it. It does not occur to women of this kind to pursue or insist on their own orgastic pleasure, and many of them would, misguidedly, think themselves egocentric if they did.

It is, incidentally, of considerable interest and importance that men and women seem to differ markedly in their attitude towards one another's orgastic capacity or lack of it. Even women who do not themselves enjoy sex feel contemptuous of men who are impotent – an attitude which can lead to a vicious circle in certain marriages. The wife's lack of interest in sex demoralizes the man, he becomes impotent and then his wife becomes contemptuous of him for being so, thereby further demoralizing him. On the other hand, men vary enormously in their attitude towards female orgasm. Some men feel deeply mortified and inadequate if their wife does not have an orgasm, a reaction which some wives deal with by simulating orgasm.

Other men seem to be indifferent or oblivious to their wife's orgasm or lack of it, while yet others feel threatened by women with orgastic capacity. This last is undoubtedly a neurotic reaction, deriving from the man's fantastic conception of Woman as a devourer and castrator.

There exist currently two incompatible explanations as to why orgastic capacity is less common in women than in men. The first, which derives from psychoanalysis, attributes lack of orgastic capacity in women to psychological inhibition. According to this theory, anatomy makes it possible for girls, but not for boys, to remain unaware of their genital equipment and its sensual possibilities, while educational pressures make them regard it as a taboo area which must not be explored; as a result, fewer women than men discover their orgastic capacity during childhood and adolescent masturbation. In addition, the sexual act is all too readily, again for anatomical reasons, initially conceived by girls as a dangerous attack, in which an enormous penis is thrust into a vagina too small to receive it; as a result, the capacity to respond fully during the sexual act may be inhibited by 'penetration anxiety', by dread of being damaged or destroyed by the penis. According to this inhibition theory, orgastic incapacity in women is always, in principle, a symptom which should be treatable by psychotherapy.

The second theory, which derives from anthropology, asserts on the contrary that female orgastic capacity is not a general, inborn potentiality but a special aptitude, somewhat analogous to musical ability, which some women have and others lack, and which some societies value and cultivate and others ignore. Proponents of this theory point out that female orgasm fulfils no known biological function, occurs in no animal other than man, and that incapacity for it seems to be compatible with normal mental health. They also assert that there are several cultures in which not even verbal recognition is given to the possibility of female orgasm, but in which none the less women are considered to enjoy sexual intercourse as much if not more than men. According to this aptitude theory, orgastic incapacity in women is only a symptom if it is accompanied by a general lack of enjoyment of sexual intercourse, and the demand that all women should have orgasm, which is current in most 'advanced' circles today, is not only doomed to non-fulfilment but may also be demoralizing for both non-orgastic women and their partners. Such couples may indeed need to be liberated from what has been called 'the tyranny of the female orgasm'.

It is generally and probably correctly assumed that psychological factors enter more into women's sexual responsiveness than into men's, but it is difficult to know to what extent this is due to biological or social factors. In our society women are markedly less interested in dirty jokes, pornographic literature and filthy pictures than men, and it is rare for a woman to assess a man's attractiveness solely in terms of his vital statistics. It is, however, difficult to know whether one should seek to explain this difference between men and women in terms of women's greater inhibitions about physical sex or men's greater tendency to sexual perversion. (Voyeurism, and indeed all sexual perversions other than lesbianism, is virtually unknown in women.) It is, however, possible to enumerate a number of reasons which probably contribute to the greater psychologization of sex in women than in men.

Firstly, women are in general smaller and physically weaker than men. This, combined with the facts that for girls the initial, childhood conception of sexual intercourse is often an alarming one and that the conventional position for it puts the woman physically at the mercy of the man, means that women have a greater need than men to trust their partner and to assure themselves that the man's vigour will be tempered by gentleness and affection. However, too much cannot be made of this point, since many men are frightened of women and require assurances that the woman they sleep with is not a bitch or a harpy, while the claim of many men that they could be potent with any physically attractive woman is often an idle boast.

Secondly, for obvious reasons women have a greater, built-in awareness than men of the connection between sexual intercourse and pregnancy. As a result, they appreciate that any man they have intercourse with is one by whom they might have a child, a consideration which is likely to influence their choice of sexual partners, and to make them attracted by men whose children they would be proud to bear. This reason for women assessing men in terms of their potential role of father to their children would cease to apply if absolute faith in the reliability of contraceptives ever became general.

Thirdly, women's self-confidence tends, in our society at least, to be based on their sense of being admired and appreciated. As a result, a woman is only likely to relax and feel sufficiently at ease to enjoy sexual relations if the man gives her evidence that in addition to desiring her physically he also loves her and appreciates her value as a person. As is well known, one of the commonest complaints made by a wife against her husband is that he takes her for granted, that he uses her as a convenience and omits to court her before having sexual relations. These complaints – and the analogous ones often levelled by husbands at their wives, e.g. that she will always insist on doing the washing up just when he feels like making love – are examples of a point I made earlier that many sexual difficulties and misunderstandings seem to arise from the fact that in our society too many people grow up and marry without acquiring any conception of what it feels like to be a member of the other sex, and are therefore unwittingly tactless and unimaginative in their intimate relations with their spouses.

Fourthly, if it is indeed true that 30–40 per cent of women rarely if ever have an orgasm, the motivation for having sexual relations for many women cannot be, as it may be for men, the conscious wish to relieve physical tension and must therefore be solely for the sake of its psychological value as an affirmation of love, and as an opportunity for intimacy and closeness.

To conclude, it cannot be over-emphasized that there is something paradoxical about orgasm and the role it plays in human affairs. On the one hand, it is a physical phenomenon, an instinctual need or appetite, which almost all men and most women crave, and which can be satisfied egocentrically either solitarily by masturbation or by exploitation of a willing or reluctant object. On the other hand, it is the psychological experience which can lead to the greatest feeling of loss of self-consciousness and union with the other of which mankind is capable. It is indeed *the* psychosomatic (body-and-soul) experience, combining in one event the most intense physical pleasure with the most spiritual sense of ecstasy, and the most lively sense of being oneself with that of transcending oneself. When, as too often happens, it is artificially divided into its physical and psychological components, it forms the central theme of, on the one hand, dirty jokes, and, on the other, of much romantic poetry and mystical literature.

1971

17

Fantasies

From an early age all human beings are capable of seeing in their mind's eye objects that are not actually present and imagining themselves doing things that they are not. Psychiatrists and psychologists call this capacity of the human mind 'fantasizing' (or 'phantasizing'), writers and artists call it 'imagination', while ordinary language possesses a wealth of terms to describe different varieties of this form of mental activity; it recognizes day-dreams, pipe-dreams, reveries, fancies, whimsies, imaginings, etc. Psychiatrists and particularly psychoanalysts also assume that there are *unconscious* fantasies at work in the mind and that night-dreams are a manifestation of their activity. They are also held to influence waking behaviour in unexpected ways.

Psychologists and the general public agree that many fantasies contain a wish-fulfilling element; that when we have day-dreams we imagine ourselves doing things that we would like to do, and, furthermore, that when we are unable to satisfy some wish by real action we are liable to attempt to satisfy it by fantasizing its gratification. Explorers who are short of food are liable to have both day-dreams and night-dreams of attending banquets; people who are failing to achieve worldly success may have fantasies in which their ambitions are fulfilled; while the sexually deprived are likely to have erotic fantasies culminating in orgasm.

It would, however, be incorrect to suppose that all fantasies are wish-fulfilling. Just as some night-dreams are nightmares and extremely alarming, so some conscious, daytime fantasies concern events which the day-dreamer would certainly dread in the actual event. These unpleasant fantasies consist typically of vivid imaginings of being punished, tortured or humiliated, of being abandoned or orphaned, or of losing all that one values. Such fantasies are inexplicable on common-sense grounds and can only be explained by recourse to psychopathology, which typically traces them to the day-dreamer's unconscious sense of guilt, so that, for instance, a fantasy of being punished or tortured is explained by postulating that the day-dreamer has other, usually unconscious, fantasies for which he believes that he deserves to be punished. Much of the clinical work of psychotherapists consists in tracing the origins of such unpleasant, *masochistic* fantasies in the patient's sense of guilt for having, usually in his childhood, entertained aggressive and murderous wishes against those whom he believed he ought to love.

There are also fantasies which are in one sense wish-fulfilling, though in another not so. There are fantasies in which we imagine ourselves doing physical violence to persons whom we in fact would not wish to injure, or humiliating persons of whom we are really very fond. Such *sadistic* fantasies are wish-fulfilling in the sense that they express anger which we, justifiably or unjustifiably, are actually feeling, but are not wish-fulfilling in as much as we would be horrified were they to be realized. Although most people on occasion have fantasies of this kind, they only constitute a serious problem to persons who suffer persistently from ambivalence, i.e. from the compulsive tendency to hate those whom they also love, and to love those whom they also hate. This tendency, which is exemplified most clearly in the illness known to psychiatrists as obsessional neurosis, originates typically in childhood, in circumstances in which deprivation or oppression have led to the development of hatred of parents and siblings side by side with love and respect.

Although most sadistic and masochistic fantasies are unacceptable to the person who has them and are experienced by him as alien, involuntary phenomena of which he would happily be rid, in a minority of people they do become acceptable. In such cases they form the basis of the sexual perversions, sadism and masochism, where the individual takes pleasure in the realization of his wishes to hurt or to be hurt, to humiliate or to be humiliated. Such behaviour belongs to the pathology rather than to the psychology of love, but it should be mentioned that one of the reasons for lack of spontaneity in love-making may be the need to repress or suppress such perverse tendencies; the individual holds himself back for fear of releasing sadistic or masochistic tendencies, thereby either injuring his partner or abasing himself. Since both sadistic and masochistic fantasies may be completely unconscious, the individual who is inhibited in this way may be utterly unaware of his motive for so restraining himself.

The fact that many fantasies are wish-fulfilling has given rise to the erroneous idea that their function is essentially compensatory, and that people only have fantasies in order to counteract feelings of frustration and disappointment. This is, however, not so. Fantasies also have an anticipatory or prospective function, since they enable us to rehearse imaginatively activities that we intend to carry out in the future. For instance, ambitious fantasies may be a response to worldly disappointments and humiliations, but they may also be the way in which we look forward into the future and decide in what direction we intend to direct our energies. A young person's decision as to what career he will embrace may be based not only on a rational assessment of the practical pros and cons of becoming a doctor, a writer, a lawyer or whatever, but also on fantasies in which he imagines himself engaging in various professional activities and discovers that one of them seems to suit or excite him most. Such fantasies will be more or less realistic, depending on how much knowledge the young person has about the various professions which occur to him, but they will also be influenced by a number of highly subjective personal factors. If he enjoys showing off, he may be attracted by the idea of becoming an actor or a barrister; if he is inquisitive about bodies, he may be attracted by medicine, with its opportunities for touching and exploring. Or he may wish to follow in the footsteps of an admired parent, uncle or teacher.

One special form of anticipatory fantasy is displayed by

creative people, who have the ability, if they are artists or writers, to construct imaginary and imaginative worlds which transcend the private quality of ordinary day-dreams and acquire a universal character which makes them enjoyable to others, or, if they are scientists or inventors, to provide novel solutions for scientific or technical problems. This form of fantasy is, however, usually called 'imagination' – or, alternatively 'phantasy', with a 'ph' not an 'f'.

The distinction between anticipatory, reality-orientated and wish-fulfilling, compensatory fantasies is particularly important, and yet often difficult to make, in the case of sexual fantasies. There are basically three reasons for this difficulty.

First, in our society at least, most people do not have sexual intercourse for several years after reaching puberty. As a result, their bodies engender sexual wishes and fantasies which they are unable to realize apart from by masturbation. Adolescent sexual fantasies are therefore both wish-fulfilling and anticipatory; they both relieve the physical tensions of the present by wish-fulfilment and rehearse the sexual relationships which the individual anticipates having in the future. The same dual function is also performed by the masturbation fantasies of mature, experienced adults who are separated from their partners or who are between marriages or affairs.

Secondly, the sexual instinct is unique in being at least partially satisfiable in the absence of its appropriate object. If we are hungry, we will fancy a meal and may indeed imagine vividly the food we would like to eat, but our hunger will not be appeased unless we eventually do have a meal. The longing for food may be controlled for a while, but it cannot be repressed, sublimated or wish-fulfilled by fantasy, and if we do not eventually have something to eat, we will die. With sex, however, things are quite different. It is possible, though usually at the cost of developing neurotic symptoms or a rigid, over-controlled character, for persons to repress their sexual needs entirely. It is possible, too, for people to canalize their sexual energies into non-sexual activities, and indeed to do so knowingly, though this process is not as easy as some traditional educationalists make out. And, lastly, it is possible to satisfy at least the physical components of the sexual instinct solitarily by masturbation, a solution which can have complicated and undesirable effects.

For instance, in predisposed persons, masturbation fantasies may lose their anticipatory quality completely, in which case masturbation will become the preferred or only possible form of sexual activity, leading to the sexual perversion of narcissism, in which the individual is in love with his own body. In other people, masturbation fantasies may become so stereotyped that, although they still regard masturbation as a substitute for the 'real thing', their sexual aim in life is to discover someone who is identical with the ideal fantasy-figure which their imagination has constructed. Such people encounter severe difficulties in adapting to the actual nature and needs of their partner, if they abandon masturbation in favour of a sexual relationship with a real, live person.

Such difficulties are compounded by the fact that masturbation fantasies are constructed before the individual has had sexual relations with the opposite sex. As a result, they are likely to contain elements which derive from the individual's pre-pubertal experience of physical intimacy and from his childhood conceptions of the nature of the sexual act. In other words, masturbation fantasies have a tendency to revolve round an imaginary figure derived from the individual's conception of his mother or sister – or, in the case of women, her father or brother – and to include details which derive from his childhood speculations about what his parents did together. This fact – that masturbation fantasies tend to contain an 'infantile' core dating back to the individual's childhood – is made use of by psychoanalysts in their search for the origins of their patients' neurotic symptoms and inhibitions.

It might be thought that men and women would resent being treated as, so to speak, real substitutes for the ideal object in their partner's masturbation fantasy, but in fact this is not always so: partly because there can be something flattering about being cast as the only star in the firmament created by the other's imagination, and partly because the desire to please may lead one partner to accommodate his or her responses to the preconceived pattern of sexual behaviour already established in the other's fantasies. According to Freud, hysterical women are educable into their husband's perversions, but this tendency seems to derive not only from the desire to please but also from the need to appease a partner who is feared as much as he is loved. The discovery by one partner that he or she has not been loved for his or her own actual qualities, but only for a willingness to act as a screen on to which the other could project his or her ideal fantasy figure, is a not uncommon cause of marital breakdown, since the realization of having been used in this way is both disillusioning and humiliating.

Thirdly, human adults, unlike small children and animals, are capable both of self-deception and of deceiving others. As a result, they are capable of persuading both themselves and others that they are feeling things that they are not. For instance, a young man eager for sexual experience may succeed in persuading himself that he is in love with a girl whom he believes to be accessible – and in persuading her too. If this happens, both partners to the relationship will develop fantasies and expectations which the actual course of events will belie; when the man has satisfied his craving for experience, both he and the girl he has deceived may be appalled to discover his complete indifference to her as a person. Similarly, but more simply, successful seducers – of either sex – have the ability to pretend to be having fantasies of a higher, more intense and more imaginative order than they in fact are, and by doing so to evoke fantasies and expectations in the other which they do not intend to fulfil.

Sexual deceit of this kind is only explicable if one assumes that there are two kinds of sexual fantasy; one of which is genuine, sincere, and stems from the ground of our being, as existentialists and theologians put it, and another which is false, insincere and 'made up'. This distinction is well recognized by writers, artists and critics, who distinguish between works of art that are 'truly imaginative' and those that are 'merely fanciful', between those that are true expressions of the artist's personality and those that are 'contrived' or '*voulu*' products consciously constructed with an eye to fashion and the market. Rather similarly, sexual fantasies may be either true expressions of the individual's sexual needs and nature or they may be contrived products designed either to enhance the fantasist's own self-image or to impress his partner.

In the previous two paragraphs I have been discussing the unconscious deceptions and self-deceptions which are made possible by the human capacity for fantasy. These are, it seems, very common. They occur, for instance, in the state of 'being in love with love', when couples build up a joint romantic fantasy which the facts of life are unable to sustain, and also in various 'collusive' relationships in which both partners fall in love with the fantastic self-image of the other and offer themselves as the other's ideal fantasy object. Such relationships can last a surprisingly long time, though the eventual disenchantment is liable to be correspondingly catastrophic. The history of such relationships has been tersely summarized in the saying, 'They lived happily together for years, and then they met.'

Of course, conscious, deliberate deceptions occur too. It is quite possible for a person to make love with one partner while imagining that he or she is making love with someone else, and I once encountered the case of a man who could only make love to his wife if *she* pretended that he was someone else. In such instances there is a gross discrepancy between the fantasies going on in one or both partners' minds and the actual physical activities they are engaged in.

The reasons for such emotional tortuosities are various. Sometimes they arise from one partner's dread of being possessed, which compels him to conjure up a second imaginary image, so that he gives himself only partially to his real partner. Sometimes it is a ruse for committing adultery without actually doing so. Sometimes it is a technique for reconciling a disappointing reality with romantic aspirations. This solution of a not uncommon dilemma is hinted at in the story of the man who was asked whether he preferred to sleep with a woman or dream of sleeping with one and answered, 'Dream of sleeping with one. You meet a better class of woman that way.' Paradoxically, sexual deceptions cease to be deceitful if they are openly admitted and accepted by both parties, since they then become games; though couples capable of such honesty with one another are unlikely to want to play such games.

1971

18

The Naked Ape Strikes Again

Although Desmond Morris's *Intimate Behaviour*,[1] the successor to *The Naked Ape*, is perhaps excessively the mixture as before, its theme – the role of touching in human relationships – its trendy, suggestive title, and its peculiar combination of accurate information with intriguing though often unconvincing biological and ethological speculation, will no doubt earn it an equal success. It will, therefore, do the book no harm if I confine myself to pointing out that its author's basic assumptions about the nature of intimacy and love are by no means as self-evident or as universally accepted as he seems to believe. These assumptions are stated with exemplary clarity in the introduction.

1. *Intimacy*. Dr Morris opens by asserting that:

> To be intimate means to be close, and I must make it clear at the outset that I am treating this literally. In my terms, then, the act of intimacy occurs whenever two individuals come into bodily contact.

In a free country one is, of course, entitled to use words as one chooses, especially if one plays fair and defines one's terms, as Dr Morris does here, but he has in fact created confusion for both himself and his readers by defining intimacy in a way that offends against common usage, dictionaries and etymology. Common usage does not equate intimacy with bodily contact – indeed it allows one to deny that one is intimate with someone despite seeing and touching them daily – but with knowing of a particular kind (*kennen* not *wissen*, *connaître* not *savoir*) which gives one an inner conviction that one understands (*ver-*

[1] Desmond Morris, *Intimate Behaviour* (London: Jonathan Cape, 1971).

stehen not *begreifen*) the other's inner mode of being. Dictionaries confirm this; *The Concise Oxford Dictionary* defines
'intimate' as 'close in acquaintance, familiar . . . essential, intrinsic', and derives it from the Latin *intimus*, meaning 'inmost';
while *The Penguin English Dictionary* gives 'closely linked by
friendship; pertaining to one's deepest feelings or thoughts'.

Dr Morris has, of course, confounded intimacy and contiguity, and by doing so has obscured from view the major
limitation to the contribution that his own science, zoology,
can make to the study of human relationships, namely that
the objective techniques it uses cannot engender concepts for
distinguishing between behaviour and the meaning of behaviour. The phrase 'intimate behaviour' is indeed a logical
bastard, since its two components belong to incompatible
frames of reference: those used by the humanities and those
used by the natural sciences. In fact, as we all know, contiguity
only gives rise to a feeling of intimacy if we feel justified
in interpreting the other's touching of us as a meaningful,
self-revelatory response to our own intentional gesture of self-
revelation. And, as we also all know, many of the tragedies,
comedies and ironies of life arise from discrepancies between
contiguity and intimacy, from misinterpretations of the meaning
of bodily contact. For one party to a kiss, it may be a formality
or a chore; to the other, an expression of passion or devotion.

Dr Morris is, it seems to me, oblivious of this distinction
between contiguity and intimacy. He describes pressing one's
hand against one's cheek in embarrassment as a form of 'self-
intimacy', and appears to believe that he has made a serious
contribution to the study of sexual intimacy by dividing the
progress from non-contact to copulation into twelve stages,
each defined in terms of the bodily organs which are being
apposed to one another. Hardly surprisingly, his discussion of
rape is peculiarly inept. It is, he says, an example of 'reduction
of the sequence', since 'the first stage runs as quickly as is
physically possible to the last stage', and is biologically undesirable since 'the rapist male, by omitting all the intermediate
stages of the sexual sequence, clearly does not allow a bond of
attachment to grow between himself and the female in question'.

In some species this 'would create no problems', but in man it is regrettable since 'our species does require this personal attachment to develop, as a means of safeguarding the successful rearing of the offspring that may result from the copulation'. Rapists with a conscience should, one infers, confine their attentions to sterile women.

2. *Love*. According to Dr Morris: 'Above all, loving means touching and bodily contact.' No one who has thought about the meaning of meaning could write such a sentence. Even if one subscribes to the view that there is some connection between loving and bodily contact, it is impossible to discern what sort of connection is implied by this use of the word 'means'. Does Dr Morris mean that loving means striving towards bodily contact, in which case he is confusing desiring and loving and would be in difficulties if he tried to explain why lovers sometimes continue to love one another after they have achieved full bodily contact? Or does he mean that loving is bodily contact, in which case he ought logically to maintain that mothers only love their children while they are actually mothering them and that lovers only love one another while they are making love?

In either case Morris is running counter to the usage adopted almost unanimously by theologians, poets and psychologists, who relate loving, as opposed to lusting and desiring, not to contiguity but to continuity, and insist, to talk Dr Morris's own language, that: 'Above all, loving means continuing to relate during the intervals between touching and bodily contact'. McDougall, one of the few psychologists audacious enough to define love, classified it as a sentiment and described it as an 'organized disposition' and an 'enduring tendency' to feel tender emotions towards its object.

To be fair to Dr Morris, he is in fact well aware that loving is a matter of continuity as well as contiguity; but the means he adopts for accommodating continuity into his conceptual framework strike me as highly unsatisfactory. This is to equate 'falling in love' with the 'pair-bonding' of animals and love with 'pair-maintenance', and then to argue that pair-bonding and pair-maintenance in both animals and man are the *result* of touching and bodily contact. He believes, indeed, that there is a specifically human tendency to form monogamous unions and that this is an evolutionary development designed to ensure that human males, unlike other primate males, act as fathers to their children; and, furthermore, that this development is correlated with the fact that men, and more particularly women, differ from the other primates in possessing hypertrophied and permanently visible sexually exciting erotic zones (e.g. breasts and buttocks), which keep pair-mates sexually attached to one another throughout the childhood of their offspring. In other words, he believes that keeping father permanently sexually aroused and attached to mother is nature's way of keeping him at home.

Although this purely physical account of loving possibly has some obscure phylogenetic sense to it, it is incapable of even beginning to account for two characteristic aspects of human loving. It cannot explain why psychologically developed people are highly selective in their choice of whom to pair-bond with, or why many if not most people experience loving as the reverse of the process described by Morris; they imagine that they touch because they love, not that they love because they touch. It also lands him in at least one ridiculous contradiction: as a good liberal Morris disapproves of arranged marriages, which he calls 'economic rape', but his theory of pair-bonding by sexual arousal could easily be used to support its traditional justification, that 'love comes after marriage'.

Morris's conception of love is indeed wholly vitiated by his inability to distinguish between behaviour and its meaning and between contiguity and intimacy. Although it may well be true that contiguity and sexual arousal enhance and sustain love, his theoretical, behavioural stance makes it impossible for him even to begin to explain why the initial attraction between future pairs is often based on shared interests and intimations of possible mutual understanding, and not on sexual stimulation, or why marriages may founder on deceit and not on sexual incompatibility. And by defining love solely in terms of visible, observable behaviour, he is compelled to write as though 'sublimated' forms of love, which transcend the physical and which depend on man's capacity to form symbols and to interact in symbolic modes, do not exist.

Finally, and in order to avoid misunderstanding, I must make it clear that I am not maintaining that intimacy and love have no connection with the fact that bodies can touch one another, nor that animal studies are irrelevant to human relationships. I am, however, suggesting that applying objective modes of thought to the study of man is a more difficult enterprise than Dr Morris seems to realize. Since the natural sciences are based on observation of visible phenomena, they lack the conceptual tools for dealing with a creature who can deceive and tell lies, who wants to understand and be understood as well as to touch and be touched, and who is concerned not only with behaviour but with its meaning. And, so it seems to me, anyone who ignores the subjective element in human experience when writing about intimate behaviour is unwittingly misleading his readers and perhaps even doing them a disservice.

1971

BIOGRAPHY
AND AUTOBIOGRAPHY

19

On Autobiography

In the early, heroic days of psychoanalysis, it would not, I imagine, have been difficult to find an analyst prepared to propound with confidence *the* psychoanalytical theory of autobiography. In a paper entitled, perhaps, *The Psychopathology of Autobiography* or *The Autobiographer as Narcissist and Exhibitionist*, the infantile fixation points and the unconscious perverse fantasies of the autobiographer would have been located and defined, and autiobiographers added to the list of those who, like children, savages, neurotics, lunatics and artists were impelled by the primitive, primary processes of their id.

But such a reductionist approach would be inconceivable today, and modern analysts are, I think, more likely to be impressed by the number of daunting problems about consciousness, self-consciousness, identity and memory that are raised by autobiographies than by the fact that particular autobiographies may provide evidence confirming, or perhaps even contradicting, particular psychoanalytical theories about human development.

The Shorter Oxford English Dictionary defines autobiography as 'The writing of one's own history; the story of one's life written by himself', thereby drawing attention to the salient and perhaps the only certain fact about autobiography: the fact that writing an autobiography is a reflexive activity, since the author and his subject are by definition the same person. Or so the ordinary conventions of thought, language and everyday life compel one to assume. But if one allows oneself to question the unity and identity of the person who writes the autobiography and the subject who is written about, and considers the possibility that neither the autobiographer nor the auto-biographee are single selves but are rather multiple sets of selves, it becomes apparent that the writer of an autobiography is engaged in an activity far more complex than the word 'reflexive' comes anywhere near to suggesting. The appropriate visual analogy ceases to be that of a painter painting a self-portrait and becomes that of someone occupying a temporal corridor of mirrors and communing in turn with images of past and present selves.

The previous paragraph is too abstract and obscure, and I must try again. It is, I am suggesting, misleadingly naive to suppose that writing an autobiography is simply a process during which a person writes down his memories of his past life, since neither the person writing the autobiography nor the person being written about is really such a simple entity as such a description would seem to imply. The autobiographer cannot be just a camera to his own past, but must (cannot but) select his memories in the light of his present conception of himself; and his memories are not just audio-visual tape-recordings of the events in his past, but are experiences pressing for (or sometimes resisting and eluding) imaginative recollection and carrying with them revivable past conceptions of both the author and his subject. The process of writing an autobiography is, I am suggesting, not one in which the present 'I' records the events in the life of the past 'me', but one in which a dialectic takes place between present 'I' and past 'me', at the end of which both have changed and the author—subject could say equally truthfully, 'I wrote it' and 'It wrote me'.

I am, of course, well aware that many books that purport to be autobiographies can fairly accurately be described as a present 'I' recalling and recording the activities of a past 'me', but such books, which are typically written by politicians, public personalities famous for being famous and actors, are really better called memoirs and recollections. Their aim is neither self-discovery nor self-revelation but, rather, self-assertion, the staking of a claim of deserving to be remembered. I shall say more about such books later, but first I must explain why as a psychotherapist I should choose to view autobiography in a way that has plunged me immediately into such obscurities as multiple selves and dialectics between past and present.

As a psychotherapist I am compelled to question both the conception of himself and the history of his life that each patient brings to me initially. If he knew himself truly and his implicit, unwritten autobiography was accurate, he would surely not seek or need my assistance. As a result, it has become natural for me to conceive of myself as an assistant autobiographer, concerned to notice and point out consistencies and recurrences that have not occurred to the patient himself, to point out biases in the direction of, typically, self-denigration or self-justification, and to discriminate between his own true voice and his learned imitations of other, typically ancestral voices. It is striking that all the various schools of psychotherapy have developed terminologies for distinguishing between true and false self, between persona (mask) and self, between assertive ego and creative unconscious, between authentic and inauthentic, expressive and defensive, spontaneous and rigid. Given my immersion in patients and the learned literature, it is, I think, hardly surprising that my own ideal conception of an autobiography should be one in which the autobiographer remains in pursuit of himself while recounting himself, and that I should betray impatience with autobiographers who are merely advertising the continued existence of a long-standing ego.

It is, however, far from certain that such an ideal autobiography has or ever could be realized. Wordsworth's *The Prelude* and Proust's *A la recherche du temps perdu* came to my mind as works in which the art is generated by the continued dialectic between the author's past and present, but although autobiographical, neither is strictly speaking an autobiography. The intention of both is something other and more than the 'writing of one's own history'. Wordsworth described *The Prelude* as 'the poem on the growth of my own mind', and, as his own mind in his own view was essentially a poet's mind, he was concerned with the growth of his poetic capacity and imagination and not with the story of all his other selves and how they interwove and interacted to create the life of William

Wordsworth, Esq., distributor of stamps for the county of Westmoreland and Poet Laureate. And Proust, if Roger Shattuck's and R. C. Zaehner's interpretation of *A la recherche* is correct, was concerned to contrast the ephemerality, the intermittence, the pointlessness of life as lived by one's (his) everyday ego with the sense of permanence and timelessness revealed by those moments in which one is (he was) touched and surprised by live memory:

> Then, immediately, the permanent essence of things which is usually hidden, is set free, and our real self, which often had seemed dead for a long time yet was not dead altogether, awakes and comes to life as it receives the heavenly food now proffered to it. One minute delivered from the order of time creates in us, that we may enjoy it, the man delivered from the order of time.

Few autobiographers, however, aim as high as Wordsworth and Proust, and the time has come for me to say something about those who aim to do no more than tell the story of their own life. Firstly, it has to be said that all autobiographies are of necessity incomplete accounts of their subject's life, since the beginning, birth and infancy, is beyond recall and can only be known about by hearsay, and the end, death, can only take place after the autobiographer has stopped writing. The fantasy of being one's own Recording Angel, who has known and understood and perhaps forgiven everything, must therefore be an illusion.

Secondly, an autobiography cannot be an accurate, complete record or chronicle of anyone's life, since it would take a lifetime to record a lifetime, and anyone who attempted to write a blow-by-blow account of his life would get caught in an infinite regress, having to spend time and words describing his autobiographizing. It has been said that history is the record of what each generation chooses to remember of its predecessors, and something analogous must apply to autobiography. It is, perhaps, a record by one's self of what all its preceding selves have chosen to remember of their predecessors, though this implies that memory is more like a filtering sieve than I suspect it really is. Autobiographies cannot but be selective, the selection being based partly on what has been registered and is available for recall, and partly on the autobiographer's intentions. Self-justification, self-aggrandizement, confession and a talent to amuse will lead to different selections being made from a nearly infinite store of memories available. Extrovert public figures and artists primarily interested in their *vie intérieure* will rather obviously recall different aspects of their lives and re-fight different kinds of battle when they come to write their autobiographies. Autobiographies are also unconsciously selective in a way that probably only doctors and psychoanalysts notice; they underestimate the part played by biological processes in the story of one's life. If anyone were to write a psychosomatic autobiography, giving equal weight to soma and psyche, not only would bodily functions play a larger role than existing autobiographical conventions allow them, but a quite different set of patterns and connections would emerge.

Thirdly, autobiography has an inbuilt tendency towards something that has, I think, to be called falsification. The process of detaching that thread, which is one's own life, from the fabric which has been simultaneously woven by those around one one introduces an inherent bias towards egocentricity at the expense of objectivity, and towards exaggeration of one's difference and alienation from others. There are, to be sure, ways in which an autobiographer may seek more or less successfully to correct this bias, notably by sharing the stage with someone or something else, e.g. his art or his profession, that he values as much as himself, but paradoxically this purchases truth (and often readability) at the cost of deviating from pure autobiography. The classic examples of the genre, e.g. Cellini's and Rousseau's, were after all written by monumental egotists.

Social historians and literary critics, e.g. Lionel Trilling, tell us that autobiography is a comparatively recent literary genre and that its rise is a consequence and manifestation of 'something like a mutation in human nature' – the phrase is Trilling's – that occurred in the late sixteenth and early seventeenth centuries. As a result of this mutation, that abstraction Modern Man came to conceive of himself as having a self, an identity, which was defined in terms of itself – and not, as previous men had defined themselves, in terms of their social role or achievements – and in terms of its opposition to, not membership of, society. As Trilling says: 'The subject of an autobiography is just such a self, bent on revealing himself in all his truth, bent that is to say on demonstrating his sincerity.' In other words, people became individuals and ceased to be limbs of the body politic, and their inner experiences, their private inner selves, became of paramount interest to themselves, and, if written down, of potential interest to others. On this view the writing of autobiographies, individualism and alienation are facets of a social, historical process that legitimizes egocentricity and makes one's own self-awareness an, perhaps even the, appropriate object of one's attention.

According to Lacan, the development of the modern '*Je*' was encouraged by the manufacture of mirrors. Blown-glass mirrors were first manufactured on a commercial scale in Venice in the early sixteenth century and plate-glass mirrors became available and cheap early in the eighteenth. So, whereas medieval man can only have had fleeting and blurred impressions of his own body, modern man can see himself clearly in mirrors and has opportunities for entrancing encounters with his own image. It is, therefore, tempting to correlate the enormous increase in the production of autobiographies in this century with the technological changes that have enabled people to make physical self-scrutiny a daily bathroom event and to see – and hear – themselves as others see them.

But maybe, as Trilling has pointed out, it was really all the other way round, and it was the 'something like a mutation in human nature', leading to greater self-awareness, that created the demand for mirrors and the impetus to invent cameras, films, and tape-recorders. In either case autobiographers are liable to become ensnared by one of the moral contradictions of our individualistic society. The pursuit of fame, cultivation of one's gifts in pursuit of self-fulfilment, searching for one's identity, writing the story of one's life, are all meritorious activities which none the less expose one to charges of egotism and vanity. Renan, who in late middle age published his *Souvenirs d'enfance et de jeunesse*, none the less wrote:

To suppose that the trivial details of one's own life are worth recording is to give proof of the pettiest vanity. One writes such things in order to communicate to others the theory of the universe one bears within oneself.

And also: 'The man who has time to keep a private diary has never understood the immensity of the universe.'

1983

20

Where I Came From

In the mid 1960s, when books by me were first going through the press, two publishers, independently of one another, asked me to write a short account of myself, on the grounds that it would help them to market me if they knew where I came from. One of them had had an education very similar to my own and had already expressed his amazement and amusement that the son of a fox-hunting country gentleman should have become a psychoanalyst; the other was a foreigner who had acquired a preposterously romanticized, idealized and inaccurate vision of the English upper classes. Although I have rewritten what I wrote then, what follows still bears the traces of my wish to entertain one and both impress and disenchant the other; and since what I wrote then was backroom work for a public-relations exercise, it contains no reference to the traumas, griefs, conflicts and confusions that were the inevitable price of coming from where I came. In any case, these were all shared by others who are still alive, and it would be impossible to describe them from my private standpoint without both abusing confidences and falsifying the facts by detaching that thread which is my own life from the fabric of which it is only a part.

I was born on the 9th September 1914, just after the outbreak of the First World War, the youngest son of Sir Richard Nelson Rycroft, 5th Baronet, and his second wife, Emily Mary, elder daughter of Colonel the Honourable William Lowry-Corry. I was my father's fourth son, and the only one not to be given one of his Christian names, and my mother's second. My two half-brothers were twenty-eight and seventeen years older than myself, and are both long dead. My one full brother is two-and-a-half years older than I am, and my two sisters are both younger than me. They are all, like myself, still alive and in good health. Although our paths and interests have diverged widely over the years, the mutual support system that existed in our childhood can still on occasion reconstitute itself.

Despite the title, the Rycrofts are really country gentry rather than aristocracy. Although the ancestry in the direct male line can be traced back to about 1400, not one of them has achieved an entry in *The Dictionary of National Biography*, and one of my father's younger brothers, who was a general in the First World War and later a Colonial Governor, is the only Rycroft ever to achieve even the slightest fame. When, as a child, I first heard of the equator, I imagined it as a wire fence that went through Uncle Bill's garden in Borneo City.

No information seems to be available as to why my great-great-great-grandfather, who was a clergyman, was created a baronet in 1784, but I have never heard it suggested that it had anything to do with merit. According to one family tradition he himself thought his ennoblement ridiculous and really aspired to a bishopric. According to another, he accepted his baronetcy as payment in kind for money won from the then Prime Minister at the gaming tables. Nor is it known in any detail how the Rycrofts, who were yeoman farmers in Yorkshire until the early eighteenth century, became rich enough by the end of it to maintain both town and country houses and to commission portraits from leading painters.

However, although the Rycrofts themselves are country gentry of, as they say, good yeoman stock, the three marriages made by my grandfather and father were all to women who undoubtedly were members of the ruling upper classes. When, in the 1850s, my grandfather asked for the hand of a plain Miss, he had, so I have been told, to overcome opposition based on the argument that he lacked the status to marry the niece of both a Duke and an Earl. According to my sisters, my mother thought she was socially superior to my father, but if she did, she never breathed a word of it to her sons. However, as a result of my grandfather's and father's marriages, I am 'well-connected', and quite a number of people in English history and even in contemporary politics turn out to be ancestors or distant relatives. As a teenager I was, I hope forgivably, impressed by these connections, but as my contact with relatives other than close ones has been slight since I grew up, they have on the whole been an embarrassment. I retain, however, a nose for the absurdities and anachronisms into which snobbery can lead people, and for the myths which families, and indeed larger social units, weave about their origins and forebears.

As my father was born in 1859, three years after Freud and six before Kipling, and as the country gentry are perhaps the most conservative class in the country, my childhood was an old-fashioned one. I can clearly remember a world which remained Victorian well into the twentieth century, one in which the rich lived in large houses often with no electricity or gas, no central heating, no bathroom – we did have electricity, and I can remember central heating and the telephone being installed, but there was no bathroom, cleanliness being achieved with hip-baths in one's bedroom – but with rows of servants, coachmen and gardeners, all of whom regarded my father not only as their employer but also as the local representative of both Church and State. He was Patron of the living and Governor of the village school, and only one house in the village did not belong to him.

And, since there were four children in the house, there was Nana, who stayed and both bullied and adored her charges, nursery maids, who left and whose love-affairs were quite instructive, and governesses who also left. I remember hating one because she favouritized me and was horrid to my brother. Since nurses and governesses – and cooks, butlers and gardeners – have domains in which they wield power, children who grow up in such an extended family receive unwittingly – unless they feel hopelessly outnumbered and confused – an education in playing one authority off against another. If Miss Muskett, the governess, disapproves of her charges reading strip cartoons, Mrs Anscombe, the cook, who hates Miss Muskett, will make a point of buying the *Daily Mirror* so that we can follow the careers of Pip, Squeak and Wilfred. If one's parents think one is still too young to learn to ride a bicycle, a gardener can be persuaded to teach one, and one's parents have to accept that one already can ride a bicycle.

The only sport my father took seriously was fox-hunting, and we were brought up to be rather contemptuous of all ball games, even though, of course, cricket and tennis helped to fill in the gap between the end of one hunting season and the beginning of the next. He had indeed been a Master of Fox Hounds for some years before I was born, as his grandfather had been before him and as later his eldest son and eldest grandson were to be. I once read an article in the *Field* which said that the name of Rycroft was 'illustrious' in the annals of fox-hunting. My mother, on the other hand, was an indoor person. She never rode or shot or played tennis or golf or went for a walk on her own account.

However, despite the fox-hunting, my family was neither barbarian nor philistine. Both men and women were expected to be well-informed about history, politics and English literature (up to about 1900), but intellectualism and its relative introspection were both suspect. Mathematics, however, was held in high esteem, and my brother and I were both years ahead of our age when we went to school. Religion was also taken seriously. My parents actually believed in the Church to which so many of their class only conformed, and while my father grounded his sons in the first principles of mathematics, my mother gave all her children religious instruction, even to the extent of explaining to us the symbolism of church architecture. I don't think it ever occurred to either of them that there was any conflict between science and religion; the enemy of both was superstition.

The atmosphere, then, was cultivated rather than cultured, and although there were good books and good pictures around, they were old books and old pictures. Music was unrepresented. Although my mother could play the piano quite nicely and had had singing lessons until she married, music played no part in our life, apart from nursery rhymes and hymns in church. I can remember relatives boasting of occasions on which they had failed to recognize 'God Save the King', as it then was, and my own ability to sing in tune was remarked upon as peculiar, if not freakish.

My father died in 1925, when I was eleven, having both looked and behaved like a young man until about eighteen months before his death. Dummer House, the mainly eighteenth-century country house in Hampshire where we had lived, was inherited by my eldest half-brother, who lived there until he sold it in 1939. My mother took her children to live in East Anglia, first with her father, who was still alive, and then in the dower house of a castle owned by an extremely remote female relative. There must, I think, have been a perhaps un-spoken contract between Cousin Beatrice and my mother, by which my mother performed the social duties of the lady of the manor, running the Women's Institute, the Mother's Union, the Girl's Friendly Society, etc., in return for living in the dower house at a reduced rent. By modern standards my father's will was most peculiar and unfair, and the principle of primogeniture was applied ruthlessly. As a result, we spent the second half of our childhoods in aristocratic poverty, enjoying the amenities of the castle, which included a lake in which we could bathe and a Norman keep in which we were allowed to rollerskate, and developing the tastes and mannerisms of the rich without the income. My mother minded her demotion to the position of poor relation very much, and for much of my teens and her forties she was what I would now describe as 'clinically depressed'.

When I was eight, I was sent to a fashionable and rather enlightened preparatory school in Dorset, where my brother had preceded me. He went on to Dartmouth and the Navy and I, at thirteen, went to Wellington, a public school with a strong Army bias. From birth it had been assumed that I would go into the Army – such a suitable career for a younger son, and two of my elder brothers were already in the Church and the Navy – but when at seventeen I decided not to, no one objected and both my mother and my housemaster, who secretly har-boured advanced views and whose wife used to lend me the books which the school authorities banned, were delighted. My mother had not felt entitled to go against my late father's wishes for me, and my housemaster, he later told me, had not dared risk his job by advising me not to go into the Army. So the decision had to be made by me alone, and it was something of an anti-climax to discover that it was being greeted with relief and not opposition.

The fact that Wellington was an Army school had one rather curious consequence. At least a fifth of the boys were the sons of Army officers who had been killed in action, and so my own orphaned state was in no way remarkable, and as I had been born in the year in which the First World War started, it was often assumed that I too was one of the *heroum filii* – the sons of heroes – for whom Wellington College had been founded. In fact, my father had fought in the Boer War, but had been too old for active service in the First World War.

Neither at my preparatory school nor at Wellington was I considered particularly bright, despite being top of every maths class I was ever in, though an occasional master thought I was interesting. I never reached the sixth form at Wellington nor became a school prefect. I was uninterested in organized games, except for a short-lived enthusiasm and glory as a wing three-quarter at rugger, but got my school colours for running, which entitled me to wear the hatband of a Gentleman of the Hunt.

When I decided not to go into the Army, I had no idea what I did want to do and so, in order to give myself time to find out, I decided to go to the University. This turned out to mean Cambridge, as Rycrofts had been going there since 1760. Looking back on it, it seems to me extraordinary that I should have had to, or been allowed to, make so many decisions alone and unaided. But in the early 1930s careers masters did not exist, and intelligence and aptitude tests were unknown.

At Cambridge things were very different. Within a few weeks of arriving there I discovered that I was thought to be a certain first and, indeed, at the end of my first year I did achieve a First Class, Second Division, in the first part of the economics tripos, and was elected an Exhibitioner of Trinity College.

Although a success at Cambridge, I was not an outstanding one. I held office in the Socialist Society, the Education Society and the Society for Cultural Relations with the Soviet Union, but I was the leading light in none of them. My left-wing interests and activities required no moral courage. Marxism was fashionable at the time, Trinity has a tradition of being advanced, and my family, with the exception of one aunt who never forgave me for wearing a hammer and sickle badge while staying with her, took the view that it was proper for young men to engage in political activity and that it was best for them to start on the left and move rightwards as they grew older. I had sloughed off all formal religious beliefs while at Wellington without much agonizing, although I upset my mother very much by doing so.

At the end of my third year at Cambridge I took a Second Class, First Division, in the modern history tripos Part II, but my supervisor, the eccentric Reverend F. A. Simpson, took the view that I should have got a first and I was elected to two studentships, which enabled me to stay up at Cambridge for a fourth year in which I was nominally doing research, though nothing worth publishing ever emerged. In retrospect it again seems to me extraordinary that I should have been elected a research student without any pointers as to what I should do research on or any suggestion that I should serve an apprenticeship assisting someone already experienced in research work.

My interest in psychoanalysis began quite early at Cambridge. Unlike several of my friends I had never heard of Freud while at school, but at Cambridge we all read him and two friends of mine applied for training at the Institute of Psycho-Analysis at about the same time as myself. We were all interviewed by Ernest Jones, and comparing notes afterwards it was obvious that he used offensiveness as a deliberate interview technique.

I cannot remember ever having had any resistance to such ideas as symbolism and dream interpretation, but for two years after first reading any Freud I did not consider the possibility of becoming an analyst myself. Although it had vaguely occurred to me that psychoanalysis was an activity for which I might have aptitude, I tacitly assumed that it was a profession reserved for Central Europeans, who at that time I believed to be intrinsically more intelligent and cultured than the English. However, during my third year at Cambridge I became friendly with a number of Bloomsbury families, who all talked about psychoanalysis a lot and believed it to be the science of the future, and I was eventually persuaded to apply for training by Karin Stephen. By that time I had, I think, read all the Freud that was then available in book form in English, but I can have had no idea what mental illness was all about and had failed to register the significance of the psychoanalytical movement. Psychoanalysis was just a fascinating new idea which looked as though it might have a contribution to make to history, sociology, medicine and the arts, and by which I might be able to earn a living. If I had known about the psychoanalytical movement's sectarianism and its tendency to engage in unedifying in-fighting, I would, I suspect, not have applied for training.

My first application was made in 1936, when I was twenty-two, and I was rejected, but told that a later application would be welcomed if I agreed to do medicine. In 1937, after having spent a further year at Cambridge as a research student and having decided that I did not want to become an academic, I applied again and was accepted. I started both my training analysis with Ella Sharpe and medicine at University College, London, in October 1937. My decision to do analysis encountered no opposition from either my family or Trinity, though both had been very dubious about the idea of my becoming a lay analyst. At about this time my mother unearthed a letter I had written to her when I was seventeen, saying that I was sure that I did not want to become either a doctor or a clergyman, and she pointed out that after a fashion I was deciding to become both.

Both my medical and analytical trainings were long drawn out, partly on account of the war and the evacuation of University College out of London. I also had great difficulty getting started on medicine and failed my First MB several times. But once I had got the hang of biological thinking, and, incidentally, of botanical techniques, I found medicine consistently interesting and daily contact with patients I found liberating. I qualified in medicine in 1945 and in analysis in 1947, having during the course of my trainings spent whatever money I had inherited and in addition accumulated an impressive debt. So in 1947 I went into full-time private psychoanalytical practice, after only eighteen months' work in general and psychiatric hospitals. I regret this, as my career has been less medical than I would have liked it to have been and gives the impression of my setting less store by medicine than I do.

Between 1947 and 1961 I sat on numerous committees of the British Psycho-Analytical Society, held several offices and wrote numerous 'scientific' papers. However, as the years went on, I increasingly came to feel that, although the Society had no objection to my doing administrative work for them, and although I received polite, sincere but often uncomprehending praise for my papers, my voice really carried very little weight in its affairs, and that the real power in the Society belonged to people of whose values I did not approve. Their analytical theories might be all right and interesting, but their ways of conducting business and engaging in controversy were entirely alien to me. I also came to feel that by Cambridge standards the analytical movement's academic level was pathetic, and that by medical standards it lacked common sense. Nor, I came to realize, did Englishmen cut any ice in it, and I was appalled by the struggle Winnicott had in order to get a proper hearing.

I therefore decided to withdraw from the Society, and over the years I have conducted a long-term strategic withdrawal such that now, in 1984, I am not a member of any psychoanalytical organization, I sit on no committees, I write for the general reader not for learned journals; but I continue to see patients, contact with whom I still find consistently interesting and liberating.

1984

21

Memoirs of an Old Bolshevik

The fact that our present Labour government is fulfilling to the letter communist predictions about the role of social democracy in prolonging the death pangs of capitalism has taken me back to the two years in the 1930s during which I was a member of a university Communist Party.

Having prematurely exhausted the amenities of my public school, I had spent the first half of 1933 in Germany, nominally learning German but in fact spending much of my time attending Nazi rallies, watching street fights and distributing banned copies of *The Times* which my brother sent me wrapped up in copies of the *Tatler*. When I went up to the university in the autumn of 1933, I was amazed to discover that it was only the extreme left-wing undergraduate organizations that were aware of what was going on in Germany and had realized that the Nazis were bent on war. I joined the communist-run Anti-War Movement soon after arriving, and a few months later I left the Conservative Association and joined the Socialist Club, of which to my surprise I was soon elected an officer.

My conversion, however, had surprisingly little effect on my daily life, which continued to be that of a young man who is treating the university as a finishing school first and as a seat of learning second. I went to sherry parties, May-week balls and point-to-points, and considered it bad form actually to be seen working. Books vanished under the sofa whenever visitors knocked on the door, and much of the necessary reading was done in the vacation so as to ensure that it did not interfere with the social round.

Many, but as we shall see not all, of the socialists and

communists I now met were quite unlike anything I had known before. They had accents and scholarships, wore polo sweaters and mackintoshes and were obviously contemptuous of anyone who appeared to take superficial matters seriously or serious matters lightly. From them I learnt that intensity, which I had previously thought a vice, was really a virtue, and also that I, poor thing, was decadent, a dilettante, a member of a dying class, precluded by the dialectic of history from ever having any understanding of the modern world or from playing any significant role in it. I was too young and innocent then to realize that passionate intensity is a sign of doubt rather than certainty or to appreciate that envy and vanity lay behind their attitude towards me. Nor did I cotton on to the fact that their theories led to the conclusion that they, the educated cadres of the proletariat, would form the ruling class of the future.

However, their patronizing but mostly indulgent attitude towards myself and my historical disabilities did not disturb me unduly. There was, I reflected, a rather satisfying combination of the romantic and the absurd in the idea that I would make a suitable exhibit in the Victoria and Albert and that my survival in the world to come would be an affront to immutable historical processes. One comrade entertained the whimsy that after the revolution some part of England, perhaps Gloucestershire, should be converted into a Social History Museum, a game reserve in which I and other valuable specimens from the *ancien régime* should be preserved for posterity.

However, even dinosaurs have their uses, and my decadence and respectability – curiously, the two terms were synonymous – were of considerable value to the movement. I looked presentable and reassuring on a platform, and could be trusted to entertain visiting liberal speakers without making it too obvious that they were supporting a cover organization. For some time, indeed, I was myself a deceived innocent, but one day, having arrived unexpectedly early for a Socialist Club committee meeting, I discovered that the other members were in the habit of meeting half an hour before the official time in order to work out the Party line in my absence.

This arrangement struck me as inefficient and eventually the

Party too decided that it was wasteful to hold Socialist Club committee meetings in duplicate merely for my sake. So a Party member, since ennobled by Mr Wilson, was told to put me on his contact list and get me into the Party. He failed, largely because he thought charm was a more persuasive revolutionary weapon than argument, but the kill was eventually made by a research student of the college who was already a full-time Party official – though he was paid by the college to do research on Balzac. Mark had rooms on the next staircase to me, he seemed to need little sleep, and I joined the Party after a marathon series of indoctrination sessions lasting far into the night. It had become a choice between joining and exhaustion.

I am, however, perhaps exaggerating his persistence and underestimating his intelligence and plausibility. He was by far the best-read person I had hitherto met and he took more trouble over me than any tutor or teacher had ever done. He also had a very ecumenical approach towards communism, which enabled him to convert people to it without requiring them to change their opinion on any important matter.

I should explain that the university Communist Party was at that time divided into two schools of thought, which were widely known as the gospels of St Matthew and St Mark, Mark being an intellectual Jesuit, Matthew a romantic puritan. Matthew believed that the bourgeoisie were damned, but that individual bourgeois could be saved if they were prepared to give up everything for the Party and throw in their lot with the working class. Ideally they should renounce their private incomes or give their capital to the Party, but failing that they should at least change their accents and their clothes and sound and look like proletarians. Matthew, who came from an upper-middle-class family well known for its high culture and intelligence, had made this sacrifice himself, but he never quite believed that anyone else had done so sincerely; in which he was perhaps right, since the romantic appeal of undergoing a class metamorphosis attracted imitators whose motives were affected rather than sincere. Among his converts there were both true and false Matthewians; the latter were camp-followers and 'camp-communists'.

Mark, on the other hand, believed that communism was the heir to all that was best in liberalism, socialism, conservatism, rationalism, catholicism and anglicanism. It was 'Forward from Everything', and he encouraged his recruits to continue to live exactly as they had before their conversion. It was, he believed, their revolutionary duty and destiny to spread the gospel from whatever station it had pleased the dialectic of history to call them to. He also held that culture was a weapon in the class struggle and that even research in aesthetics was a legitimate form of revolutionary activity. Prolonged meditation on the foot of a Chippendale chair would, I once heard him say, bring a Marxist to a closer understanding of the class structure of eighteenth-century England.

Mark's view of communism suited me down to the ground. I continued to hunt during the vacation and justified doing so by displaying in my rooms in college a poster issued by the Society for Cultural Relations with the USSR advertising the facilities for fox-hunting offered by the Georgian Soviet Republic. Nor was I alone in being attracted by Mark's all-embracing interpretation of the nature of revolutionary pastoral activity – which was, I now realize, the Marxist equivalent of St Augustine's 'Love God and do what you will.' Such an opportunity for having everything both ways was too good to be missed, and it became fashionable in my college to join the Party. Doing so became, indeed, a recognized form of social climbing.

Matthew's and Mark's converts were, naturally enough, suspicious of one another. The differences in outlook and income between Matthew's working-class, grammar school followers and Mark's public schoolboys led to mutual embarrassment, contempt and envy, which were compounded by the fact that both groups contained members who aspired to belong to the other. Matthew's group contained social climbers who angled for invitations to stately homes, while some of Mark's converts celebrated their induction into the Party by buying themselves trousseaux of working-men's clothes.

If Matthew had been in control of the university Party, it would have been a single-minded body without internal tension and discord, but it was Mark who had the ear of King Street (the national headquarters). He was, therefore, allowed to introduce his own ingenious solution of the problem, which his catholic interpretation of communism had created. This was the division of the college cell into two, an 'A' cell containing the *haute bourgeoisie*, and a 'B' cell containing the grammar school types. Nominally, 'A' was the privileged cell; its members were supposedly the *crème de la crème* of the liberal intelligentsia, too original and gifted to be subjected to Party discipline, to be expected to toe the Party line – its members were allowed, for instance, to have doubts about the validity of Marxist ideas in the subject they themselves were reading – and it was understood that their contribution to the class war would be made not at the barricades but on the cultural front. Their historic tasks were to infiltrate senior combination rooms, the corridors of power, Bloomsbury and Mayfair, and to hold themselves in readiness to reestablish cultural life after the chaos of the revolutionary period.

In fact, however, as we discovered to our shame and embarrassment, quite other considerations had been in the Party's mind when it created the 'A' cell. Its purpose was to segregate the decadents and protect the simple-minded proletarians from contamination and corruption by contact with unreliable elements. It was to enable the Party to keep a closer eye on us and to retain the Party members whose family connections were of use to it but who were themselves regarded as irredeemably middle class. Several of us were deeply mortified to discover that our exclusive, apparently privileged position was in reality a form of quarantine, and that, so far from being admired or envied by the rank and file, we were being contemptuously referred to as 'social pansies' and our cell was known as the 'scabs' group'.

(In the event, Mark's solution proved to be a failure, since to the best of my knowledge only one member of the 'scabs' group' continued to be a communist after going down; but the later careers of his converts show that Mark was a remarkably skilled talent spotter. Most of his disciples have since made their names, mostly in the academic field.)

Despite our segregation, we scabs all had our moments of

inspiring contact with the genuine working class. My bedmaker was one of the only two proletarian members of the local Party – the other was her husband – and she understandably made a favourite of me, in particular protecting me from the Fascist machinations of an Hon. who had rooms on the same staircase. He, so she believed, went through the contents of my wastepaper basket daily, so she impressed upon me that it was my revolutionary duty to burn all discarded documents and keep all possessions under lock and key. One day she disappeared. I later heard that she had been admitted to the local mental hospital as a case of paranoia.

Another contact with the working classes was provided by a visit we made to a Welsh mining village, which contained, so it was said, 2 Party members and 600 ex-members. I stayed with a miner's family who treated me like royalty, except for Mum, who decided that I was all skin and bones and insisted on my eating enormous meals. Our hosts found our presence puzzling, and even a little flattering, but I doubt whether we did anything to advance the class war; indeed I suspect that unwittingly we did an excellent public-relations job for the very people we were nominally working against. Despite good will on both sides an insuperable barrier seemed to exist between us and our working-class comrades, a barrier which not even a shared ideology could bridge; I remember once being flummoxed by a comrade who asked me to explain the psychological reasons for the fact that he always fell asleep whenever he picked up Lenin's *Imperialism*.

There was, of course, a working-class district nearer to hand than South Wales, but our contacts with industrial Oxbridge were confined to occasional marches through it in support of strikers. On the occasion of a bus strike one of us composed a revolutionary song beginning 'What's wrong with us is/The bosses own the buses,' which enjoyed a certain vogue, but as most of the revolutionary songs we knew were in either German or Italian, I doubt whether our revolutionary ardour made much impact.

There were also mass rallies in Hyde Park and Trafalgar Square, which provided a welcome opportunity to visit London.

Here again the issue of the two gospels raised its head, one school arguing that our solidarity with the working classes should be expressed sartorially, the other insisting that we should dress like gentlemen in order to demonstrate the extent to which even feudal elements were throwing in their lot with the working classes during the decline of capitalism. I must have belonged to the latter school of thought, as I can remember dropping out of a march down Pall Mall in order to have tea at the Reform Club and joining the march again later.

Looking back on it all, I don't think we did either ourselves or anyone else much harm. Perhaps we should have worked harder at our academic studies or read more widely in the classics and less deeply in Marxism, but as the Party's exam results were always excellent, even the charge of wasting time does not stick. I can, incidentally, remember taking part in a policy-making discussion as to whether the Party should admit an applicant who had only got a third and who was only a commoner of his college. Nor, I think, were we really corrupted by totalitarian ideas. Most of us entered before the Radek trial of 1935 and had left – 'lapsed' is the jargon term – before Russia's equivocal role in the Spanish Civil War had shown to what extent it was still an imperialist power. I certainly learnt a lot about the dynamics of small groups and, in particular, how to spot when a committee is being manipulated by a faction within it, a piece of knowledge which has been invaluable throughout my professional career. Nor, despite the absurdity of some of our activities, were we wrong to bear witness to the presence of evil and to believe that it should and could be opposed. But everything seemed simpler then.

1969

22

On Ablation of the Parental Images, *or* The Illusion of Having Created Oneself

I wrote the original version of this essay in 1965 and offered it for publication first to the *International Journal of Psycho-Analysis* and then to the editors of the International Psycho-Analytical Library, who were at the time preparing my volume of collected psychoanalytical papers, *Imagination and Reality*, for publication. It was rejected by both, not, I understand, because the thesis it proposed was thought to be untrue or misguided, but because it was thought to be impolitic to publish an essay which discussed some of the psychopathological reasons which may lead people to become psychoanalysts. Since then, however, three things have happened which make it unlikely that anyone will today consider its publication offensive or ill-advised.

Firstly, several, perhaps thirty, psychoanalysts have read or heard me read this essay and most of them have agreed that it describes a type of person with whom they are clinically familiar – though I have no reason to suppose that any of them would endorse every idea expressed in it.

Secondly, some change in the intellectual climate has occurred which makes psychoanalysts more willing than they used to be to admit publicly that analysts have, or have had, their 'problems', and has made it no longer necessary for psychoanalytical organizations to present a front of pretending that all their members are, and always have been, paragons of mental health.

An example of this change in the climate is the fact that psychoanalytical journals now find it possible to print papers suggesting that certain aspects of psychoanalytical theory are better regarded as reflections of Freud's personal psychology than as objective statements of general validity. For instance, the *International Journal of Psycho-Analysis* recently published a paper (Needles, 1973) suggesting that Freud's conviction that human beings always strive for reduction of instinctual tension – an idea which runs counter to such easily observed facts as that human beings may seek out excitement and that '*l'appétit vient en mangeant*' – was the theoretical reflection of Freud's own 'idiosyncratic sexual experience' of becoming totally unconscious during the sexual act. It is interesting to note, however, that Needles felt it necessary to express the hope that his readers would not hold him guilty of committing *lèse-majesté* by advancing such a hypothesis.

Thirdly, clinical experience during the last nine years has convinced me that the type of person I describe in this essay is much commoner than I realized when I first wrote it, and that it was only the contingencies of my own practice which led me to notice it first among people who aspired, sometimes successfully, to become psychoanalysts. I now think that the ten–dency, or temptation, to deal with conflicts with parents, and all that they stand for, by disowning them and denying that they affected one at all is widespread, and that people who exemplify this tendency are common in all social movements which repudiate the past and claim that it is possible to start again and afresh from scratch – in contrast to those social movements which rebel against the past or hold that all hopes for the future lie with some already existing social group or class which has a historical destiny to fulfil.

At the present time, the ahistorical tendency characteristic of ablators of parental images seems to me to be most clearly exemplified by those heterogeneous social groups or anti-groups which are collectively known as the 'alternative society' and the 'counter-culture'.[1] These groups display, it seems to me,

[1] See Theodore Roszak, *The Making of a Counter-Culture* (London: Faber, 1970).

precisely the same ambiguities I describe below as characteristic of individuals who, during their individual development, deal with conflicts with their parents by pretending that they never had any. On the one hand they approach life with admirable freshness and are prepared to envisage and act upon quite novel solutions of all problems of living inherent in the human condition; on the other, by ignoring the experience of the past and by rejecting the possibility that there may be such a thing as traditional wisdom, they run headlong into problems, notably in relation to jealousy and privacy, which could in fact have been anticipated.[2]

Alternative society groups, anti-psychiatric therapeutic communities and communes also display another ambiguity similar to one I describe as being characteristic of individuals who ablate their parental images. Although their avowed aim is to establish self-created groups outside and alternative to existing society, economic considerations compel them to adopt a parasitic relationship to what they in principle reject, and psychological necessities compel them to seek out 'ideal' intellectual ancestors to replace the actual ones they have dismissed. These chosen ancestors typically come from cultures remote both geographically and in style of thinking from that in which they and their actual parents were reared (e.g. Eastern sages) or are safely dead and therefore in no position to repudiate them (e.g. Wilhelm Reich); alternatively, the degree of intellectual indebtedness is blurred over by understatement and oversimplification; R. D. Laing's indebtedness to the work of Gregory Bateson is much greater than anyone unfamiliar with it would ever appreciate, and Bateson, a loyal representative of Cambridge high culture, is far from being an anti-establishment figure.

It can generally be assumed that as children patients – and,

---

[2] See David Cooper, *The Death of the Family* (London: Allen Lane, 1971), for an extreme statement of the view that self-awareness and a sense of one's own identity can only be achieved by 'de-population' of one's psyche, i.e. by total extrusion of all those figures who have been internalized during childhood, and that all existing institutions, including even happy families, are enemies of the self.

indeed, all human beings – have had intense feelings about both their parents, and that as adults they never become entirely indifferent to them, but retain them as living images in their minds, both as living persons who are to some extent still loved or hated and as internal figures whose behaviour and ideals are still used as models to be copied or defied.

It would seem, however, that in some people the parental images suffer a different fate. Instead of remaining a living part of the patient's personality, they are, or appear to be, ablated or destroyed, so that the patient appears to lack parental introjects. Such patients impress their analysts by the fact that, unlike most patients who seek analysis, they neither follow in their parents' footsteps nor rebel against them, seem not to use their parental introjects as internal points of reference, but on the contrary seem to be indifferent to them and to find their physical proximity meaningless. Sometimes, indeed, they may have no idea whether their parents are alive or dead, have no wish to find out what has happened to them, and have adopted life-styles from which all traces of their parents and their parents' values have been expunged. Such patients convey the impression that it is strange, almost unbelievable, that they are their parents' child and constitute apparent exceptions to the saying that the child is father to the man.

This apparent psychological discontinuity is, of course, in the last resort an illusion and a piece of unconscious self-deception, explainable by postulating the massive use of such defence-mechanisms as repression and splitting, which exclude the parental images from consciousness and from the patient's self-image and which divest all memories of father and mother, and of the self's childhood with them, of all meaning. As a result, there is a break or caesura in these patients' biographies, before which all remembered events seem unreal, strange, trivial and alien and only after which does real life, real selfhood seem to have begun.

The phenomenon I am describing can also be explained as the result of an unconscious fantasy that the parents have died. Several such patients have told me dreams in which one parent, usually the father, is dead and his body is being transferred from deathbed into coffin, or in which the coffin is being nailed down. Characteristically, in such dreams the father is represented as having died, not as having been killed, and they are concerned not with the dreamer's emotional reaction to the idea that his father has died but with the purely practical task of disposing of his body.

Characteristically, too, the dreamer's father is, in fact, still alive, but the dreamer has lost touch with him or, if he does see him on occasion, regards his physical presence as an irritating nuisance, as a foreign body who merely intrudes upon his life without forming part of it. If the father does die, such patients take good care not to be around when it happens, think up preposterous excuses for not attending the funeral, and feel relief rather than grief afterwards. The fact that these patients have to dream of disposing of their father's dead image is, of course, an indication that they have not been as successful in dismissing him as a dead loss as they would like to believe.

The same process of ablating parental images can also be seen in delusions. The schizophrenic man whom I described in a paper first published in 1959 ceased when he was five to believe that his father really was his father. He suspected that various strangers took turns to impersonate his father, and as an adult he instated a series of distinguished mathematicians, philosophers and soldiers as his father. During analytical treatment he entertained similar doubts about the reality and uniqueness of his analyst, who might, he believed, quite likely be a set of people who took turns to impersonate one another or be Bertrand Russell or General Eisenhower in disguise. His ablation of the maternal image was even more thorough; he never once spontaneously mentioned his mother, and women played no part whatsoever in his delusional systems.

One must, I think, presume that as children such patients, both those who as adults become psychotic and those whom one has to diagnose as 'character disorders', suffered some emotional catastrophe, some gross breach in communication with their parents, which they dealt with by withdrawing all interest from their parents and by divesting their images of all meaning; and that they 'recovered' from the resulting state of despair and disillusion by a process similar to that described by Freud in his paper on Schreber. Schreber, it will be remembered, extricated himself from a state of utter despair and hopelessness by asserting that all the actual people he had dealings with were merely 'miracled-up' and 'cursorily improvised', and by developing delusions in which he enjoyed a special relationship with God and was the child not of his actual parents but of the Margrave of Tuscany and Tasmania. Rather similarly, the patients I am describing seem to me to have 'recovered' from their infantile catastrophe by constructing a mythical 'false self' which is conceived to owe its origins to some source other than their own actual, physical parents. As a result, they are not consciously ambivalent towards their parents – though one must presume that they once were – but have disowned them, have withdrawn all interest from them and have ablated their images.

I have the impression that as children these patients were not deprived but humiliated. They were not underfed or under-protected or exposed to long periods of separation from their parents, but were either totally misunderstood, so that their assets and potentialities were entirely unrecognized, or were treated as things, as possessions of the parents, who felt it unnecessary to be either considerate or truthful to them. They come from families in which toys are thrown away without the children's permission being asked and in which the parents make it clear that the home belongs to them and that the children are there on sufferance. In some cases the parents' attitudes towards one another was so morbidly close that they experienced the arrival of their own children not as additions to the family but as intrusions by a stranger, and it would be as true to say that the parents ablated their children *in statu nascendi* as that the children ablated their parents. Morton Schatzman has shown that Schreber's father, who was a pae-diatrician and educationalist, set out to break his children's will from infancy onwards and confined them in mechanical restraints, invented by himself, in order to nip all signs of man's 'innate barbarity' in the bud.

In adolescence these patients did not go through an identity crisis of the kind described by Erikson in his *Childhood and Society*,[3] but instead made a fresh start without relying on either the straightforward support of internalized parental approval or even the more complex support that can be derived from espousing precisely those ideals of which the parents disapprove. Typically, they developed interests and ideals, and adopted occupations, which were outside their parents' ken and of which they could neither approve nor disapprove.

However, the purpose of this essay is not to discuss the causes but the effects of ablation of the parental images and to suggest that these may be paradoxical; that a person for whom it is not totally catastrophic, ablation of the parental images may be at one and the same time imaginatively liberating in a way that can be creative and also productive of an element of falsity and dishonesty of character which throws suspicion on the value of their creativity. Furthermore, I intend to suggest that persons of this kind may be drawn to psychoanalysis and the psychoanalytical movement in a way that may, perhaps, be beneficial to them but is harmful to psychoanalysis.

The creativeness, the falsity and the dishonesty all derive from the same source. If the natural parents are disowned, the patient acquires an illusion of choice about precisely those aspects of himself that are given and unalterable; his parentage, his identity, his physical and mental constitutional endowment. If his parents are psychologically dead to him, he can choose other parents and therefore his identity. Or he can deny that he ever had any parents and claim to be self-made in the most absolute sense imaginable. Or he may arrogate to himself attributes which he claims to derive from parents who he himself claims to have discovered. This last possibility is, short of delusion, only open to people with considerable intellectual development, who can then claim that their only really significant ancestors are the philosophers, prophets, mystics or psychoanalysts whom they themselves have discovered.

This process of re-creation of the self can be regarded as imaginative and creative, but it is also false, since it can only be

---

[3] E. H. Erikson, *Childhood and Society* (New York: W. W. Norton, 1950).

squared with the dreary truth by suppression of some facts, by distortion of others and by subordination of memory to mythopoeisis. Such people indeed do not recall their childhood; they create a myth about it which is designed to support whatever vision of themselves they have in the present. For instance, a woman patient, who before she was five had openly expressed the wish to be an orphan, applied for training as a psychoanalyst. Quite wrongly, as it turned out, she decided that she would be accepted for training and one day came out with the statement that she had always known that it was her destiny to become a psychoanalyst, and that, when she had first encountered psychoanalytical ideas, she had felt that she had known them all before. As I had never heard this story before, I asked her how old she had been when she first encountered psychoanalytical ideas. She replied that it had been when she was at college. I then asked her from whom she had first heard about psychoanalysis. She said that she could not remember and that, on second thoughts, it must have been at her secondary school. I then reminded her that one of her many complaints against her secondary school was that it had never given her any contact with new ideas, and she then said that it must have been from books she had borrowed from the public library during the holidays, but what these books were she could not remember, except that they were not by Freud. Now this patient was not, I think, trying to recall the origins of her interest in psychoanalysis, but was constructing a myth of herself as a self-created analyst. She was indebted to no living person or even any remembered book for her interest in psychoanalysis, and in any case she had known all about it before and had always known that to become a psychoanalyst was her destiny. She was doing for herself what society has always tended to do to those who produce ideas which transform its vision of reality; she was creating a myth of her analytical virgin birth and claiming that her vision was autochthonous. In asserting her right to become an analyst, she explicitly repudiated any indebtedness to Freud, whose books she had *not* read, and implicitly denied me, her analyst, any part in her future birth. We were not even being allowed to be Josephs.

Such people are not only false but dishonest, since their new self involves a betrayal of the ideals derived from the physical parentage they have disowned. They have not struggled with, or rebelled against, the ideals and values for which their parents stood, have not fought their way through to new insights of their own. They have simply erased the past and started afresh. As a result, the original parental values continue to operate unconsciously in an unmodified form. This unconscious survival of the consciously ablated parental images is responsible for the paradoxical picture such people often present to the world; messianic in their advocacy of their own self-created ideas, but shifty and ill at ease in their way of presenting them. If they write scientific papers their acknowledgements are either scanty or obscure, or, contrariwise, so extensive that their real indebtedness is hidden as successfully as a needle in a haystack. They are uniformly anti-historical, or rather ahistorical, and their writing and thinking lacks any implicit awareness that the answers they give to the problems they claim to have solved are contributions to a discussion which has been in progress ever since mankind became self-conscious. They project their own psychic discontinuity and act as though the world of thought began when they, or rather their own new self, did.

This underlying sense of betraying something, even and indeed especially when they feel that they are being creative, explains, I think, why such people not infrequently dream about espionage and double agents, since the world of espionage is one in which every action is ambiguous, in which physical courage may be linked with moral cowardice and in which the hero and the traitor may be one and the same person.

Another result of the ablation of the parental images is that patients who have done so never spontaneously tell their analyst which of their parents they physically resemble nor which relatives they take after or have shown signs of possessing the 'gifts' to which they themselves lay claim. The word 'gifts' indeed signifies precisely what these patients deny; according to their own view of things they have been given nothing, have inherited nothing, but have made or discovered everything they have. Furthermore, nothing is held to be 'given' in the sense of being sacrosanct, unalterable or unquestionable. It is this latter aspect of their denial of indebtedness which makes them creative. Since nothing is unalterable or unquestionable, their minds are open to new solutions even of problems which appear already to have been solved or which have been proved to be insoluble. The schizophrenic patient whom I mentioned earlier persuaded himself that he had discovered a general solution for equations of the fifth degree, this despite the fact that, or rather because, one of his 'hypothetical' fathers, the mathematician Abel, had demonstrated that no general solution was possible. Since not all received ideas are true, since human knowledge is as yet far from being complete, and since the worlds of art and literature can always accept novel solutions of their formal and expressive problems, less ill patients may prove themselves creative in ways that, so far from being delusional, are either scientifically true or artistically valid. This is perhaps most easily exemplified in the case of literature. Whereas schizophrenics produce neologisms to which only exceptionally empathic people can attach any meaning, poets and writers can stretch and force words and rhythms into playing unfamiliar roles which are, none the less, comprehensible and effective. It is this fact that justifies Shelley's apparently arrogant claim that 'Poets are the unacknowledged legislators of the world,' but it is the underlying sense of betrayal and of possessing 'thefts' rather than 'gifts' which made him and other poets feel haunted by the myth of Prometheus. Shelley's physical ancestors were, in fact, 'acknowledged legislators', having been landowners, Members of Parliament and magistrates for many generations, and his education – private preparatory school, Eton and Oxford – was designed to produce a Whig statesman or politician rather than a poet. However, so far as I can discover, Shelley was not an ablator of his parents but a rebel against them, who derived his ammunition for attacking what we now call the Establishment from within the cultural tradition in which he was educated, not from esoteric and remote sources.

Jean-Paul Sartre's autobiography *Words* contains an illuminating even if horrifying account of the development of someone whose father was ablated for him. Sartre's father died when he was a few months old, before he could possibly have begun to know and love, or hate, him. His mother returned to her family, who behaved as though his father had never existed. *Words* consists of an ironic account of the various poses which the young Sartre adopted, some with his relatives' approval and connivance and some without, and of his alienation from his body and from his real self. It also records his later disillusionment in his false self and his belated discovery that bodies and things are more real than words. I have discussed Sartre's self-disillusion elsewhere in an essay entitled 'Look Back in Loathing', and here I intend only to give a number of quotations from *Words* which illustrate vividly the remarkable way in which words can replace objects and in which despair evoked by the absence of a living paternal image and by alienation from the body can be warded off by self-idealization.

A Platonist by condition I moved from knowledge to its object; I found ideas more real than words . . . I met the universe in books . . . I never scratched the soil or searched for nests, I never looked for plants or threw stones at birds. But books were my birds and my nests, my pets, my stable and my countryside; the library was the world trapped in a mirror.

A father would have ballasted me with a few lasting prejudices . . . he would have dwelt in me; this respectable tenant would have given me self-respect, I would have based my right to live on this respect.

This would have been fine if I had got on all right with my body but it and myself formed an odd couple . . . I fulfilled my alimentary duties and God sometimes, rarely, sent me that grace which permits you to eat without disgust.

Since no one claimed me seriously I set up the pretension that I was indispensable to the universe . . . to escape the desolation of created things I prepared for myself the middle-class solitude for which there is no cure, that of the creator . . . I was born from writing, before that there was only a reflection in the mirror, by writing I existed. I escaped from the grown-ups.

The creative capacity of these parent ablators makes it impossible for me to cite detailed clinical data as extensively as I should wish. Of the ten men and three women whom I have had in mind while writing this essay, all except three have received some public recognition of their abilities, either before or after analysis, or are, it seems to me, likely to do so in the future. As a result I can only offer impressions, generalizations and an occasional unrevealing, i.e. discreetly revealing, detail. They all displayed schizoid, manic and obsessional traits, but not one was hysterical or phobic. None of them were impotent or frigid, but 'fore-pleasure' meant little to them – it was endured for the sake of their partners – and they all showed obvious signs of being alienated from their bodies and lacked the conviction that the most unalterable, inescapable and obviously mortal part of themselves really was part of themselves. Only one was an only child and all save one had had urban child-hoods.

All of them had fathers who survived well into their adult lives and only one had lost a mother in childhood. They are indeed quite unlike people who have really lost a parent in childhood. Whereas the truly orphaned are capable of grief, are prone to sadness and nostalgia and tend to pine for parental substitutes, the ablators are incapable of grief, are unsentimental, and unwilling to admit dependence on anyone. In ten of the thirteen cases, ablation of the father was more marked than that of the mother, though I suspect that the proportion would have been different if the series had contained more women, schizophrenics and male homosexuals. All of them had dreams in which the latent content seemed to be undisguised. This, I think, must be due to the fact that in persons for whom words have become more real than their referents – in whom there has been a massive shift of cathexis from unconscious object-representations on to word-representations – images in dreams may be iconic representations of ideas and not symbols of objects. And wishing to get one's parents out of one's system is perhaps subject to less guilt than wishing to kill them.

One male member of my series, who is now long dead, presented himself to the world as a perfect, indeed all too perfect, English gentleman. His clothes were Savile Row, his umbrella was always rolled, he spoke impeccable Oxford English and always pronounced foreign words and phrases such as volte-face in the accent appropriate to their language of origin; e.g. 'voltay fachay'. In fact he was an American who as a child had known great poverty and he had only come to England in his early thirties, after losing, or rather breaking, all contact with his parents and six brothers and sisters; and he neither knew nor cared whether they were still alive. Now, Americans who hate all things American and become more English than the English are by no means rare – Henry James and T. S. Eliot are perhaps the two most famous examples – but there was something peculiar about this particular one. He had recurrent dreams of buildings in which the architecture was all wrong. Either the buildings could not possibly have stood up or, more usually, they were stylistically impossible unless they were fakes. For instance, they might have a Palladian sixteenth-century ground floor and Norman, romanesque upper floors. These buildings represented, I thought, his attempt to construct a new self for himself, one which was grounded not at all on the foundations of his actual lowly American upbringing but on European high culture. For him Europe and its past was, paradoxically, the Newfoundland in which he hoped to be able to escape from his own American past. But in his dreams he had to confess to himself that this self-construction was artificial, a fake and a façade, and inherently unstable, even though superficially it worked well enough and enabled him to earn an enormous income. By becoming the patient of an English analyst he hoped, of course, to acquire at least a flying buttress for his English, European new self, but in the event he encountered something very different; a situation in which he was compelled to establish connections between his childhood and his present.

Ablators of the parental images are drawn to psychoanalysis for both genuine and corrupt reasons. On the one hand, they sense that something is amiss with them and that they are in a way inhuman and incapable of enjoying the simple and minor pleasures of life. They feel, too, that their personalities are houses built upon sand, and at certain crises in their lives they become fearful of disintegrating and of suffering self-disillusionment. For these reasons they may genuinely seek help – and may succeed in getting it, particularly if they come into analysis when they are in a state of crisis.

On the other hand, there are certain aspects of the psychoanalytical situation and movement which appeal to ablators because they seem to them to be designed to enhance the myth of self-creation and to provide opportunities for strengthening, not dissolving, their defensive system.

First, under conditions of private practice patients can persuade themselves that they have chosen their analyst and have, therefore, acquired a parent whom they themselves have discovered. A woman patient, who had in fact been referred to me through the usual channels and who had never heard of me before, reversed the expected roles by insisting, despite abundant evidence to the contrary, that she was my first patient and that, therefore, any competence I might eventually acquire would be entirely her creation. As a child she had done the same thing to her parents; she had found their dependence on her appreciation of presents they gave her infinitely touching. Another patient set out deliberately to teach me her own privately constructed system of psychopathology, so that I would acquire the ability to analyse her – and, incidentally, eventually be able to enjoy much better mental health than could have been vouchsafed me by my conventional Freudian training. Patients and student analysands who do in fact succeed in being analysed by the analyst of their own choice often, it seems to me, become proselytizers of their analyst's theories as much out of personal vanity as out of genuine appreciation and gratitude for his understanding and skill. In such cases, the patient or analysand patronizes his analyst, while basking in the reflected glory of someone whom he has himself elected to idealize and whom he believes he has discovered; thereby reversing the humiliating biological fact that he did not choose his own parents.

Secondly, psychoanalysis is still a young science and even if the ablator has been compelled reluctantly to admit his need to acquire a symbolic parent, the line of ancestors simultaneously so acquired is only a short one, and the burden of the past to be submitted to, and perhaps eventually superseded, is also only a short one. Whereas in medicine, philosophy, law and the arts there is a line of distinguished forebears and a set of traditions and precedents stretching back into the remote past, the first analyst was still alive in the ablator's own lifetime, or if not in his at least in his father's. And it is possible, by appropriate manipulation of the concepts 'science' and 'knowledge', to argue, while remaining this side of madness, that nothing was known about human nature before Freud. As a result, ablators who develop an interest in psychoanalytical theory are indifferent to the prehistory of psychoanalysis and are uninterested in the various physicians, philosophers and artists who anticipated many of Freud's ideas and in the social and intellectual milieu in which Freud worked; they prefer to believe that psychoanalysis arose as an autochthonous idea in the mind of the genius they have discovered. In adopting such an ahistorical approach towards psychoanalysis they are, incidentally, aided and abetted by two curious features of the psychoanalytical movement; firstly, the fact that several psychoanalytical ideas do indeed derive from Freud's own self-analysis and appear therefore to have originated in an unconscious source external to the history of ideas; and, secondly, the fact that the first generation of psychoanalysts were eager to hive off psychoanalysis from the various medical and scientific groups to which it could arguably have remained attached.

Thirdly, psychoanalysis is a theory about mental processes and has not greatly concerned itself as yet with the constitutional aspects of personality. As a result ablators can use it to justify their belief that their own personality is entirely the creation of their own experience and to ignore what they have inherited from their parents. In extreme cases they can attribute the whole of their post-analytical personality and achievement to the solely mental rebirth which they underwent while in treatment with the analyst of their own choosing.

Thirdly, another attraction of psychoanalysis for ablators is that it affords infinite opportunities to be ambiguously creative. Since its limits and limitations are as yet unknown and the criteria for deciding whether any creative work in it is valid or not are uncertain, it offers a field in which it may be impossible to decide whether work is spurious or not. This is true both of clinical and theoretical psychoanalytical work. Clinically, this is demonstrated quite simply by the mere existence within the British Psycho-Analytical Society of three – or is it more? – different schools of theory and technique, all of which claim to have better therapeutic results than the others. For such a bizarre situation to have arisen and to be still existing, some people must be deceiving themselves, some people must be idealizing their own ideas and work or that of their analysts, and objective criteria for deciding what kinds of patients are suitable for treatment and what sort of results should be deemed successes must be entirely lacking. I am, I hope, not being unduly cynical in suggesting that, in such a nebulous, ill-defined field, inauthentic, spurious characters can survive and flourish.

Theoretically and intellectually, pathobiography – the psychoanalysis of artists, writers and historical characters – provides a good example of an activity which is ambiguously creative. On the face of it, psychoanalytical studies of the dead are spurious, since they involve making interpretations about people who are not present to confirm or reject them and making inferences about precisely those aspects of their lives about which there is the least likelihood of finding documentary confirmation. And, furthermore, they are likely to miss the point, since to demonstrate that a creative person suffered from neurotic conflicts or the results of infantile traumata is to highlight the extent to which he resembles rather than differs from others. On the other hand, there is no reason to suppose that a psychoanalytical biography might not itself be a valid work of art or that it might be used as a vehicle for communicating important but difficult general truths. Erikson's study of Luther seems to me to be an example of such creative use of pathobiography. Rather similar considerations apply to psychoanalytical studies of works of art and fictitious characters. Analysing Hamlet's Oedipus complex is, on the face of it, a ridiculous undertaking, since there was in fact no Hamlet to have an Oedipus complex, but such an exercise could, indeed did in Jones's essay, provide a means for getting across some important general insights into human nature.

In this respect psychoanalysis resembles much modern art. Changes in technology and social structure have undermined the traditional representational function of art – there is no longer any need for anyone to employ artists as craftsmen to record events or the appearance of people – and as a result there has arisen a search for new functions and new techniques, and a concern with formal relations, which provide openings for both the creative and the phoney. And who is in a position to decide now who will later prove to have been the genuine innovators and who were merely tricksters, who are the truly imaginative and who the merely facile? The point I am making here is that psychoanalysis, a psychological theory about the vicissitudes of bodily instincts which conforms to the canons of neither the natural sciences, the humanities nor the arts, has a special attraction for people whose own relationship to their bodies and their past is ambiguous and whose own inner frames of reference are ill-defined.

Now, although these fictitious and adventitious attractions of psychoanalysis can in principle be analysed and the process of ablation be revealed as a defence against remembering the hatreds, humiliations and guilts of childhood, so that the analysand is enabled to discover himself as a unique person with a specific endowment located in his own body, occupying a prescribed position in the history of mankind and possessing that freedom which is the knowledge of necessity, it seems to me that in fact this does not always happen. As a result, the psychoanalytical movement contains, and from its earliest days contained, a not insignificant number of people who tend to suborn psychoanalytical theory to fit their own need to deny important 'given' parts of themselves. And this group of people is, and has been, I believe, large enough to introduce a number of biases and falsifications into psychoanalysis.

Firstly, it leads to idealization of the training analysis and of the so-called 'apostolic succession', and to a tendency to believe that an analyst's competence derives solely from his personal analysis. And yet many analysts have had extensive relevant experience before they were analysed, many have shown themselves to be able and gifted people before becoming analysts, and some at least must have had parents who treated them with insight and understanding in their childhood. But these obvious facts tend to be obscured by the need of some analysts to disown their actual parents and pretend that they started afresh when they went into analysis. The dislike that some analysts have of entering the public arena is, I suspect, sometimes due to the fact that their creative espousal of psychoanalysis is linked with a sense of having betrayed their pre-analytical past. As a result they use their practices as hiding places and can only feel at ease in the presence of those whom they believe to have made a similar betrayal. This is, I believe, one of several factors which contribute to the social isolation of psychoanalysts.

Secondly, if an ablator becomes an analyst, he will inevitably become a dedicated, compulsive analyst who is incapable of forgetting his analyst's self-image. He is then liable to incur a sense of guilt arising from the fact that the creative energy he puts into his work is being taken away from his ordinary human commitments to parents, spouse, children and friends and that he is infringing the elementary principle that charity begins at home. This sense of guilt will force him into a vicious circle of increasing analytical activity designed to relieve the guilt by reparation. Although this may in some cases be the best possible solution of a particular human predicament, its effect on the psychoanalytical movement as a whole is unfortunate, since it contributes to the tendency to regard psychoanalysis not as a profession but as a calling. The driven enthusiast inevitably sets the pace and establishes a convention of intense absorption in theory and practice which is good for neither, since it leads to staleness of mind, and bears heavily on analysts whose professional motivation is more straightforward. The resulting group phantasy that the psychoanalytical movement is an elite of special people is another contributing factor to the social isolation of analysts.

Thirdly, since the self-created self is inevitably a mental construct, the presence of ablators in the analytical movement encourages the neglect of the connections of psychoanalysis with biology and genetics. In this country at least, analysts rarely discuss psychosomatic illness – though this is not so true now as it was when I wrote the original version of this essay in 1965 – and have made next to no use of the abundant evidence suggesting that personality and temperament are in some way correlated with physique. But stock-breeders, biologists and experimental psychologists, who breed strains of rats with high or low endowments of aggression, have no doubt that such a correlation exists, and it can only be idealization of the self-conscious psyche which leads some analysts to write as though they believed that the whole of human personality is ontogenetically determined. Psychoanalysis is, incidentally, the only discipline which uses the word genetic to mean ontogenetic; all other disciplines use it as the adjective referring to genetics, the study of heredity and phylogenesis. Another significant minor detail is that one of Freud's earliest distinctions, that between psychoneuroses due to psychological conflict and 'actual neuroses' which are physical reactions to misuse and over-use of the sexual organs, has been largely forgotten.

Fortunately, the increasing acceptance of Winnicott's distinction between the 'true self' and the 'false self' has now made it possible for psychoanalysis to take cognizance of hereditary and constitutional factors without appearing to undermine its own contribution to the understanding of personality. It is, of course, the 'true self' which is the depository of what the individual inherits from his parents and can elaborate into something which is truly and uniquely himself, whereas it is the false self which harbours the defences, the disguises and the pretensions.

1965
1973

23

Miss Y: The Analysis of a
Paranoid Personality

I

Recently, on rereading my paper on 'The Function of Words in Psycho-Analytical Treatment', I noticed for the first time that almost all my clinical examples were taken from one patient, a woman whom I had in analysis from 1948 to 1952. In this present paper I shall give some account of this patient and describe certain aspects of her analysis.

There are, of course, disadvantages in reporting a case six years after the end of treatment, but these will, I hope, be compensated for by my having in the meantime acquired sufficient distance to be able to present both her and my contribution to the analytical relationship with reasonable detachment. As Miss Y was a person who tended to evoke very strong reactions in everyone who had dealings with her, the detachment given by the passage of time is perhaps of particular value in the present instance. I have, however, made no attempt to conceal my own emotional reactions, as I believe that by including them I shall give a truer account of the dynamics of the analytical process than I should were I to present myself as having been a detached observer throughout.

II

The story of Miss Y's analysis begins two years before she came to me for treatment. She was at that time in her mid thirties, an unsuccessful actress living an insecure and Bohemian existence. Quite suddenly she became depressed and withdrew completely from her previously very sociable life. During her 'breakdown', as she called it, she experienced various peculiar changes in her moods and perception of reality. These she observed and recorded, using them as the material for a self-analysis which she conducted for the next year. As her guides she relied on the only two books on psychoanalysis she had ever read, Theodore Reik's *Ritual* and Wilhelm Reich's *Character Analysis*. She also occasionally talked on the telephone with two doctors whom she had known when they were medical students and who both had shown a passing interest in psychoanalysis. On the basis of her introspective findings, armed with what we should consider somewhat inadequate theoretical support, she undertook not only an independent self-analysis but also the construction of a new system of psychopathology. Unfortunately, she never put down on paper any definitive statement of her system, but during the first few months of her analysis with me I came to know it intimately. So far as I could see, it was entirely logical and self-consistent and, apart from it not being true, I could only find three flaws in it. Firstly, it was based on only one case. Secondly, it attached no significance to any experiences after the age of three months. Thirdly, it took no cognizance of guilt. In all other respects it conformed to the usual pattern of recognized psychopathological theories and took account of both internal and external reality, of stages of libidinal development, and of libidinal fixations and the transformation of infantile libidinal drives into non-sexual social and artistic activities. Her three stages of libidinal development were (*a*) uterine, in which the relation to the mother was mediated by auditory, tactile and postural channels; (*b*) birth, which was a 'traumatic' stage leading to 'paranoid' anxieties particularly associated with visual and thermal sensations; and (*c*) oral, in which the relation to the mother was mediated by the mouth and all other bodily organs with the exception of the genitals. The phenomenon of love was associated with this third stage and under ideal conditions of development played no further part in human relations after this stage was passed. This, to her mind, was her one really original contribution to psychoanalysis, the discovery that all love is 'infantilistic', as she put it. In her view, really mature sexual relationships contained no trace of love and in her own sexual relations fore-pleasure was only permissible as a regrettable concession to the immaturity from which her partners, all unfortunately unanalysed, inevitably suffered. Sexual relations were, however, not purely sensual acts – sensuality was, indeed, in her view masturbatory – but were experiences of 'transcendental harmony' produced by the interchange of electrical energy. It would, I think, be a mistake to dismiss these ideas of hers as nonsense. Once one has cut one's way through the semantic confusion centring round her use of the word 'love', one can see that she was struggling to formulate an insight about the qualitative difference between genital and pregenital love. Her theories had extensive ramifications, but for the moment I shall give only two other details. Firstly, she held that all sublimations have their origin in some specific aspect of one or other of her three stages; music, for instance, being derived from the primary pleasure of listening to the pulsations of the umbilical cord. Secondly, she had discovered the existence of psychically real internal figures; these she called 'effigies', for reasons which will become apparent later. Miss Y had absolute conviction in the essential truth of her system, and this conviction had exactly the same basis as has ours in *our* analytical theories: her experiences during her own personal analysis.

After about a year Miss Y came out of her depression and decided to have treatment with a psychoanalyst. She knew that analysts, like all other bourgeois professional people, charged exorbitant fees for their services, so she set to work to save money and to find a well-paid job acting, with a view to seeing an analyst during the middle of the day, when, she surmised, they probably have difficulty in filling their vacancies. After a year she had saved about £150 and had a part for which she was paid £25 a week in a show that promised to have a long run. She then contacted one of the doctors I mentioned earlier, who referred her to me with a diagnosis of phobia.

Her conscious reason for seeking analytical treatment was *not* that she had realized she was seriously ill. On the contrary, she believed that she had much more to give analysis than analysis had to give her. The reasons she gave during the first few weeks of analysis were:

Firstly, she wished to become a child analyst, believing that the insights she had obtained during her self-analysis would enable her to make original contributions to the theory and practice of child analysis.

Secondly, she intended to become physically immortal. She had discovered that physical illness and ageing were caused by the 'paranoia' engendered by a traumatizing and hostile infantile environment, and she therefore concluded that thorough analysis of her reactive sadism and conflicts would eliminate the otherwise inevitable tendency to decay and death. She rather reluctantly admitted her inability to carry out unaided the complete analysis necessary to ensure immortality, so she decided to enlist the help of a classically trained analyst, fully realizing, of course, that *his* limitations would have to be made good by what *she* taught him. Since the ultimate goal was physical immortality, she could afford to envisage an almost interminable analysis. However long it lasted, it would be short in comparison with the ultimate reward of life eternal – for the analyst as well as herself. She had never encountered anyone who was prepared to take these ideas of hers seriously, but she did not herself consider them particularly outrageous or original. She thought she was merely drawing an obvious logical conclusion which conventional analysts, with typical bourgeois cowardice, had been too frightened to face. So far as I know she was unacquainted with the notion of the death instinct; the pathogenic factor which she hoped to eliminate by complete analysis was the paranoia induced by the sadism of the infantile environment.

Thirdly, she wished to be relieved of a pain she experienced during sexual intercourse. This pain was unilateral and occurred only with deep penetration. She had already been informed by a competent surgeon that it was indubitably of organic origin and that it could be relieved by a lower abdominal operation. She was not, however, prepared to accept this, the whole idea of surgery being anathema to her.

Miss Y did not mention her ideas about physical immortality

during her initial consultation, quite consciously withholding them until she felt I was fully committed to continuing her treatment. At the time I accepted the referring physician's opinion that she was a suitable case for psychoanalytical treatment without question. My first impressions of her were of her determination to have analysis, her tremendous tenseness, and her bewilderingly complex mode of speech, which last I shall describe in detail later.

III

Two details of the initial consultation proved later to have contributed significantly to the dynamics of the analytical relationship, even though at the time they passed unnoticed by me.

When we came to discuss fees she told me about the money she had saved and that she was at present earning £25 a week. I then asked her how long she expected the show to last and how much of the year she usually spent 'resting', thereby using the common stage euphemism for 'unemployed'. She said perhaps six months a year, so I suggested we discuss fees on the assumption that she earned £12 not £25 a week. I had correctly guessed that £25 a week was considerably more than she was accustomed to earn, but I entirely failed to realize that I had confronted her with an attitude towards money which ran counter to all her preconceptions about professional people. She had assumed without question that analysts were ruthless in their pursuit of fees, and that I would fix hers without any regard to her circumstances. The fact that I inquired carefully into them and took account of them when deciding on the fee I should charge had, therefore, the effect of undercutting one of her most cherished grievances.

I became aware of another significant feature of the initial consultation when I found it necessary to investigate my own counter-transference. I then realized that Miss Y had very effectively dared me into undertaking her analysis. By presenting herself as a difficult case and as having made strenuous exertions to make treatment possible from her side, she had appealed both to my sporting instincts – a phrase, incidentally, she would have found highly offensive – and to that counter-phobic tendency which makes one determined to undertake a task just because it has been presented as difficult. I learnt later that games of daring had been carried to hair-raising lengths in her childhood and that she had retained into adult life an exceptional capacity to accept physical risks. At one time she had earned her living in a circus riding on the pillion of the motor cycle that circles the Wall of Death. By daring me in this way she evoked a determination to penetrate her defences which, in alliance with her own determination to be analysed at whatever cost, helped to overcome her equally great determination *not* to abandon any of her defences. The importance of this lies in the fact that her analysis turned out to belong to the not uncommon category which raises the question of why the analyst commits himself to the treatment of a patient from whom he cannot expect the usual economic reward.

IV

Miss Y was small and slight but her marked presence made her appear taller than she was. She was strikingly good-looking, though the effect was marred by her tense expression and posture. She spoke in a low, harsh or husky voice. Her clothes were either untidy to the point of sluttishness – my receptionist nicknamed her 'the Gypsy' – or exotic to the point of being bizarre. She was intensely interested in her effect on other people, but made no attempt to appear smart or fashionable.

At first I often had considerable difficulty in understanding her highly individual mode of speech, and I had therefore to analyse it in some detail. It contained the following five peculiarities: (*a*) she made her own choice of prefixes and suffixes, always, for instance, saying 'comatic' not 'comatose'; (*b*) she gave words private meanings that were remote from and yet obviously somehow related to their accepted meaning: 'comatic', for instance, meant lethargic, intellectually lazy, unawakened; (*c*) she had a number of favourite words which she used in unusual or old-fashioned senses: one of these was 'reactionary', which meant sensitive or responsive; (*d*) she had invented new words and appropriated a number of already existing words to signify various intrapsychic phenomena she had encountered during her self-analysis and for which she had had no words in her pre-breakdown vocabulary: the most striking example of this was the word 'effigy' to describe an internal object; (e) she preferred abstract to concrete modes of expression and avoided metaphor, preferring to restrict her vocabulary to words which have lost all apparent connection with any concrete object or activity. This was the crucial disturbance and its cause became clear in the light of her reactions to the use of metaphor by myself. It then became obvious that she had difficulty in distinguishing between the literal and metaphorical meanings of words, and between words and the concrete objects they signify. If, for instance, I used the phrase 'getting something off one's chest', this evoked the sensation of something on her chest weighing her down, not the idea of unburdening herself. My use of this phrase was taken as a sadistic attack, a deliberate attempt to make her feel a weight on her chest. I am not sure to what extent this difficulty existed in her everyday life or how much it was exacerbated by regression during the analytical session.

She herself tried to maintain that the difficulties in verbal communication that sometimes arose between us were due to her American upbringing and that she was unfamiliar with idiomatic English. This last was quite untrue, as for various reasons I insisted confidently from the beginning, and I later learned that all the significant figures in her childhood had been brought up in England and had all clung militantly to their English middle-class accents despite long residence abroad. The real reason for her conviction that she could not understand English and that I could not understand her expatriate speech was her unconscious belief that there had been an irreparable break in the channels of affective communication between herself and mother-figures which no words, not even those of her mother tongue, could ever bridge.

Although I became in time familiar with the idiosyncrasies of her speech and knew, for instance, that 'reactionary men have no sense of structure' had nothing to do with politics but meant that sensitive men are incapable of lasting personal relationships, I deliberately refrained from making more than the minimum amount of accommodation to them for fear of becoming involved in a linguistic *folie à deux* which might make it harder for her to work through her hostility to the uncomprehending mother-image. I am not altogether sure that I was right in adopting this policy.

Some of her neologisms were amusing, but quite unintentionally so. A 'lowerarchy' was a hierarchy viewed from above – those of us who are not at the top, of course, usually view hierarchies from below. She once, again quite seriously, said, 'Annoyed? I was paranoid.' I have, of course, been describing an early stage in a schizoid thought-disorder, the result of a regressive disturbance in symbolic thinking and of the confusion created by her attempt to master unaided the disordered perceptions of her breakdown. This thought-disorder cleared up completely during the analysis. During the period of recovery she used to make up jokes based on metaphor being taken literally. Some of them were used as captions for a volume of humorous drawings made by a friend of hers.

In line with her belief in her capacity to analyse herself without external aid was her faith in her own untrained creative powers. At the age of ten she had decided to become the female Shakespeare; at the same age she also decided to become a ventriloquist. At seventeen she wrote a poem identical with one by Verlaine and a melody identical with one by Rachmaninov. At the age of thirty she had been told, so she said, by a ballet teacher that with a few weeks' practice she could reach the standard of a ballerina. She also claimed telepathic powers. The only artistic gifts to which she made no pretensions were painting and drawing. It is not surprising that one of her reports at Dramatic School – acting was the only art for which she had any formal training – described her as exceptionally talented but quite incapable of learning from anyone. A dream she had in the first year of analysis depicted the omnipotent character of her belief in her genius. It also shows her failure to deny *completely* her need for external support.

Dream I. She was demonstrating to a group of stuffy bourgeois professors her ability to dance without touching the ground. She had, however, to keep one finger touching a round tea-table in the middle of the room.

Her determination to deny any need to be dependent on others was also shown in her attitude to external dangers and difficulties. Not only was she physically fearless, she also seemed without social anxiety. She was never shy or overawed by anyone, and was quite incapable of accepting any offers of patronage that might have helped her professionally. She also denied any anxiety about the economic insecurity in which she habitually lived. During a phase of the analysis in which she was penniless she refused unemployment relief and tried to persuade herself that hunger pains were psychogenic. Nor did she admit that any dangers attach to sexual promiscuity.

She would not have used the word promiscuous about herself, but it would be hard to find another word to describe the bewilderingly rapid series of transient encounters that comprised her sexual life. In her view it was a search for an ideal partner with whom she could experience complete sexual harmony uncontaminated by either love or sensuality. Occasionally, or so she said, her search was successful, when she found a 'reactionary' man, but then, alas, they always proved to have no 'sense of structure'. The others always proved 'comatic'. Rather inconsistently, I thought, she referred to her sexual partners as lovers.

It will already have become obvious that Miss Y was counterphobic rather than phobic and that in many ways her character was paranoid. In the last section of his paper on Schreber Freud observes that the familiar principal forms of paranoia can all be represented as contradictions of the single proposition 'I (a man) love him (a man),' and goes on to show that projection cannot be the essential mechanism in paranoia. Although Miss Y certainly used the mechanism of projection extensively, her defensive personality seemed to be based on a massive contradiction of her unconscious wishes and fears rather than on denial and projection. Her heterosexual promiscuity contradicted her underlying attachment to the mother and her fear and hatred of men. Her pretensions to genius, an example of what Freud called sexual overestimation of the ego, contradicted her unconscious need for object-love, this being reinforced by her ideological rejection of love as infantile. Her imagined discovery of a means by which death could be eliminated was a contradiction rather than a denial of death. Similarly, her conviction that almost everyone other than herself was sadistic was as much a contradiction of her need for love as a projection of her own sadism. This was shown by the fact that it was just those classes of persons whose occupation it is to care for others and whose care she needed that were in her view most sadistic. She considered all doctors, especially women doctors and psychiatrists, to be sadists. In principle psychoanalysts were not, though during the first year of analysis most of my interpretations were considered to be deliberate sadistic attacks. In charitable moods she attributed my sadism to the contamination I had suffered while acquiring a medical qualification. All mothers she met were scrutinized closely and any mistakes or awkwardnesses they showed were attributed to sadism; when possible she interpreted this to them.

Her need to love and feel loved had, however, found one outlet. She kept cats – several of them, which she had saved from being put down. She was devoted to them and fondly believed that they were dependent on her. Fortunately she decided early on in the analysis that I too was fond of cats. That cats were part of an *external* reality about which she had normal emotions and in which her usual omnipotent defences did not operate was shown by the fact that the first open, naive expression of anxiety in the analytical situation occurred in relation to one. One day the housekeeper's cat went to sleep under the analytic couch, from which it emerged during the middle of the session. When Miss Y suddenly noticed it stalking towards the door, she leapt off the couch on the opposite side. I remained seated. I am convinced that if a man, not a cat, had emerged, she would not have batted an eyelid.

Another feature of her personality, which was, I think, manic rather than paranoid, was that her appearance and whole demeanour could alter so much that it was hard to believe that the different characters presented to one were in fact aspects of the same person. In one character she was hard, aggressive, querulous and argumentative, and usually sluttishly dressed. In another she was transfigured and radiant, absolutely confident in her ability to charm everyone she encountered. In such moods everyone in the street stared at her appreciatively as she passed and complete strangers came up and talked to her. It was an important step in the analysis when she compared this to the way passers-by will stop to talk to a happy baby and, though still flattered, recognized it to be an intrusion on her privacy. These changes in mood at first occurred independently of the analysis and were remarked upon by others than myself; later they became associated with changes in the transference.

In describing Miss Y's character I have already used the terms counter-phobic, paranoid and manic, and the question arises, I think, as to whether she was, *psychiatrically* speaking, psychotic. She certainly displayed incongruity of affect. This was well described by one of her lovers, who once remarked to her: 'It's the glorious irrelevance of you. You look at the sugar-bowl with intense hatred and talk of the weather with an expression of ecstasy.' I am fairly sure that at first she was terrified that I would decide she was mad and was more than relieved that I never in any way treated her as such.

Since Miss Y often behaved and spoke in a way that in everyday life one might be inclined to dismiss as pretentious, absurd and bizarre, I must mention explicitly that very early on I decided that she was in fact a very gifted, though profoundly disturbed, person, and, in particular, that she had an unerring aesthetic sense. It would be hard to justify such an impression by citing examples that would be generally convincing, and I shall only say that her sensibility often manifested itself negatively. No one could have hated Rembrandt as passionately as she did without a profound though denied insight into his understanding of ageing and death.

So far, I have presented Miss Y's character and ideas without relating them in any way to the childhood experiences which alone make them comprehensible. My reason for having done this is that during her analysis I had to learn to feel at home with the defensive personality she presented to the world before

I could learn the bare facts of her childhood, let alone acquire any imaginative understanding of it.

V

Miss Y was the youngest child of the only English-speaking family living in a small village in America, both her parents having emigrated from England. They were converts to Catholicism and five children followed each other in rapid succession, first a boy and then four girls. The whole family's life was overshadowed by a series of deaths which occurred before Miss Y was ten years old. Her mother died when she was just over two. An aunt then came to keep house and care for the children; she died when Miss Y was four and a half. The children next had a governess who was committed to a mental hospital when Miss Y was ten and who died there soon after admission. Miss Y had some recollection of all three deaths. In her early teens her father remarried. Her stepmother found Miss Y unmanageable and both parents became very strict in their attempts to control her adolescent interest in boys. She reacted by becoming more and more defiant. In her late teens she was put for a while into a reformatory run by nuns, and later, after failing to hold down a number of office jobs, she was shipped back to England to live with some distant relations in a small provincial town. She soon found the aspidistras and antimacassars unendurable, and before she was twenty-one she ran away and got a job with a circus. From then on she lived a precarious, unsettled and nomadic existence, her only contacts with her family being very occasional letters to her sisters and appeals for financial help to her brother. Under these circumstances no confirmatory external evidence about her childhood was available, while her own description of her treatment by her father and stepmother bore all the hallmarks of paranoid distortion. The idea she had at the beginning of her analysis that both her father and brother had attempted to abuse her sexually was, fairly certainly, a delusion. I suspect that her father was a moody and difficult man who was often at his wits' end as to how to handle five motherless children. They ran wild, and a lot of their hostility and resentment was worked out on each other in bullying and spitefulness, with my patient, as the youngest, bearing the brunt of a lot of it. I think, too, that to begin with she was her father's favourite child. She owed to him her interest in poetry and acting and was the only one of the children to be infected by his passion for Shakespeare. His getting rid of her, first to a reformatory and then to England was, I suspect, the action of a man bitterly disillusioned in his idealized favourite daughter rather than that of a crude disciplinarian. What her precise dismeanours were I never discovered. The other children have all made conventional adjustments to the American way of life.

Although these facts about her childhood are very scanty, they are enough to make her unconscious longing for the mother, her conscious hatred of her father, and her fear of death, all imaginatively comprehensible. They offer, however, no explanation of the paranoid twist to her personality, of the fact that her infantile traumata led not to repression, impoverishment of the ego and symptom-formation but to the development of an ego itself based on active contradiction of her pathological, unconscious impulses. One consequence of the fact that she emerged from her childhood not with a psycho-neurosis but with a paranoid, manic character was that energy which in a neurotic is dissipated in symptom-formation or held in leash by repression was available to her organized ego, though at the price of a partial break with reality. This was the basis of the forcefulness of personality which was one of her most striking characteristics.

VI

Miss Y's analysis lasted for over four years. I shall not attempt to describe its course fully, but shall confine myself to giving a general picture of the three phases into which the analysis fell and to describing in more detail a number of crucial episodes. Miss Y was a prolific dreamer of remarkably undisguised dreams, which I shall use extensively as illustrative material without reporting her associations, which were in general more confusing than illuminating.

The three phases into which the analysis fell were:

1. A phase of resistance, in which Miss Y fought to prevent

disintegration of her omnipotent and narcissistic defences.

2. A phase of regression, in which she re-experienced the despair and depression that had necessitated construction of these defences.

3. A phase of recovery, in which she acquired sublimations and reconstructed her defences on a less omnipotent and narcissistic basis.

Since the phase of regression had a rapid onset and ended suddenly during one of my holidays, this division into three phases corresponds closely to the clinical facts and is not a theoretical construct introduced to facilitate exposition. The phase of regression was, however, foreshadowed more than once during the phase of resistance and I shall describe one instance of this in some detail.

VII

The phase of resistance lasted for just under two years. The preceding sections of this paper have in the main been based on impressions and information acquired during this first phase. It was characterized by long periods of intense hostility towards me alternating with short periods of complete harmony. During the hostile periods she attacked me on almost every possible count. I was held to be sadistic, insensitive, stupid, lacking in understanding and a legitimate target for her hatred of all things English – English conventions, English snobbery, English doctors, English food, English cooking and English weather. All attempts to interpret this hostility were taken as indicating my approval of what she was attacking and therefore as further proof of my insensitivity and stupidity. Alternatively, I was thought to be deliberately provoking her by affecting to approve the obviously intolerable conditions by which she was daily traumatized. Now although most of this hostility was undoubtedly transferred, the accusation that I was lacking in understanding did at times and in certain respects have some validity. There were two reasons for this: one unavoidable, the other the result of a failure in discrimination on my part.

The unavoidable reason was the confusion created by her highly individual habits of speech. *She* used a language I had yet to understand, while *I* used a language that to her meant lack of understanding, since to her mind it was inherently incapable of describing her inner feelings and was full of phrases designed to disturb her by evocation of painful imagery. She had furthermore a hatred of language itself since, in her view, it only exists because human beings fail to understand each other. Her repudiation of her mother tongue and her attempt to replace it by a private language was, as I have already mentioned, an indication of her despair about the possibilities of affective communication.

The avoidable reason was that I failed to discriminate sufficiently sensitively between different types and sources of aggression. Evidence of penis envy and oral frustration was only too obvious in her attacks on doctors and on English food and weather, and it was true that she envied me for being a man and felt frustrated by the mother country which gave her neither food nor warmth; but her dreams – as I only realized much later on when I had reason to abstract them from my notes – suggested that her envy and aggression were not primary and instinctual but were part of her defence. Her repudiation of her need for love and her attachment to internal objects from whom she derived her sense of omnipotence had imprisoned her in her internal world and her fundamental demand on me was that I should help her take the risk of abandoning her self-sufficiency and trust an external object. Having made this demand on me, having instated me as someone by whom she could hope to be rescued, her anxiety compelled her to hate and fear me. Just because I was the person she had chosen to liberate her from her internal objects I inevitably became the person who threatened to destroy her sense of omnipotence. Just because I was the person she had put into a position in which I could prove myself trustworthy and make her aware of her need for love, I became the person it was most necessary to prove hateful, insensitive and without understanding. Further-more, she had to test out that I could continue to be benevolent, however venomous she might be. Interpretations of her hostility in terms of envy and oral aggression lost sight of all this and, in particular, lost sight of the fact that her whole aggressive attitude towards me was an attempt to contradict the impression she had gained in the initial consultation that I was a person to whom she could trust herself.

I shall now recount some of her dreams which illustrate this and depict her narcissistic attachment to internal objects and her sense of imprisonment by this attachment.

Dream II. She was masturbating by rubbing her legs together as though there were a penis between them.

Dream III. She was trying to suck her own breast. Then she decided to masturbate, but desisted when she remembered she would have to tell her analyst ... She was escaping from a prison.

Dream IV. She was in a medieval castle. She and an old woman walked out over the drawbridge. The moat was full of drowned 'effigies', the corpses of her former lovers. Then she tried to reach the sea but her way was blocked by a wall of ice.

Dream V. She was escaping from the Soviet Union in a boat. In the middle of the sea she found a trap door. She opened it and found a Post Office Savings Book.

Dream VI. Her clitoris was elongated and tubular. She was alone on an island except for one other person, whose sex was uncertain.

These dreams depict very clearly, I think, her attempt to sustain herself by a narcissistic attachment to internal objects and the resulting sense of loneliness and imprisonment. The sense of omnipotence which constituted the illusory gain from her attachment to internal objects is strikingly presented in her dream, which I have already related, of dancing before the bourgeois professors and also in the image of the enlarged vaginal–phallic clitoris.

During the phase of resistance there were three ways in which she could temporarily lose her sense of being trapped. One was with her cats. Another was in her sexual promiscuity. The third was in her phases of harmony with me. During these she felt that I understood her completely and absolutely, everything I said was wise and right. My consulting-room was always beautifully warm and the weather perfect. However, all this was resistance too. She came late for sessions and only welcomed my interpretations enthusiastically by reading into them her own preconceptions about herself. These ecstatic, manic moods were identical with the transfigured, radiant moods I described earlier. That they were based on a fantasy of union with the analyst as mother is shown by the following dreams.

Dream VII. She and her analyst are in a studio. She is at peace.

Dream VIII. The analyst is sitting beside her as she lies on the couch. She falls asleep. When she wakes up he asks her whether all her friends are homosexual. Then he feeds her with salad.

I have already mentioned that the phase of regression was foreshadowed on more than one occasion during this first phase of resistance. The most impressive of these occurred near the end of the first year of analysis and was precipitated by circumstances external to it. She had been persuaded, partly by myself, to have a surgical operation for her dyspareunia and went into hospital during one of my holidays. The operation was planned to take place three days before I returned to work. I was therefore surprised and disturbed when she telephoned to tell me that she would be coming to her session despite having had the operation only three days previously. When she arrived she walked straight to the couch without looking at me or greeting me in any way. She lay down and went completely limp, in striking contrast to her usual very tense posture. She remained silent and uncannily motionless. I assumed, rightly, that she had discharged herself from hospital almost immediately after the operation and knowing that she had had a lower abdominal operation feared that she might have had a haemorrhage. Her absence of colour did nothing to reassure me and I remember entertaining for a moment the idea that she had come to die on the couch. I was therefore more relieved than distressed when I noticed that she was weeping silently. After a while she tried to speak but failed, and I helped her off the couch on to a chair. She then told me what had happened. She had had the operation with much less pain and distress than she had feared and had been coping successfully with the barbarous conditions in an English hospital until a small child had been admitted to the ward. This child had cried all night and she had been as much upset by the indifference of the nursing staff as she was by the crying itself. Next morning she could endure it no longer and after a row with the ward sister and house physician had discharged herself from hospital. I hardly needed to point out that she was re-experiencing her own desolation after the deaths in her own childhood and that her indignation on the child's behalf was born of her own need for consolation.

VIII

During the months following this episode she began to change. She stopped being promiscuous and became preoccupied with her memories of a young Frenchman, half her own age, with whom she had had a short affair. She lost her job after a quarrel with the producer and then sabotaged every audition she went to by her unaccommodating attitude. Her savings were nearly exhausted. She became increasingly aware of her dependence on me and stopped attacking me incessantly. She began to have anxiety dreams in which I featured as a benevolent and protecting figure.

Dream IX. She is climbing a cliff to reach the analyst. On the way she passes a thug or policeman. The analyst had become very wise and intelligent and she realized that his sadistic treatment of her had all been play-acting done for her own good.

Soon after this dream she became regressed. By this I mean that she entirely dropped her defensive attitude towards me, that instead of lying tense and over-alert on the couch she became relaxed and absorbed, and that instead of arguing with me and producing masses of highly intellectualized material in a loud, harsh voice she started describing simply and quietly what she felt it must have been like to have been a child and infant. She became so absorbed in the analysis that the question of her working did not arise and she spent most of her time continuing the analysis in her imagination, sleeping, or day-dreaming about the young Frenchman. To my mind this Frenchman was clearly an idealized representation of myself, but interpretations to this effect were always unacceptable to her.

The actual content of the sessions during this phase is difficult to describe. With one exception her reconstruction of the experiences and emotions of infancy corresponded closely with the picture of infancy painted by contemporary analytical research. The exception was her complete rejection of the idea that an infant can feel anger or hatred towards its mother and that it can be disturbed by its own destructive fantasies. Interpretations of dreams which seemed to me to depict this aspect of infancy were either brushed aside or reacted to with such anxiety that I eventually decided to let her take her own time discovering the importance of infantile aggression.

The emotional atmosphere of this phase is even harder to convey. This is partly because it contained two elements which are logically incompatible and which yet coexisted without apparent contradiction. One was a feeling that I was bored, tired, ill and indifferent, while she was listless, despairing and overcome with a sense of futility; it was as though she was re-enacting a mother–infant relationship from which all life had been withdrawn. The other was her belief that I *could* be trusted to see her through, could be a support until she succeeded in gaining access to her own sources of vitality. At times the only evidence of hopefulness in her was the regularity and punctuality with which she attended sessions. She paid no fees during this period, living entirely on borrowed money. However, despite her helplessness and absorption in the analysis, her dependence on me and surrender to me as an introjectible good object never became fully explicit, largely, I think, owing to her fear of the destructive implications of her incorporative fantasies, her fear that she might turn me into an effigy. As a result, she never asked me to lend her money and deflected some of her longings on to the Frenchman, who by living abroad remained out of range of her aggression and could do nothing to disillusion her.

She dreamed much less during this phase and I shall only relate two dreams.

Dream X. A female producer did not want to give her a part . . . She was hurt to find that there were no photographs of her in Mrs X's album. Here we see the feeling of being slighted by being unwanted and unremembered by her mother, who, as she then felt, would not have died if she had really loved her daughter, but the dream contains no hint of anger or resentment.

Dream XI. She pressed her breasts against a wall. Although her breasts were anatomically hers, they were also someone else's.

It is this dream which justifies my interpretation of Dream III, in which she was trying to suck her own breast, as an internalized object relationship and not as an autoerotic activity. This last dream depicts her acquisition of insight into the object dependence implicit in her narcissism. It also represents her primary identification with the analyst as breast.

Eventually, however, aggressive feelings began to emerge unequivocally. Firstly, she remembered a gardener in her childhood who had always kept the vegetables locked up and how determined she had been to steal some of them. Then she had openly sadistic dreams which shocked her profoundly.

Dream XII. She is in a butcher's shop buying meat. She takes his carving knife and starts cutting up two white cats. Then she is in my consulting-room, where I am analysing a lesbian friend of hers. I look as though I am going to work off some of my aggression on the lesbian but instead I show her (i.e. Miss Y herself) a drawing done by a poet friend of hers. It is very chaotic but I assure her that he has also done some very 'integrated' drawings.

In the first part of this dream it was, of course, the cruelty to cats which shocked her so much. In the second part she depicts her dawning insight into the intimate connection between creativity and aggression, but does not yet dare locate either within herself. The integrative processes which were already occurring within her have therefore to be represented as taking place off-stage, at one remove from the analytical situation.

Dream XIII. She is forced down a cul-de-sac by a lorry. Then a workman is lying unconscious on the ground. She can only presume that she herself must have attacked him.

Here she depicts the feeling that she is being forced into a position in which she will no longer be able to deny her aggression.

IX

Dream XIII was dreamt at the end of November 1950. To her first session after my Christmas holidays Miss Y brought some drawings that she had done. I was very struck by their strict realism and classical technique; they were 'integrated', to use the word she had herself used when recounting Dream XII. I also felt there was something frightened and overcautious about them. As I put it in the notes I made at the time: 'Her drawings show a fear of being too violent, e.g. very gentle lines on paper that would tear easily.' The best drawings were all of cats. During the session she told me how she had come to start drawing. Over Christmas she had been with a friend to visit the friend's mother. The mother and daughter were not on good terms and the atmosphere had been tense. On one occasion her friend lost her temper with her mother. Miss Y's sympathies were with her friend and she suddenly found herself wishing to murder the mother. This feeling came like an illumination and with it many things that I had said to her about hostility and ambivalence fell into place. Later, when she got home, the idea of trying her hand at drawing occurred to her; she sat down with pencil and paper and found she had no great difficulty in drawing her cats and other objects in the room. Since then she had spent much of her spare time drawing.

Drawing was one of the few arts about which Miss Y had had no pretensions, and her attitude towards her newly acquired aptitude was in striking contrast to her previous tendency to refuse all help and guidance and to rely defiantly on her own inner genius. She took evening classes in drawing and seemed quite prepared to learn from her teachers. Indeed, her only complaint about the art class was that she found her tendency to flirt with the male students interfered with her work. It was also very striking that she had no objection to spending hours copying the work of old masters and seemed concerned only to acquire a realistic technique. She was quite uninterested in abstract or 'advanced' forms of art.

She also began to write poetry again. Here too she expressed herself in simple traditional forms, and she never showed me a poem which was not comprehensible on a single reading. In a series of poems about her childhood she worked through her grief and described her recovery of the internal image of a loving mother and the resulting loss of her inner sense of isolation. I regret that I am unable to quote any of these poems.

Miss Y's need to draw, and, in particular, her need to draw the external world as it is, was an expression of her drive to escape from the prison of her introversion and to re-establish contact with the world of everyday reality, which she used her hands and eyes to master and rediscover. On the same day that she first showed me her drawings she asked me how much longer I thought the analysis would last, and shortly afterwards she began to concern herself with the problem of earning a living. As she decided that acting was not her *métier* and had no other training and qualifications, the remaining eighteen months of the analysis were to some extent disorganized by her search for suitable work and it was partly for economic reasons that she terminated analysis four years after beginning treatment.

I do not intend to describe in any detail this last phase of recovery. Much of it consisted in working over again material I have already presented, but with the difference that she was capable of operating the normal split in the ego which enables psychoneurotic patients to observe and reflect upon the material they present instead of becoming totally immersed in it. There were also periods in which development seemed to be occurring spontaneously and in which my function was confined to providing a setting in which insight could increase and to being ready to intervene when she seemed to be losing her way. I have no doubt that in view of the emotional insecurity of her childhood and the social insecurity of her adult life the mere continuity of the analytical relationship had a therapeutic effect. I think, too, that the sudden emergence of a sublimation and, with it, of a firmer grasp of reality indicates that a normal, non-defensive ego-organization must have already been present when treatment began, however overshadowed it may have been by her highly defensive 'personality'. The last phase of her analysis was a phase of recovery, not only in the sense that she recovered from her regression, but also in the sense that she

recovered certain faculties and potentialities which had previously been dissociated and, therefore, inaccessible. In the last
resort this was based on recovery of the belief in the possibility
of affective communication, a belief which had been shattered
by the traumatic experiences of her childhood. The most obvious example of her becoming more in touch with, more at home
in outer reality was her changed habit of speech – I remember
being amazed when she first came out with such an ordinary
word as 'flirt' – but much more than this was, of course,
involved.

In April 1951 Miss Y received a telegram telling her that her
father had died. After unsuccessful attempts to find a friend to
stay with her, she rang up and asked me to come and see her.
The sense of urgency was obvious in her voice and I went at
once. When I arrived, almost the first thing she said was that
in a sense I need not have come at all; all she had needed was
the certain knowledge that I had appreciated the urgency of her
call and that I was willing to come, though of course, she added,
the only way I could show this was by actually coming. What
she needed was that her grief should be recognized, otherwise
she was in danger of denying it. Miss Y had realized this danger
herself, hence her call to me. After talking about this for a little
while she gave me a cup of tea and I returned home. My reason
for reporting this incident – the only occasion on which I
stepped out of the analytical role – is to give an example of the
sensitivity and perceptiveness which she had kept hidden behind
her narcissistic defences, a perceptiveness which made her
realize how easy it would have been to recall only the grievances
of her adolescence and to maintain that she had always hated
her father and recognize immediately how urgently she needed
a witness for her grief. It did not, of course, require much
imagination on my part to appreciate that someone who had
lost three mothers in her childhood and who as an adult had
had to fabricate theories denying the inevitability of death
needed endorsement of her threatened insight when confronted
with the fact of her father's death.

Miss Y had in fact identified with her father in many ways,
and I have already given material, without commenting on

it, which shows how extensively a phallic organization was interwoven with her omnipotent defences. During the last months of her analysis she became markedly more feminine, a process which began shortly after she first admitted hostility towards the mother. A fortnight later she had the following dream.

Dream XIV. She is in a room belonging to a beautiful girl. At first she thinks the girl is not there but to her surprise she finds her asleep in bed.

A few days later she expressed concern on my behalf for the first time. She was worried, she said, about the aggression I must have to put up with from my other patients. During the same hour she said she had just realized how much she always wanted to be the centre of attention and how hard she found it to tolerate the idea that it was unrealistic of her to expect me always to be able to understand immediately what she was getting at. A few days later she remembered how slighted she had felt following her father's second marriage. One can perhaps detect in this sequence a hint of the conflict she must have had as a girl between the *fantasy* of being her father's devoted wife, concerned about the demands made on him by all the other children, and the *knowledge* that she was still one of them herself; and then the mortification of discovering that she was not cast for the role of her father's daughter–wife.

Her earlier sexual promiscuity had been homosexual in the sense that her idea of eliminating love from sex involved denial of specifically masculine and feminine emotions. She now began to express quite simple feminine anxieties. She complained of her compulsion to flirt. She admitted to being frightened when walking alone through dark streets at night. She dreamt that a man tore open her blouse and then broke one of her vases. When she set up house with a man she was appalled at her tendency to nag him. Fairly soon before the end of the analysis she had the following dream.

Dream XV. In the middle of a party a girl squats down to urinate. She has a penis which she tries to push back into its proper place as a vagina. She fails to do it herself so she enlists the aid of a man, who pushes it in with his penis.

In this dream we see depicted the reversal of another of the contradictions on which her defensive 'personality' was based. Instead of accepting her femininity, as a normal woman would, or denying her lack of a penis, as a hysteric would, she had tried to contradict her anxieties about being a woman and not a man by asserting that her vagina was really a penis. This contradiction involved her in an untenable break with reality and the dream epitomizes her return to reality through analysis, depicting first her attempt to return unaided and then the acceptance of help. What it leaves out is her resistance to the required invagination, her struggle to retain her omnipotent bisexual penis–vagina, which she could only begin to relinquish after she had tested out during the phase of regression that it was safe to rely on someone other than herself and had achieved some degree of inner security through acquiring an internal image of a mother whose 'legacy of gentleness could cool her even when the fire of hatred burnt within her'. I am here paraphrasing one of her poems.

This dream, which is the last that I shall quote, was a wish-fulfilment, since it depicted as completed a process which in fact remained incomplete. Unlike the actual surgical operation she had, which was an outstanding success, her analysis was only partially successful. Although she became a much softer person, she remained in many ways narcissistic and schizoid, and there was, I think, a manic element in the partial recovery she made. In so far as this can be attributed to a failure in technique rather than to limitations inherent in her pathology, the fault lay in my failure to bring certain relations directly into the transference, notably her idealization of the young Frenchman and her impulse to murder her friend's mother. As a result the dynamic changes which occurred when she recognized her hostility and found she could draw took place by a sort of manic intrapsychic manipulation conducted under my aegis, as it were, rather than directly within the transference relationship.

Although Miss Y's analysis ended prematurely, she had a proper last session. During it she said, 'Well, I see it all now. It wasn't their fault, and it wasn't mine either,' and then turning round to look at me she added, 'Though why in the hell didn't you say so at the very beginning?' This was meant half-humorously, but perhaps she had a point. Perhaps if I had started from the assumption that she must have been through some experiences too painful to be assimilated and that she was seeking a relationship secure and sensitive enough for her to abandon her protective defences and risk suffering again, things might have been easier and quicker. But perhaps she would not have understood what I was talking about, and could not have done so until she had unburdened herself of much of the aggression with which she had become overcharged.

1959

ART AND PSYCHOANALYSIS

24

Psychoanalysis and the Literary Imagination

Psychoanalysts differ widely among themselves as to which aspects of Freud's theories they wish to remember and commemorate. For his theories, so far from constituting a unitary, fixed structure which either stands or falls as a whole and which analysts subscribe to in its entirety, are really more a collection of miscellaneous ideas, insights and intuitions propounded over a span of fifty years. Freud derived them from three disparate sources – his clinical experience, his self-analysis and the biological theories current in his lifetime – and they have proved capable of development and elaboration in several different and apparently, perhaps even actually, incompatible ways. There exist today in this country at least three different schools of psychoanalysis, all claiming to be Freudian and all capable of showing that their ideas can indeed be discovered, albeit often in embryonic form, somewhere in Freud's writings. The fact that these writings have proved to be more a quarry than an edifice, then, makes it necessary for me to state explicitly at the beginning of this essay which aspect of Freud's thinking I consider most important and which particular group of Freudian concepts I shall be using while developing my argument.

Now, it so happens that my own view in this matter coincides with Freud's. To his and my mind the most important, the most seminal and the most revolutionary idea that Freud ever had was his idea that the human mind is capable of thinking in two different ways or modes; that there are, to use the title of one of his papers, 'two principles of mental functioning', one of which is characteristic of our waking life, the other characteristic of dreaming and neurotic symptom-formation; and that it is possible to define and describe these two modes by presenting them in antithesis to one another, so that each can be conceived of as possessing characteristics which are the opposite of the other.

Freud termed these two antithetical principles or modes, to my mind misleadingly, the primary and secondary processes; the primary processes being those characteristic of our dream-life, the secondary processes being those characteristic of our waking thought. The primary processes, in Freud's terminology, are *condensation*, by which mental images tend to fuse with one another, and *displacement*, by which they tend to replace and symbolize one another; they ignore opposites and the categories of space and time, and they are wish-fulfilling. The secondary processes, on the other hand, respect the differences between images, obey the laws of grammar and formal logic, take cognizance of opposites and of the categories of space and time, and are adapted to the 'realities' of the external world. To use a terminology which Freud himself did not use, the primary processes are iconic and non-discursive, the secondary processes verbal and discursive; the meaning of primary process utterances – if one can call a dream or a symptom an utterance – being ascertainable only by teasing out items and threads from the total agglutination, amalgam or fuzz that constitutes the dream, and the meaning of secondary process utterances being ascertainable by reference to the dictionary definitions and syntactical rules of the language which the waking speaker or writer is using. Furthermore, it was Freud's view that the primary processes in some sense come before the secondary processes – hence, of course, the nomenclature – and are, therefore, more infantile, more primitive and less adaptive than the secondary processes, which are learned during the course of each individual's development from a primitive, phantasizing infant to a civilized, adapted adult.

Now, as a method of approaching the main theme of this present lecture, I intend to make a number of introductory comments on Freud's idea, or discovery, of the existence of these two principles of mental functioning.

First, Freud unwittingly became involved in an inherently paradoxical activity when he tried to formulate in words the nature of a type of thinking which is essentially non-verbal and which is, therefore, of necessity falsified by being put into words. But as a rationalist and a scientist he really had no option but to try. Utilization of already available techniques for handling unverbalizable, ineffable experiences and phenomena, such as the *via negativa* of the mystics and the apophatic mode of argument of the theologians, would have seemed to him to be a betrayal of his ideal – the creation of a truly scientific psychology – and of one of the basic assumptions of his generation: the assumption that the only real truths are scientific truths.

Let me try to clarify this comparison with theology. Freud asserted that one of the major characteristics of the primary processes is that they are unconscious, and in his initial formulations he located them in a fictive space or area, which he designated negatively as the unconscious. And even when he changed this area's name to the id, as here in *New Introductory Lectures on Psycho-Analysis*, No. 31, his description of it consists largely of what it is not:

It is the dark inaccessible part of our personality; what little we know of it we have learnt from our study of the dream-work and of the construction of neurotic symptoms, and most of that is of a negative character and can be described only as a contrast to the ego. We approach the id with analogies; we call it a chaos, a cauldron ... It is filled with energy reaching it from the instincts, but it has no organization, produces no collective will ... the logical laws of thought do not apply ... contrary impulses exist side by side without cancelling each other out ... There is nothing in the id that corresponds to the idea of time ... The id, of course, knows no judgements of value; no good and evil, no morality.

Now, so far as I know, the only other example of anyone proclaiming the existence of something profoundly important by asserting that it can only be approached with analogies and that it is not anything that can be defined and asserted positively is to be found in negative or apophatic theology, which argues that human language, when applied to God, is inevitably inexact and that it is therefore less misleading to use negative language about God than positive: 'to refuse to say what God is, and to state simply what He is not'.[1] Curiously enough, the one positive attribute of God which negative theologians assert can be known about God is His energy, which again corresponds to Freud's account of the id. However, my reason for mentioning negative theology here is not to discuss the parallels that can be drawn between the theological concept of God and the psychoanalytical concept of the id, interesting though it might be to do so, but to prepare the ground for arguing later that there is something about the literary imagination that can only be stated in negative terms.

Secondly, Freud formulated his theory of the primary and secondary processes in a cultural milieu very different from our own. Freud was born in 1856, he was fifty in 1906, and his formative years were, therefore, pre-Einstein, pre-Picasso, pre-cubism, pre-Ezra Pound, pre-James Joyce. As a result it was natural for him to assume a much closer relationship between the verbal, the rational and the realistic on the one hand, and the non-verbal, the irrational and the imaginary or imaginative on the other hand, than any thinker can today. He formulated his ideas before the visual arts had ceased to be representational and before literature had begun to explore the possibilities of fragmenting and manipulating the syntactical structure of language. He was therefore able to assume that when painters painted pictures they were depicting objects and scenes that could, in principle, also be described in words, and that when writers wrote books, they were using language in the same sort of way as scientists do when they write learned treatises. As a result there appeared to him to be – and indeed given the historical context there was – nothing incongruous in assuming that, of the two types of mental functioning, one (the verbal, rational mode) was characteristic of the ego, of consciousness, of health, and of successful adaptation to reality, and the other (the non-verbal, irrational mode) was characteristic of

[1] See Timothy Ware, *The Orthodox Church* (London: Penguin Books, 1963).

dreamers, neurotics, lunatics, infants and primitive people; and that the capacity to use the former was dependent on repression of the latter.

In the event this idea that the primary processes are unconscious, primitive, neurotic, archaic, etc., and are normally subject to repression, was to cause psychoanalysis considerable trouble, both in its theorizing and its public relations, since it soon became evident that there was some similarity between the imaginative activity displayed by artists and writers and the primary processes described by Freud as characteristic of dreaming and symptom-formation. Given the clinical origins and bias of psychoanalysis, the easiest, the most tempting way of explaining this similarity was to assert that artists and writers are neurotic and that works of art are analogous, or homologous, to dreams and neurotic symptoms; and that the techniques of psychoanalytical interpretation can be transferred without modification to artists and their works.

This idea is still around today, despite Freud's rather belated disavowal of it in 1928, when he wrote: 'Before the problem of the creative artist analysis must, alas, lay down its arms.' It owes its vitality, I suspect, to four disparate sources. Firstly, to envy – we are all a bit envious of creative people and it is comforting to entertain the idea that they are not, after all, so very different from ourselves, and that their gifts may not truly be gifts but by-products of their neuroses. Secondly, to the pecking order that exists among academics and the intelligentsia generally – if scientists, and psychoanalysts almost universally claim to be scientists, could explain creative activity, could analyse the literary imagination, and could slot it neatly into the scientific scheme of things, they would have one-upped the artists and increased their own prestige. Thirdly, to the rise of Eng. Lit. as an academic study and the resulting expansion of the Ph.D. industry, which has led to a demand in academic circles for new techniques to apply to the victims of literary thesis-writers – and what more tempting than to add to literature's own critical armoury a few, mostly character-assassinating weapons borrowed from psychoanalysis? And fourthly, to the fact that there is indeed some similarity between

the creative imagination and the oneiric, dream-producing faculty, a similarity long recognized by artists and writers themselves, and that it is, therefore, legitimate to discuss what the
nature of this similarity is. But, and it is a big 'but', discussion
of this similarity is queered from the outset if one assumes, as
most of the early analysts seem to have done, that in healthy
people the primary processes are repressed and that people in
whom they are not repressed are *ipso facto* neurotic. The whole
idea that artists and writers are neurotic stems, I am suggesting,
from one simple but fallacious assumption, namely, that the
primary and secondary processes are mutually antagonistic, and
that the former have, in health, to be relegated by repression to
a curious underworld, the id or the unconscious. If this were
true, then painters who can imagine what they intend to paint
with quasi-hallucinatory, eidetic vividness, and writers who can
conjure up characters who seem to take on an independent life
of their own, would indeed be neurotic and psychotic.

But if one starts from another assumption, namely that the
primary and secondary processes coexist from the beginning of
life and that under favourable conditions they may continue
to function in harmony with one another, one providing the
imaginative, the other the rational basis of living, creative
people may be conceived to be those who retain into adult life
something of that imaginative freedom which healthy children
display openly but all too many grown-ups in our present
rationalist, bourgeois culture lose when they enter the adult
world. According to Freud in his paper of 1915, 'The Unconscious', 'A sharp and final division between the content of the
two systems does not, as a rule, take place till puberty.'

It may seem that I am being perverse in first asserting that
in my opinion Freud's most important contribution was his
formulation of the distinction between the primary and secondary processes and then going on to qualify this statement by
arguing that in one vital respect his formulation was misguided
and requires modification. I must, therefore, defend myself
briefly from this charge by making three points. Firstly, hints
of the possibility of modifying Freud's theory in the direction I
am suggesting can be found in Freud's own writings, particularly

if one allows oneself to reverse statements he made, e.g. his remark in the same paper that 'a total severance of the two systems . . . is what above all characterizes a condition of illness'. Secondly, I am far from being alone among analysts in rejecting the idea that the primary processes are archaic and maladaptive; in this country Winnicott, Bowlby, Marjorie Brierley and Marion Milner have all in their different ways done so. And thirdly, attempts to reconcile Freud's position with a positive, non-reductionist attitude towards imaginative activity always seem to lead to formulations which are tortuous and obscure but still leave the central mystery unexplained. For instance, Heinz Hartmann, the distinguished American psycho-analyst, who is on record as having subscribed to 'the theoretical ideal of rational action' and to the view that healthy develop-ment leads to 'alienation of the id from reality', was forced into using such phrases as 'regressive adaptation', 'detours through the archaic' and 'regressions in the service of the ego' when writing appreciatively about art.[2] The attempt to explain im-aginative activity in terms of a theory primarily designed to explain neuroses without impugning either its value or its healthiness seems to me to amount to no more than asserting that creative people possess some knack for getting round the repressions assumed by the theory to be normal and then finding some impressive-sounding verbal formula to describe this knack.

The next point I have to make is that Freud's conception of the existence of unconscious primary processes was, in Freud's own view of the nature of science, profoundly unscientific. The unscientific nature of this part of his theory seems only to have struck him forcibly when he came to consider the actual details of the imagery used by the primary processes and came to recognize the importance of symbolism in general and of sexual symbolism in particular. It is not, I think, generally known that the original 1900 version of *The Interpretation of Dreams* had no section on symbolism in it and cites only one dream

---

[2] See H. Hartmann, *Ego Psychology and the Problem of Adaptation* (New York: International Universities Press, 1958).

exemplifying sexual symbolism, that it was only in the 1914 edition that a section on symbolism appeared for the first time, and that in the present Standard Edition that section accounts for only 55 of its 623 pages. Of course, the embarrassing, unscientific nature of symbolism arises from the fact that symbolic interpretations can be arrived at intuitively and, as Freud himself put it, intuition 'is exempt from all criticism and consequently its findings have no claim to credibility' (Freud S. SE vol v p. 350.). Although this is a very respectable scientific opinion, it is hardly applicable to the subject of symbolism, since symbolism is a form of metaphor and, as Aristotle said, 'a good metaphor implies an intuitive perception of the similarity in dissimilars' (*Poetics*, ch. 22).

As a result of Freud's understandable rejection of intuition, objective evidence in support of symbolic interpretations of dream-imagery had to be culled from sources remote from the natural sciences on which Freud had hoped to build psychoanalysis; he had to turn to myths, to folk-lore, to anthropology, to etymology, to jokes both clean and dirty, all 'soft' subjects from a natural-scientific point of view.

If Freud had lived today, he would not, I think, have had to be embarrassed by the apparently non-scientific nature of this aspect of his discoveries, since the emergence of linguistics as a scientific discipline would have enabled him to use that science as a model instead of neuroanatomy. Instead of constructing, as he did, a mental anatomy in which the primary processes were located in one part of a mental apparatus and the secondary processes were located in another, he could have formulated a paralinguistic science, which might perhaps have been called oneirics, with iconic, structural and semantic branches, containing sets of rules governing both the translation of oneiric, iconic statements into phonetic, verbal utterances and the setting up of obstacles against translation. In other words, the rules would have to be able to explain why, and under what conditions, dreams can be understood and interpreted to the mutual enlightenment of both interpreter and analysand, and why, and under what conditions, they sometimes cannot be. Another set of rules would have (had) to account for the fact that imagery related to biological destiny, which includes birth and death as well as sex, seems to occupy a central position in oneiric structure – and perhaps in language structure too. (See ch. 4, 'Is Freudian Symbolism a Myth?')

I have suggested that there are indeed similarities between the literary imagination and the faculty of dreaming, and I would now like to discuss in detail what these similarities are. I must, however, first emphasize that there never seems to have been any doubt among poets and writers themselves that some important connection exists between their creative activity and dreaming. It would be possible to cite innumerable examples of writers using their dreams as the initial source of their inspiration, of their claiming, sometimes untruthfully, to have composed poems in their sleep, of their including dreams they have had in the text of their novels, of their claiming specifically to be 'dreamers of dreams'. These facts are, however, so well known that it would be mere padding on my part if I were to spend time citing them, so instead I shall give just one quotation from Charles Darwin.

> The Imagination is one of the highest prerogatives of man. By this faculty he unites former images and ideas, independently of the will, and thus creates brilliant and novel results. A poet, as Jean-Paul Richter remarks, 'who must reflect whether he shall make a character say yes or no – to the devil with him; he is only a stupid corpse'. Dreaming gives us the best notion of this power; as Jean-Paul again says, 'The dream is an involuntary kind of poetry.'

This quotation is from Darwin's *The Descent of Man*, which was first published in 1871. Darwin borrowed the quotations from Jean-Paul Richter from a book by Henry Maudsley, the English psychiatrist who provided the money with which the London County Council built the Maudsley Hospital. Note that both Darwin and Richter emphasize imagination's independence of the will, a point to which I shall return later.

The first and most striking similarity between dreams and works of literary imagination is that they can be granted or refused meaning according to the predilection of their viewer, hearer or reader – English seems to lack a word which would embrace a person viewing his own dream, a person listening to an account of someone else's dream and a person reading a poem or novel. Now, this statement is obviously true in the case of dreams. Despite Freud, it is probably still true that the majority of educated people in this country, though perhaps not in the United States, do not attribute any meaning to dreams, and, on the face of it, it is a matter of personal bias or temperament whether anyone sees meaning in dreams or regards them as, say, analogous to the 'noise' made by electronic equipment when it is switched on but not actually working. It is, however, less obvious that it is possible to deny meaning to poems and novels. Most people, I expect, can think of acquaintances who are literate but literal and not literary, who do not really get the point of novels and poems and who are flummoxed by the fact that the realm or order of reality to which they should be assigned is not readily defined or located; who are flummoxed, indeed, by precisely that element of fiction in fiction which makes it impossible to read novels simply as disguised biography or disguised sociology, and who do not really understand why poems need to be laid out on the page in such a wasteful, extravagant manner.

There would, I think, have been something facetious about my having drawn attention to the fact that dreams, poems and novels can all be regarded as meaningless were it not for the fact that, if one does attribute meaning to them, they immediately acquire not a single meaning, but multiple and manifold meanings. Unlike factual statements, like 'The Battle of Waterloo took place on 18 June 1815' or 'Arsenic is a poison,' which have only one meaning, poems, novels and dreams either have no meaning or several meanings. Once one has recognized or decided that they have meaning, they become open to interpretation, and characteristically several not mutually exclusive interpretations can be made of them. And characteristically, too, exegesis of these interpretations takes up more space, and uses more words, than does the dream, poem or even the novel itself. This is due, of course, to the fact that the imagination unites, to use Darwin's word, or condenses, to use Freud's word, numbers of images and themes into a unitary whole, which therefore takes up less space than the individual items do if enumerated in series. To take two examples. The first dream that Freud ever 'submitted to a detailed interpretation', that of Irma's injection, which he himself dreamt in 1895, took him two-thirds of a page to recount and fourteen pages to interpret. And, secondly, in a volume of essays entitled *Interpretations*,[3] it takes Dennis Ward thirteen pages to answer the question 'What did the sonnet "The Windhover" mean to Gerard Manley Hopkins?' (i.e. just under a page to a line). Furthermore, his answer involves him in mentioning at least ten verbally distinguishable meanings for one of the poem's two central images, the falcon – the other central image is the air or wind which sustains it in flight – even though these ten meanings unite in the poem itself to form one meaning which it is artificial to dissect into sub-meanings.

Interestingly enough, neither Freud nor Ward suggest interpretations of a kind that we nowadays think of as being specifically psychoanalytical, and Freud's interpretation of his own dream does not include any mention of any underlying overall meaning. But anyone reading it today with hindsight can see that it has one, though it is not clear, to me at least, whether or not Freud saw this meaning and suppressed it for reasons of tact and delicacy. I shall have reason to return to Hopkins' 'The Windhover' later.

Although it is, I understand, accepted practice for literary critics to proffer multiple but interconnected meanings for literary works they interpret, psychoanalysts are not uncommonly criticized for doing precisely the same thing when they interpret dreams – and are indeed sometimes themselves unhappy about doing so. The difficulty here is, I think, based on a confusion between causes and meaning. If one asserts that the cause of A is X, then one is in difficulties, though not always insuperable ones, if one also asserts that its cause is Y and Z; but if one asserts that a meaning of A is X, there are no objections to asserting that it also means Y and Z, since there is no rule that utterances, other than scientific statements, should have only

---

[3] John Wain, ed., *Interpretations: Essays on Twelve English Poems* (London: Routledge & Kegan Paul, 1955).

one meaning. Unscientific utterances can, and indeed usually do, have double meanings, implied meanings, unintended meanings, and can hint and insinuate, and may indeed mean the opposite of what they apparently mean, especially if they are said in a certain tone of voice. Here again we have an example of psychoanalysis being caught in a trap created by its own history, of laying itself open to attack for being unscientific, when it has in fact entered a field where it has no need to claim to be scientific.

A third similarity between dreams and imaginative works is that their production is independent of the will. We do not make up or construct our dreams; they occur or happen to us, and while we are dreaming we do not recognize the dream as a creation of ourselves. The same seems to be true of at least the initial idea or impetus of any literary work; it just comes to the writer or poet. A necessary precondition of all imaginative activity seems to be what Keats called 'negative capability', the ability to allow oneself to be 'in uncertainties, mysteries, doubts, without any irritable reaching after fact and reason'; in other words, the ability to abandon Hartmann's 'theoretical ideal of rational action' and to stop trying to 'master reality' in favour of letting oneself happen. And, at least for some writers, the execution as well as the conception of a work of art may also be largely independent of the will. Coleridge claimed that 'Kubla Khan' came to him in his sleep, though he must have decided after awakening that it was worth writing down, and Enid Blyton has left a vivid account of how her characters took over while she was writing her books.[4]

I shut my eyes for a few minutes, with my portable typewriter on my knee – I make my mind a blank and wait – and then, as clearly as I would see real children, my characters stand before me in my mind's eye. I see them in detail – hair, eyes, feet, clothes, expression – and I always know their Christian names but never their surnames . . . I don't know what anyone is going to say or do. I don't know what is going to happen. I am in the happy position of being able to write a story and read it for the first time, at one and the same moment . . .

[4] See Barbara Stoney, *Enid Blyton: A Biography* (London: Hodder & Stoughton, 1974).

Sometimes a character makes a joke, a really funny one, that makes me laugh as I type it on my paper – and I think, 'Well, I couldn't have thought of that myself in a hundred years!' And then I think, 'Well, who *did* think of it then?'

Although I have no particular wish to sing Enid Blyton's praise, it must be admitted that her question 'Well, who *did* think of it then?' is an extremely good one, and that she was far from being what Jean-Paul Richter called a stupid corpse who had to reflect whether she should make a character say yes or no. This curious fact that the literary imagination is independent of the will, of the self-conscious ego, is presumably the reason why poets and writers before the rise of psychology could believe literally in their inspiring Muse. It is also the reason why we do not accord full artistic authenticity to works of art which strike us as contrived or '*voulu*'.

But despite these similarities between the ways in which the imagination manifests itself in dreams and in works of literary art, there are, of course, numerous differences. Quite apart from the obvious fact that most dreams are more like moving pictures than the printed word, dreams are in general less organized, less unified, indeed less condensed than works of art; they more often resemble someone who is groping for the appropriate metaphor than someone who has found it. If one accepts Richter's dictum, quoted earlier, that dreams are an involuntary kind of poetry, one has to add that they are, usually, also an uncompleted kind of poetry. Something would still need to be done to them before they could be transferred from the private sector of experience to the public, before they could acquire universality. This something-still-to-be-done must, I think, be something more than just the translation of visual, non-discursive imagery into verbal, discursive language; in other words the transformation of a dream or unconscious fantasy into a work of literary imagination cannot, I think, be analogous to the process of interpretation as practised by psychoanalysts; it must rather comprise the casting of the central meaning in symbols which are part of the shared iconography of the culture of which the poet or writer is a member, and which, therefore,

carry a heavy charge of shared, public associations and resonances.

Gerard Manley Hopkins' 'The Windhover', for instance,
fuses images derived not from his private experience but from
ornithology, falconry, skating, chivalry and Christianity – all
public images with which any literate person could well be
familiar – to make a personal statement about the relationship
between divine inspiration, symbolized by the wind, and human
aspiration, symbolized by the hovering falcon. Interestingly
enough, if it were permissible to equate Hopkins' God with
Freud's id, it would be possible to interpret 'The Windhover'
as a statement about the dynamic interdependence of the ego
and the id, though a lot would be lost by doing so.

But I have stated my last point positively when I should have
stated it negatively. It is not that the poet or writer actively
masters the iconography of his times in order to be able to
universalize his private emotions, but that one aspect of his
'negative capability' is an exceptional sensitivity and receptivity
to the iconographical network that constitutes the culture of
his time, that makes it natural for him to express his private
emotions in universal terms – or, indeed, perhaps not to distinguish between the individual and the universal, between the
microcosm and the macrocosm.

It may already have become clear that I have no wish to dilate
on the psychodynamics of the literary imagination. I must,
however, state my impression, my conviction, that people who
possess negative capability to a high degree seem not to conceive
of themselves as opposed to an alien environment which they
have to master by 'irritably reaching after fact and reason', but
rather as a part of the universe which is capable of absorbing
the whole into itself and then re-creating it by distillation in
imaginative works; in other and psychoanalytical words, their
relationship to 'external reality' remains identificatory, without
any drawing of impermeable ego-boundaries between themselves and other people and other things. And, secondly, they
seem to be refreshingly free from the conventional notion that
activity is masculine and passivity is feminine and can therefore
oscillate between active and passive states of being without

feeling that their identity is threatened by doing so. As a result they can, for instance, imagine themselves into characters of the opposite – or rather other – sex as readily as into characters of their own. This identificatory relationship with the outside world and this freedom from the conventional masculine–active and feminine–passive dichotomy can, of course, be used as evidence in favour of the view that artists are neurotic, and no doubt has been, but it could equally plausibly be used to prove the opposite – since drawing ego-boundaries between oneself and others could be regarded as a symptom of alienation; and rejection of the masculine–active feminine–passive dichotomy could be regarded as a healthy immunity to indoctrination by cultural prejudices. It all depends on which part of the Freudian quarry one chooses to excavate.

Although I have been emphasizing the healthy core of imaginative activity, I have, of course, no wish to deny that mental creative processes may be interfered with by inhibitions, symptoms and anxieties analogous to those which may impede biological creative activities. But it is, I think, as much an error to suppose that these disturbing factors are an essential part of imaginative, creative activity as to suppose that sexual hang-ups are an intrinsic part of orgastic capacity, a capacity which can indeed itself be conceived to be a form of negative capability.

There are, then, intrinsic, inherent limits to the amount that can be said about the imagination in general and much of what can be said can only be stated in negative terms; hence my initial reference to negative theology and my citation of Freud's statement that most of what we know of the id is of a negative character and can only be approached with analogies. I should like to suggest that there are three reasons for thinking that there are three intrinsic limits to the amount that psychoanalysts in particular can say about the specifically literary imagination.

First, literary studies seem to be largely concerned with questions of value and quality, i.e. with the question of why, and in what sense, some poems and novels are better than others, whereas psychoanalysis, to the extent that it remains attached to Freud's ideal of a scientific psychology, can have nothing to say about value. Erik Erikson, the psychoanalyst who has most concerned himself with problems of meaning, value and ethics – even to the extent of introducing the word 'virtue' into his psychoanalytical vocabulary – has, as Yankelovich and Barrett point out, been more engaged in 'rediscovering prescientific truths' and absorbing them into psychoanalytical theory than in extending psychoanalytical theory so that it can contribute anything new to history, literature and moral philosophy. And, as Yankelovich and Barrett also point out, Erikson has consistently 'blurred the extent of his divergence from the psychoanalytical movement' and the extent of his dependence on a philosophy at odds with that of Freud. Although I sympathize with Erikson's motives and agree with much of what he says, it must, I think, be admitted that the creative traffic goes in the opposite direction to that in which it often appears to go, and that psychoanalysts have more to learn from historians, literary critics and philosophers than they have to teach them.[5]

Secondly, since imaginative activity is a classic example of the self as agent, to use John Macmurray's phrase, accounts of the self that dreams, imagines and creates are inevitably vitiated by the fact that the dreaming, imagining, creating self is not open to inspection or introspection. If the self tries to observe itself while creating, it inevitably fails, since the self-as-agent must, willy-nilly, become located in the observing, introspecting self and not in the part of itself that it is trying to observe. In other words, self-scrutiny and negative capability are mutually exclusive states of mind. Another way of putting this point is to say that the self that dreams, imagines and creates is intrinsically nominative and can only be the subject of verbs, can only be 'I' and never 'me', and that it does a disappearing trick if one tries to push it into the objective, accusative position. It is indeed somewhat similar to the concept of time, of which St Augustine wrote that he knew what it was so long as no one asked him what it was, but that if he was asked he did not know.

Thirdly, it is, I think, open to doubt whether there is such

[5] See D. Yankelovich and W. Barrett, *Ego and Instinct* (New York: Vintage Books, 1971).

a thing as a *literary* imagination which can be isolated and differentiated from other forms of imagination. My reason for this doubt stems from two sources: first, from the fact that our original knowledge of language is not of seeing words and sentences printed on paper but of hearing them spoken, and that, for instance, our first encounter with poetry is hearing nursery rhymes recited or sung to us by our mothers, not reading poems in books. As a result there must, it seems to me, be a phonetic and musical substructure to the literary imagination, which must be an elaboration or special case of some wider form of imagination which is essentially auditory and musical, and I suspect that this is as true of prose as it is of poetry. And, secondly, since literature, like music, is a discursive art which proceeds through time, the literary imagination must, I suspect, contain some reflection of the rhythms and harmonies which the body uses to sustain itself as an organized entity through time. According to Walter Pater, 'all art constantly aspires towards the condition of music', and Henry Maudsley, whom I mentioned earlier, must have had a similar thought in mind when he stated that the roots of the imagination lay in 'the multitudinous infraconscious vibrations of organic nature'.[6]

Finally, I must acknowledge my overwhelming indebtedness to Coleridge, whose thinking has been at the back of my mind while writing almost every paragraph. This essay can indeed be regarded as an attempt to marry Coleridge's theory of the poetic imagination and Freud's concept of the primary processes — without, I hope, doing too much violence to either.

1975

---

[6] See L. S. Hearnshaw, *A Short History of British Psychology* (London: Methuen, 1964).

RELIGION AND MORALS

25

On Continuity

As soon as I accepted James Mitchell's invitation to write about 'The God I Want',[1] I realized that I should have to reverse the habits of two decades. As a psychoanalyst my experience has been in elucidating the needs, desires and fears of others, and it would have been easy for me to suggest reasons why others want a God and to write a learned and plausible paper describing how some people want a paternal God whom they can revere and feel protected by, how others would like a maternal God who would enfold and nourish them, and how yet others would like a phallic Goddess before whom they could abase themselves, and so on through all the mental disorders, listing the kind of God most apt for their psychopathology.

However, such erudition is not what James Mitchell required, nor would such a display be strictly truthful, since it would not really be based on clinical experience. The fact is that very few religious people seek an analysis, particularly from an analyst trained in the Freudian school, and those few who do either have no need to expose their beliefs to clinical scrutiny – it has become what contemporary analytical jargon calls an 'autonomous function of the ego' which is 'conflict-free' and remains outside the scope of the analysis – or make it clear from the outset that their religious beliefs are a way of affirming their belief in love; an affirmation which only requires analysis in those cases in which it turns out to be a denial of their disbelief and despair, when it forms part of what the jargon calls a 'manic defence' against depression.

[1] This essay was originally a contribution to *The God I Want*, ed. James Mitchell (London: Constable, 1967).

The distinction between beliefs which simply affirm and those which affirm in order to deny the despair which arises from knowledge of the incapacity to affirm is indeed crucial, and is, I suspect, independent of the language in which the affirmation is made. Those who have had a religious upbringing will tend to affirm in religious terms, while those who have had a secular upbringing will do so in secular terms, but I doubt whether those who affirm in one mode differ essentially from those who do so in the other – though those whose beliefs and doubts are stated in the secular mode will only have a hundred-year-old tradition of thought in which to formulate their dilemmas, while those who use the religious mode will be able to call on the experience of millennia.

Although these introductory paragraphs lay me open to the charge that I am still concealing myself behind a mask of professional anonymity and that I am ducking the question by suggesting that the religious quest can be restated in terms of health, depression and manic denial of depression, I have in fact already revealed some of the things for which I do *not* want a God. Having said that to my mind religion is concerned with the affirmation of love, I am placing God in the realm of feelings and am making it clear that I do not want Him to explain the universe for me or to invoke him as a First Cause or Prime Mover. That things have been happening since long before I was there and will continue to happen for long after I cease to be here, and that this creates problems as to whether the universe ever began, and if so when and how, is mysterious enough; to my mind it only compounds the mystery still further to assume that the Creation was the act of Someone who then allows His creation to run according to the rules which He then established.

I do not, then, want a God who will provide me with a cosmology, and I am, therefore, dispensing with Him in the role for which until recently he was most often wanted. In the cosmological sense God is, to my mind, dead, and had indeed been dead for some time before my professional progenitor, Freud, wrote the essay in which he argued that God is a wish-fulfilling illusion, a projection of the worldly father whom every child reveres and wishes to feel protected by. This essay

led his one Christian disciple, the Swiss Pastor Pfister to remark
that his rationalism was 'basically the idea of the eighteenth-
century Enlightenment in proud modern guise' and has led some
latter-day analysts to wonder why, if God is a projection of
childhood wishes, he remains persistently masculine despite the
fact that our patients nowadays are mother-fixated, and why,
if as other parts of Freud's work lead us to think it is the
capacity to love which makes us feel good, mankind should
have created the illusion of Someone who loves us. Surely it
would not have been beyond the wit of man to devise an illusion
which enhanced his belief in his own capacity to love instead
of one which left him dependent and beholden to the love of
Another.

Here again I am stating something for which I do not want
God. I do not want Him as a father-figure, nor as a mother-
figure. Not only do I not want to return to childhood, or to
retain an enclave in which childhood is preserved, but I am also
sceptical as to whether this desire is really the reason why even
those who believe in God in a most literal, concrete sense as
Someone up there or 'out there' do so. And even if I did
want a God who restored me to childhood, my professional
conscience would not allow me to endorse such a wish; it
would be impossible to hold a belief knowing that it could be
demolished by one's own professional expertise, which could
demonstrate that it was a symptom of one's own private psychopathology.

The God I want must, therefore, be immune to interpretation,
and cannot be one who either recreates for me the blissful
security of childhood or who compensates me for the bliss
which I perhaps never enjoyed. One of the difficulties of the
neurotic projection theory of God is that it does not tell one
whether God is a projection of what one once did experience
or of what one did not, whether it recreates a past that once
really was or whether it creates something entirely fictitious.

As I do not want a God who will explain the universe for me
or who will provide me with a substitute for one of the reassuring figures of childhood, the God I want will have to be Someone
who never came into Freud's field of vision – at least when he

was writing about religion. This is perhaps why I find Freud's *The Future of an Illusion* curiously dated and irrelevant. It seems to miss the point and is in some ways reminiscent of the attitude taken up by many psychiatrists towards the so-called 'delusions' of psychotics. Having satisfied themselves that some statement of a patient is neither scientifically nor historically true, they label it a 'delusion' or 'false belief' and then attempt to explain it, according to their theoretical predilections, as the manifestation of either some primitive infantile fantasy or some biochemically determined thought-disorder, without stopping to ask whether it was ever intended to be taken literally as a factual statement or whether it might make sense if interpreted in some other mode.

In fairness to both Freud and the psychiatrists, it must be added that psychotics are themselves confused about the logical status of their utterances and that the spokesmen of organized religion have often shared with Freud the idea that the scientific and religious modes are in competition with one another, and that loyalty towards or even comprehension of one necessitates contemptuous dismissal of the other. As Eliot has observed, ever since the seventeenth century man has suffered from a 'dissociation of sensibility' which compels him to change his stance perpetually and to shift uneasily from participating emotionally in life and adopting the pose that he is above and outside the system which he is observing objectively. However, the solution of adhering consistently to one stance and ignoring the other involves letting more than one baby out with the bath-water. Those who adhere to the scientific stance can find no place in their philosophy for art or intuition; those who adopt Eliot's own solution can make nothing of technology; while those who adopt the psychotic solution of jumbling the two stances together become confused, bewildered and incomprehensible to their fellow men. The God that is really wanted, as opposed to the God I personally want, is one Who would annul this 'dissociation of sensibility' by an act of synthesis. I doubt, however, whether any self-conscious attempt to synthesize such a deity would be any more successful than those of the God-creating schizophrenics, who usually, for reasons that will emerge later in this essay, end by asserting that they themselves are God.

When Galileo advocated a heliocentric cosmology, the objections of the Church seem to have stemmed not from any intrinsic objection to any particular facts which he adduced – indeed, according to de Santillana the Jesuits in the Rome Observatory were busy confirming his astronomical findings at the very time that the Dominicans were charging him with heresy – but from the fact that he was taking up an attitude towards the universe which implied that he was above and outside it: a position which in the Church's view could only be occupied by God. As de Santillana puts it, the charge against Galileo was that he was 'necessitating' God, in that he was asserting that the universe must be the way it looked to him when he put himself in God's position, and was committing hubris by imaginatively usurping God's place and telling Him how He must have created the universe.

The charge that the scientist is arrogant in claiming absolute and exclusive validity for the view of the universe which arises when he imagines himself to be an observer external to it was also being made by Pfister when he remarked that Freud's view of religion was eighteenth-century rationalism in 'proud modern guise'. Since recent developments in both physics and psychopathology have shown that the idea of a detached observer, whose own position and nature can be ignored, is a myth, Freud's scientific but pre-relativity analysis of religion can be regarded as the assault on one illusion by another, as the attempt of one claimant to expose the pretensions of another, or even as an attempt by the promoter of a new commodity to impugn the credentials of a rival. And it remains to be seen whether Freud, or Jung, or Klein, really does wash whiter than religion.

Although this last paragraph may seem unfair to Freud, it must be remembered that he once described himself as a conquistador, that he founded a movement with its own hierarchy and its own form of the Apostolic Succession and the Laying on of Hands – the training analysis means that all Freudian analysts can trace their descent from either Freud himself or one of his original 'disciples', and that he devised a

new set of myths and symbols which bid fair to replace the
traditional Christian iconography.[2] Philip Rieff, in his *The
Triumph of the Therapeutic*,[3] suggests that this has already
happened in the United States, and I know of one analyst who
writes poetry in the language of Freudian metapsychology. Nor
is it hard nowadays to find people who believe that they consist
of an id, ego and super-ego with the same literalness as the
traditional Christian believes that he has a body, a mind and a
soul, and who take equally literally the Freudian metaphor of
layers of personality arranged in geological strata.

Most analysts seem puzzled by the idea that they and the
Churches are competing for power and dominion over the same
territory and that the achievement of psychoanalysis may lie
more in the introduction of a new set of meaningful images
than in having added to scientific knowledge. There is, however,
a growing body of literature which suggests that there may be
something intrinsically paradoxical about the enterprise of applying the scientific method to human beings, about the observer
observing the observer, and that the point of psychoanalysis may
lie not in its capacity to elucidate the causes of human behaviour
but in making sense of it. Orthodox analysts tend to react to this
idea with the same bewilderment and anxiety as the religious
establishment did to the idea that the value of the Bible might lie
in something other than its accuracy as a historical document,
and that the Church's teaching about the meaning of life could be
dissociated from the assumptions about the nature of the physical
world which were contained in its literature.

And yet it seems obvious – once one has noticed it – that
psychoanalysis and pre-scientific theology resemble one another
in consisting of a mixture of ideas which are of differing logical
status and which cannot, therefore, be integrated into a single
system of thought. Just as the Bible contains both statements
which are allegedly or apparently factual, such as the statement

---

[2] I am not suggesting that this is necessarily a bad thing. Perhaps all
movements concerned with the dissemination of a particular way of looking at
reality require an organization of this kind.

[3] Philip Rieff, *The Triumph of the Therapeutic: Uses of Faith after Freud*
(London: Penguin, 1973).

that the world was created in seven days, and others which are moral and evaluative, such as 'Honour thy father and mother, that thy days may be long in the land which the Lord thy God giveth thee' and 'Blessed are the meek: for they shall inherit the earth,' so the psychoanalytical literature comprises both allegedly factual statements about human psychological development, as in its theories of infantile sexuality and ego development, and others which refer to the preconditions for attaining mental health, such as statements about the need to resolve the Oedipus complex or to reach the depressive position. (I have deliberately chosen examples which run parallel to one another. Resolution of the Oedipus complex clearly has something to do with honouring one's father and mother, while reaching the depressive position involves abandoning infantile omnipotence and self-centredness and being able to admit the possibility that one is in the wrong.)

In both cases the former class of statements, the theological ones about cosmology and the psychoanalytical ones about infantile development, are in principle verifiable or falsifiable by non-theological or non-analytical means. That the world was created in seven days or that there was a Flood are factual statements which can be either proved or disproved by application of the scientific method. They are amenable to objective assessment since, among other reasons, the distance between the relevant facts and the observer is so great that the principle of relativity can be ignored. Similarly, psychoanalytical theories about infantile development can be proved or disproved – and, indeed, are being so – by direct observation of infants and by the application of ethological techniques, derived in the first instance from the study of animal behaviour. The first class of statement can be handled by the scientific method without raising awkward problems about meaning or value.[4]

---

[4] It is, incidentally, not an accident that psychological theories about infants, children and adolescents are easier to come by than theories about the middle-aged and old. Most established psychologists and analysts are themselves middle-aged or old and are, therefore, capable of feeling sufficiently remote from their subject matter not to worry unduly about problems of observer error.

Such problems are, however, raised by the second class of statement. Honouring one's father and mother, becoming meek, resolving the Oedipus complex and reaching the depressive position are all phrases which refer not to the morally neutral physical world which one can safely regard as other than oneself but to something which we and people like ourselves either do or should or might do; and their consequences – living long in the land which the Lord thy God giveth thee, inheriting the earth, achieving maturity – are states of mind or being or grace which elude objective definition. They are, indeed, meaningless phrases if taken objectively and only begin to make sense if one feels entitled to interpret them in the light of one's own subjective experience. And just as religious people do not always agree as to what is meant by meekness or inheriting the earth, so psychoanalysts do not always agree as to what is meant by maturity or resolving the Oedipus complex. Some, for instance, would interpret the latter negatively as a process by which one ceases to be fixated on one's parents, while others would regard it as a positive process by which the parents are discovered as real people undistorted by infantile fantasies and wishes. Similarly health, which is both a medical and a religious concept, may be defined in terms either of conformity to some ideal of virtuous or mature behaviour or of the attainment of an inner state of wholeness.

This resemblance between religion and psychoanalysis – which should not be used as an argument against either – derives, I think, from the fact that both consist of a core of insights into the human condition which becomes surrounded by an accretion of ideas from other sources.

First, there are those which derive from the fact that insight cannot be formulated directly and has therefore to be expressed in terms of metaphors, parables and paradoxes which are liable to be taken literally.

Secondly, there are the ideas which arise from the use of mythopoiesis as an expository device. The resulting myths again tend to be taken literally. Even though Freud prided himself on being a scientist, his insight into the importance of Oedipal guilt led him to formulate an anthropological theory about the

murder of the Primal Father which he himself described as a
'just-so' story, and to invoke a Greek myth as an expository
device for getting across what children feel about their parents.
These expository devices, both in religion and psychoanalysis,
tend to be taken as explanatory hypotheses for those who fail
to get the message intuitively.

Thirdly, there is the tendency to confuse the subjective, metaphorical language of insight with the objective language we use
when dealing with the impersonal. This confusion is enhanced
by the fact that one of the major insights of both religion and
psychoanalysis is that the realm of insight and the personal is
much more extensive than those without insight like to admit;
that, for instance, much physical illness is not due simply to the
mechanical failure of the body's organs but to a malaise of the
whole personality, and that apparently trivial gestures and
mannerisms are messages of profound import.

My reason for using the last few paragraphs to draw attention
to the similarities between religion and psychoanalysis is partly
that, as an analyst who spent his childhood in a moderately
devout Anglican home, I am personally concerned to establish
some continuity between my past and my present, and partly
because, unlike, I hope, other contributors to this book, I have
practical and almost daily experience of patients trying to turn
me into The God They Want. This indeed occurs so frequently
that in some moods the God I want is one who would relieve
me of the pressure of patients who try to manipulate me into
acting as their God.

That the study of human nature is an activity which differs
radically from other scientific disciplines is perhaps shown more
clearly than anywhere else in the response of psychoanalysis's
raw material to the experience of being studied. Quasars show
no tendency to bow down and worship the astronomer, nor do
they try to persuade him to adopt any particular interpretation
of the shift he observes. Light itself shows no preference for the
wave or particle theory and makes no attempt to inveigle the
physicist into opting for one or the other. But this is what
patients do to their analysts all the time. Not only do they deify
him in the sense of worshipping him – 'idealization' is the

technical term – but they also try to persuade him to explain themselves in the light of whatever available theory of the origin of neurosis appeals to them. Those who wish to be pitied and like to believe that it is all other people's fault try to get him to opt for one of the deprivation theories of neurosis, while those with a romantic imagination try to persuade him that they have brought ruin and destruction down on themselves and that their neurosis is the result of their own death instinct or innate envy. In doing this they are deifying him by regarding him as the creator of the natural laws of psychology to which they are subject, and their choice of an analyst of a particular school is analogous to the religious person's choice of a particular sect or interpretation of Holy Writ.

By deifying the analyst the neurotic is behaving like the religious person whose beliefs include the idea of a God, external to himself, who set up the rules by which both the impersonal world and human beings are governed, who knows all about him, and who was there at the beginning and will still be there at the end. And yet, it seems to me, the only person who is really in a position to know one's own nature is oneself, and the only person who both was there at the beginning and will be there at the end is oneself. The neurotic and the believer in a God 'out there' is, in fact, preserving his own sense of conti-nuity and his innate self-knowledge by attributing it to Someone other than himself – to his God or his analyst. This procedure is presumably only necessary to those who have lost contact with themselves and who feel that they have become fragmented. Integrity, wholeness, health and insight still exist but are located in Another, from whom, however, it may be recovered, either by psychoanalysis or by communion with God.

Here I have, rather to my surprise, I must admit, come to a position which resembles Jung's view that God is an objectifica-tion of the self, though, as those familiar with recent ego-psychology will realize, my route has been strictly Freudian.

It follows from what I have just said that the analyst is subject to a professional hazard to which other scientists are not ex-posed, that of being seduced by his patients into accepting the role of God. If this happens, he comes to believe that he is the sole fount of insight, wisdom and light and that his patients can only acquire health if they incorporate him and become his disciples, eternally nourished by, and grateful to, the immanent internal image of the analyst with whom they once communed. The patients of such analysts are cured by conversion, and instead of returning after analysis to their own lives, they become proselytizers of the analyst or the theories to which they owe their salvation. Analysts who succeed in resisting this temptation enable their patients to rediscover themselves and attribute their successes to the *vis medicatrix naturae* which reasserts itself once he has succeeded in exposing their defensive self-deceptions. The ability to do so depends on a technical knowledge of psychopathology and some capacity to distinguish truth from falsehood – more modest gifts than those required to found a new sect or school.

By this time it has become obvious to me that the God I want would not ordinarily be recognized as one; or, to put it the other way round, and perhaps more honestly, I do not want a God in any sense in which that word is ordinarily understood. It has become clear to me that some kinds of God have become unavailable to me, since my professional training and conscience would compel me to interpret them as wish-fulfilling illusions or as parts of myself which are better kept to myself. It has also become clear to me that, although I value both insight and self-awareness, I feel no need to objectify the self; that although I recognize that my mental life needs monitoring, I also think that it is best done by myself; and that, although I feel at home in that realm of thought and feeling which is traditionally occupied by religion, I feel little or no need to systematize this feeling into anything that could be called a religion. I belong, in fact, to that small group of Englishmen who actually enjoy going to Church and who can attach meaning to almost every-thing they hear there, but who cannot imagine themselves subscribing to any institutionalized or systematized formulation of religious beliefs.

This attitude is, I suspect, the logical conclusion of the Pro-testantism in which I was reared. It combines setting a high value on integrity, believing that even the apparently trivial should be treated sacramentally, distrust of the propensity to codify and ritualize, and insistence on my right to think for myself and be the custodian of my own conscience. In my attitude towards psychoanalysis it has led me to view with misgiving the tendency of some analysts to organize their insights into complete systems of theory which claim to embrace the whole of human experience – such systems are at best premature, since psychoanalysis is still a young science, and at the worst stultifying dogmas – and to engage in controversies which are to my mind scholastic. The present controversy about the rival merits of ego-psychology, instinct theory and object relations theory seems to me to be based on the assumption that it is possible to decide whether the essence of a sentence lies in its subject, verb or object, whether agent, action or object should occupy the central position in theory. Rather similarly, the tendency to standardize analytical technique seems to me to involve the risk that it may become a ritual which is practised without being understood, and the dissemination of definitions of normality and maturity, which imply that they can be achieved by conformity to a known pattern of behaviour, to involve the risk that the letter and not the spirit of the law will be obeyed.

In addition to having a prejudice against systematizing religious ideas and feelings, I find that I am also reluctant to take one particular intellectual step which seems to be necessary if one is to engage in the game of God-making. This is the shift from lower to upper case, and all that it implies, which is involved in converting private and personal statements like 'I value love' or 'reason' into public and authoritative affirmations like 'I believe in Love' (or Eros or Agape or Logos: for some reason translation into Greek raises the tone of such utterances still further). This procedure, which undoubtedly comes quite naturally to many people, seems to me to be dangerous since it tends to reverse the proper power relationships existing between words and man. Words were created by man – 'In the beginning was the Word . . .' cannot literally be true, though the passage from which it comes makes sense if it is taken to refer to the birth of self-awareness – and their function is to act as his tools and servants. When, however, they acquire the status of proper names and are reified, personified and deified, they cease to be tools and become masters. And when men cease to think of themselves as the users of words and start instead to regard themselves as their servants, they become slaves of language and capable of inhumanity. As both religious and political history show, men who in their private lives may be kind and tolerant are prepared to kill, persecute and engage in heresy-hunting at the behest of abstract nouns, whether these be God, Liberty, Equality, Fraternity, the Fatherland or the Party. Indeed, much of the behaviour which is adduced as evidence that man is an intrinsically aggressive, destructive and sadistic animal can also be interpreted as a consequence of his liability to lose contact with the sensuous reality of persons and things and to invest ideas with absolute and dogmatic value. When he does this, the social virtues of loyalty, devotion and integrity become destructive and inhuman.

As a result, God-making is not only a game but also a potentially dangerous one, particularly if it is accompanied by the messianic wish to provide God with worshippers additional to oneself. However, if I were compelled to take some idea and deify it, I should, I think, choose Continuity. Although Its name might occasionally be taken in vain to justify Luddite attacks of machine-breaking, It would on the whole, I believe, prove a comparatively harmless Deity, whose rites would only rarely clash with those of other better-established members of the Pantheon, Eros, Agape and Logos. And if It ever decided to go into the Church business, it would find a market already ripe for exploitation among those sightseers who, despite having no great interest in history, architecture or religion, already make their pilgrimages to our cathedrals and stately homes; and among those in whom new towns induce a feeling of desolation, among those who feel ill at ease in rooms which have been designed for them by some fashionable interior decorator and who insist on living in homes which reflect their own lives, and those who feel that the Bible in modern English is not quite as good as the one authorized by King James. All these, and many more, are potential worshippers of Continuity. And there would be more recruits to my new religion were it not for the fact that the sense of continuity is one of the commodities already established by longer-established religions, and by such cults as genealogy, the monarchy and the family.

But Continuity is not only past-seeking, and it should not be confused with either nostalgia or traditionalism. Continuity implies growth and change and, if deified, it would be two-faced, looking forwards as well as backwards. But since the future has not yet arrived and has yet to create its symbols – though nature will presumably continue to act as a symbolic bridge between past and future – the worshipper of Continuity can only feel awe towards one of its faces. Towards the future he will have to have faith that something will continue for ever to be as it was in the beginning.

1967

Complete Bibliography

Essays marked with an asterisk are included in the present volume.

1951
'A Contribution to the Study of the Dream Screen'. *Int. J. Psycho-Anal.*, vol. 32, and *Imagination and Reality*, pp. 1–13.

1953
'Some Observations on a Case of Vertigo'. *Int. J. Psycho-Anal.*, vol. 34, and *Imagination and Reality*, pp. 14–28.

1956
'Symbolism and Its Relationship to the Primary and Secondary Processes'. *Int. J. Psycho-Anal.*, vol. 37, and *Imagination and Reality*, pp. 42–60.

1957
Review of *Peter and Caroline: A Child Asks about Childbirth and Sex*. *Int. J. Psycho-Anal.*, vol. 38 by Sten Hegeler.

1958
'An Enquiry into the Function of Words in the Psycho-analytical Situation'. *Int. J. Psycho-Anal.*, vol. 39, and *Imagination and Reality*, pp. 69–83.
Review of *On Shame and the Search for Identity* by Helen Merrell Lynd. *Int. J. Psycho-Anal.*, vol. 39.
Review of *Neurotic Distortion of the Creative Process* by Lawrence S. Kubie. *Int. J. Psycho-Anal.*, vol. 39.

1959
Review of *The Quest for Identity* by Allen Wheelis. *Int. J. Psycho-Anal.*, vol. 40.
'The Luther Case'. Review of *Young Man Luther* by Erik Erikson. *Observer*, 13 December.
'The Disciples of Freud'. Review of *Freud and the Post-Freudians* by J. A. C. Brown.
Review of *The Integrity of the Personality* by Anthony Storr. *Observer*, 10 July.

1960
*'The Analysis of a Paranoid Personality'. *Int. J. Psycho-Anal.*, vol. 41. (Published in this volume as 'Miss Y: The Analysis of a Paranoid Personality'.)

'Scream from the Grave'. Review of *Fear, Punishment, Anxiety and the Wolfenden Report* by Charles Berg. *Observer*, 3 January.

'Married Couples in Conflict'. Review of *Marriage: Studies in Emotional Conflict and Growth*, ed. Lily Pincus. *Observer*, 28 January.

1961

*Review of *Personality Structure and Human Interaction* by Harry Guntrip. *Int. J. Psycho-Anal.*, vol. 42. (Published in this volume as 'Fairbairn and Guntrip'.)

'Problem Children'. Review of *Delinquent and Neurotic Children* by Ivy Bennett. *Observer*, 5 February.

*'In Our Time: The Kleinian Viewpoint'. *Observer*, 9 April. (Published in this volume as 'Melanie Klein'.)

'Freud as a Father Figure'. Review of *Letters of Sigmund Freud 1873–1939*, ed. Ernst L. Freud. *Observer*, 18 June.

1962

'On the Defensive Function of Schizophrenic Thinking and Delusion-Formation'. *Int. J. Psycho-Anal.*, vol. 43, and *Imagination and Reality*, pp. 84–101.

'Beyond the Reality Principle'. *Int. J. Psycho-Anal.*, vol. 43, and *Imagination and Reality*, pp. 102–113.

'Discipline for Young Children – at Home. By a practising psychoanalyst'. *Where*, Summer.

'Leonardo Psychoanalysed'. Review of *Leonardo da Vinci* by K. R. Eissler. *Observer*, 8 April.

'Naivety of Melanie Klein'. Review of *Our Adult World and Other Essays* by Melanie Klein, *Observer*, 1962.

'Priest, Philosopher and Physician'. Review of *Three Hundred Years of Psychiatry 1535–1860*, by Richard Hunter and Ida Macalpine, *Observer*, 1963.

1963

'Corrupted by a Mystique?'. Review of *The Feminine Mystique* by Betty Friedan. *New Society*, 6 June.

'Psychiatric Orthodoxy Contradicted'. Review of *A Study of Brief Psychotherapy* by Dr D. H. Malan. *New Society*, 3 October.

'Freud and the Romans'. Review of *Problems in Psychoanalysis: A Symposium*. *New Society*, C. Batten, 17 October.

'Freud and the Pastor'. Review of *Psycho-Analysis and Faith: The Letters of Sigmund Freud and Oskar Pfister*, ed. Heinrich Meng and Ernst Freud. *Observer*, 15 December.

1964

'Analysing Freud'. Review of *Freud* by Reuben Fine. *Observer*, 16 February.

'Post Freudian'. Review of *Introduction to the Work of Melanie Klein* by Hanna Segal. *Observer*, 5 April.

'Beyond the Panel'. Review of *Fringe Medicine* by Brian Inglis. *New Society*, 30 April.

'To Touch Us'. Review of 'Art as Communication', an exhibition of art by psychiatric patients at the ICA. *New Society*, 14 May.

'"Improvements" in Psychiatry'. Review of *Psychotherapy: Purchase of Friendship* by W. Schofield. *New Society*, 20 August.

'The Cave of the Insane'. Review of *The Indications of Insanity* by John Conolly. *Observer*, 23 August.

'The Emergence of Psychology'. Review of *A Hundred Years of Psychology* by J. C. Flugel and *A Short History of British Psychology* by L. S. Hearnshaw. *New Society*, 17 September.

'Therapist and Patient'. Review of *An Introduction to Psychotherapy* by Sidney Tarachow. *New Society*, 26 November.

'Books for Christmas: Look Back in Loathing'. Review of *Words* by Jean-Paul Sartre. *New Society*, 3 December.

1965

'The Effect of the Psychoneurotic Patient on his Environment'. *The Role of Psychosomatic Disorder in Adult Life*, ed. J. Wisdom and H. Wolff. Oxford: Pergamon Press, 1965. See also *Imagination and Reality*, pp. 129–35.

'Being Changed by Language'. Review of *Linguistic Change in Present-day English* by Charles Barber. *New Society*, 21 January.

'Two Sides of Eysenck'. Review of *Fact and Fiction in Psychology* by H. J. Eysenck. *Observer*, 21 March.

'A Conspiracy of Victims'. Review of *Pedophilia and Exhibitionism* by J. W. Mohr, R. E. Turner and M. B. Jerry. *New Society*.

'The It and the Id'. Review of *The Wild Analyst* by Carl and Sylvia Grossman. *Observer*, 13 June.

'Friend of Freud'. Review of *The Freud Journal of Lou Andreas-Salome* by Stanley A. Leavy. *Observer*, 15 August.

Review of *Contemporary Schools of Psychology* by Robert S. Woodworth in collaboration with Mary R. Sheeham. *New Society*, 25 September.

'Even Patients are Human'. Review of *Introduction to Psychology for Medical Students* by R. R. Hetherington, D. H. Miller and J. G. Neville. *New Society*, 16 October.

'Guide to Freud'. Review of *What Freud Really Said* by David Stafford-Clark. *Observer*, 21 November.

'A Disease of People'. Review of *Hysteria: the History of a Disease* by Ilza Veith. *New Society*, 23 November.

*'On Ablation of the Parental Images'. Unpublished article, rev. 1973. (Published for the first time in this volume.)

1966

*'Causes and Meaning'. *Psychoanalysis Observed*, ed. Charles Rycroft. London: Constable, 1966, and Harmondsworth: Penguin Books, 1968: pp. 7–22.

'Cheering Up Freud'. Review of *A Psychoanalytic Dialogue: The Letters of Sigmund Freud and Karl Abraham 1907–1926*, ed. Hilda C. Abraham and Ernst Freud. *Observer*, 21 January.

'Should Inauthenticity be Punished?' Review of *One in Twenty* by Brian Magee. *New Society*, 2 April.

'A Foray against Ghosts'. Review of *Eliminating the Unconscious: A Behaviourist View of Psychoanalysis* by T. R. Miles. *New Society*, 30 June.

'Striptease with the Clothes On'. Review of *If Hopes were Dupes* by Catherine York. *New Society*, 7 July.

'In Abstract-Cuckooland'. Review of *The Triumph of the Therapeutic* by Philip Rieff. *New Society*, 11 August.

'Sleeping Like a Baby'. Review of *Medical and Dental Hypnosis and its Clinical Applications* by J. Hartland. *New Society*, 11 August.

'Man and Superwoman'. Review of *Jean-Jacques Rousseau* by J. M. Guéhenno. *New Society*, 1 September.

'Light on Jung'. Review of *What Jung Really Said* by E. A. Bennet. *Observer*, 11 September.

'The Origins of Fighting'. Review of *On Aggression* by Konrad Lorenz. *New Society*, 15 September.

'Ashes, Old Boy – Just Ashes'. Review of *The Life of Ian Fleming* by John Pearson. *New Society*, 1 December.

'Grassroots Oddities'. Review of *The Social Psychology of Social Movements* by Hans Toch. *New Society*, 22 December.

1967

*'The God I Want'. *The God I Want*, ed. James Mitchell. London: Constable, pp. 25–41. (Published in this volume as 'On Continuity'.)

'Knees under the Table'. Review of *ESP: A Scientific Evaluation* by C. E. M. Hansel. *New Society*, 9 March.

'Patients in Prison'. Review of *Psychopathic Disorders and Their Assessment* by M. Craft. *New Society*, 26 January.

'Muddle in Massachusetts'. Review of *The Boston Strangler* by Gerold Frank. *New Society*, 16 February.

'The Games Society Chooses'. Review of *Being Mentally Ill* by Thomas J. Scheff. *New Society*, 20 April.

'Lost Children'. Review of *The Empty Fortress* by Bruno Bettelheim. *New Society*, 4 May.

'Priest and Psychotherapist'. Review of *A Fortunate Man* by John Berger. *New Society*, 11 May.

'The Necessity of Anxiety'. Review of *Psychology and the Human Dilemma* by Rollo May. *New Society*, 27 July.

'Awful Warnings'. Review of *The Anxiety-Makers* by Alex Comfort. *Observer*, 30 July.

'Avoiding the Stigmata'. Review of *The Clock of Competence* by Robert B. Edgerton. *New Society*, 17 August.

'Of Mice and Men'. Review of *The American Male* by Myron Brenton. *New Society*, 7 September.

'The Growth of Humanism'. Review of *You Shall be as Gods* by Eric Fromm. *New Society*, 14 September.

'Holons and Hierarchies'. Review of *The Ghost in the Machine* by Arthur Koestler. *New Society*, 19 October.

'Biography: Brotherly Hatred'. Review of *Friendship and Fratricide* by Meyer A. Zeligs. *TLS*, 9 November.

'Uninhibited'. Review of *The Use of Lateral Thinking* by Edward de Bono. *TLS*, 30 November.

Review of *Two Wise Children* by Robert Graves and *Gertrude's Child* by Richard Hughes. *New Society*, 7 December.

'Prospectors of the Unconscious'. Review of *Freud and his Early Circle* by Vincent Brome. *Observer*, 24 December.

1968

Imagination and Reality: Psycho-Analytical Essays 1951–1961. Intro. M. Masud R. Khan and Joan D. Sutherland. London: The Hogarth Press and The Institute of Psycho-Analysis.

A Critical Dictionary of Psychoanalysis. London: Nelson; reprinted in paperback 1972.

Anxiety and Neurosis. London: Allen Lane.

'Doctor's Psychotherapy'. Review of *Sexual Discord in Marriage* by Michael Courtenay. *New Society*, 28 March.

'Grande Dame'. Review of *Selected Problems of Adolescence* by Helene Deutsch. *New Society*, 23 May.

'Non-accidental Injuries'. Review of *The Battered Child* by Ray E. Heffer and Henry Kempe. *New Society*, 20 June.

'Drugs for the Mind'. Review of *Psychopharmacology*, ed. C. R. B. Joyce. *TLS*

'Ouch!' Review of *Disease, Pain and Sacrifice* by David Bakan and *Individuality in Pain and Suffering* by Asenath Petrie. *NYRB*, 11 July.

'The Victims'. Review of *Death in Life: The Survivors of Hiroshima* by Robert Jay Lifton. *New Statesman*, 30 August.

'Why War?' Review of *Sanity and Survival: Psychological Aspects of War and Peace* by Jerome D. Frank. *New Society*, 3 October.

'The Suicidal Society'. Review of *Negations* by Herbert Marcuse. *New Statesman*.

'Under Stress'. Review of *Violence, Monkeys and Man* by Claire Russell and W. M. S. Russell. *New Statesman*, 8 November.

1969

*'All in the Mind'. Review of *Analytical Psychology: Its Theory and Practice* by C. G. Jung. *NYRB*, 16 January. (Published in this volume as 'Carl Jung and Analytical Psychology'.)

'Marriage Lines'. Review of *Marriage and Personal Development* by Rubin Blanck and Gertrude Blanck. *New Society*, 23 January.

'Mnemonists Never Forget'. Review of *The Mind of an Mnemonist* by A. R. Luria. *TLS*, 20 February.

'On Tape'. Review of *The Twisting Lane* by Tony Parker. *New Society*, 20 February.

'Life Without Father'. Review of *Society Without the Father* by Alexander Mitscherlich. *Observer*, 9 March.

'Yes with Everything'. Review of *Individual Morality* by James Hemming. *New Society*, 27 March.

'What's So Funny?' Review of *Rationale of the Dirty Joke: An Analysis of Sexual Humor* by G. Legman. *NYRB*, 10 April.

'Psychology and Science: Playing at being Us'. Review of *The Presentation of Self in Everyday Life* by Erving Goffman. *TLS*, 8 May.

'Painful Subject'. Review of *The Spectrum of Pain* by Richard Serjeant. *New Society*, 15 May.

*'Out of the Way: Memoirs of an Old Bolshevik'. *New Society*, 29 May. (Published in this volume as 'Memoirs of an Old Bolshevik'.)

'Unattainable Aims of Psychoanalysis'. *TES*, 13 June.

'Analysing the Analyst'. *TES*, 20 June.

'A New Religion?' *TES*, 27 June.

'Psychoanalytical Insight'. *TES*, 4 July.

*'The Origin of Love'. Review of *Attachment and Loss*, vol. I: *Attachment* by John Bowlby. *TLS*, 14 August. (Published in this volume as part of 'Bowlby: Attachment and Loss'.)

'Freudian Slip'. Review of *Eros and Civilisation: A Philosophical Inquiry into Freud* by Herbert Marcuse. *New Society*, 25 September.

'The Royal Affliction'. Review of *George III and the Mad-Business* by Ida Macalpine and Richard Hunter. *Observer*, 16 November.

'The Case of Wilhelm Reich'. *NYRB*, 4 December.

1970

Anxiety and Neurosis. Harmondsworth: Penguin Books.

'Airy Thinking'. Review of *The Mechanism of Mind* by Edward de Bono. *TLS*, 12 February.

'Freudian Triangles'. Review of *Brother Animal: The Story of Freud and Tausk* by Paul Roazen. *Observer*, 26 April.

Review of *Human Sexual Inadequacy* by William H. Masters and Virginia E. Johnson. *Nature*, 25 July.

1971

Reich. London: Fontana.

'Among the Flower Children'. Review of *The Human Be-In* by Helen Perry. *New Statesman*, 1 January.

*'The Psychology of Orgasm'. *Man and Woman*, 14 April.

'Noes, Noses, Nonsense'. Review of *The Death of the Family* by David Cooper. *Guardian*, 25 May.

*'Not So Much a Treatment, More a Way of Life'. Review of *The Wolf-Man by the Wolf-Man*, ed. Muriel Gardiner. *NYRB*, 21 October.

*'A Feeling in the Air'. Review of *The Naked Ape* by Desmond Morris. *New Statesman*, 15 October. (Published in this volume as 'The Naked Ape Strikes Again'.)

'Ritual Joy'. Review of *Encounter Groups* by Carl R. Rogers and *Joy* by William C. Schutz. *New Society*, 11 November.

'Sampling Sex'. Review of *Sex and Marriage in England Today* by Geoffrey Gorer. *New Statesman*, 26 November.

'Madhouses'. Review of *The Trade in Lunacy* by William L. L. Parry-Jones. *New Statesman*.

1972

'Why Psychiatry is an Intrinsically Odd Profession'. Unpublished lecture first given at Bristol University Medical School, 25 January.

'Roots of Love'. Review of *Love and Hate* by Irenaus Eibi-Eibesfeldt. *New Society*, 10 February.

'Closed System'. Review of *Beyond Freedom and Dignity* by B. F. Skinner. *New Statesman*, 17 March.

'Unthinkable'. Review of *The Roots of Coincidence* by Arthur Koestler. *New Statesman*, 11 February.

*'A Great Mother's Helper'. Review of *Playing and Reality* and *Therapeutic Consultations in Child Psychiatry* by D. W. Winnicott. *NYRB*, 1 June. (Published in this volume as 'D. W. Winnicott'.)

'Still Outside'. Review of *New Pathways in Psychology* by Colin Wilson. *Spectator*, 27 May.

'You Never Can Tell'. Review of *Psychological Probability* by John Cohen. *New Statesman*, 23 June.

*'Doctoring Freud'. Review of *Freud: Living and Dying* by Max Schur. *NYRB*, 10 August. (Published in this volume as 'Freud: Living and Dying'.)

'The Artist as Patient'. *TLS*, 22 September.

'Hybrid Monster'. Review of *Pornography: The Longford Report. TES*, 29 September.

'Stages of the Transference'. Review of *Freud* by Jonathan Miller. *Spectator*, 7 October.

'The Anatomy of Violence'. Unpublished lecture first delivered at the Social Responsibility Conference organized by The Bishop's Council for Social Responsibility, Coventry Cathedral, 4 December.

1973

'Agents and Patients'. Review of *Ideology and Insanity* by Thomas S. Szasz. *New Statesman*, 23 February.

'Theory Games'. Review of *Encounters* by Erving Goffman. *TLS*, 1 March.

'Psychology: Tragic Romances'. Review of *Incest* by Herbert Maisch. *TES*, 2 March.

'Bions and Phantasies'. Review of *Wilhelm Reich: The Evolution of His Work* by David Boadella. *TES*, 30 March.

*'Life with Father'. Review of *Soul Murder* by Morton Schatzman. *New Statesman*, 30 March. (Published in this volume as 'Soul Murder'.)

'Dead or Injured'. Review of *Violence in Human Society* by John Gunn. *New Society,* 21 June.

*'Psychology: Experience, Not Fantasies'. Review of *Attachment and Loss*, vol. 2: *Separation: Anxiety and Anger*, by John Bowlby. *TES*, 29 June. (Published in this volume as part of 'Bowlby: Attachment and Loss'.)

'Dog Beneath the Skin?' Review of *The Mind Possessed* by William Sargant. *Observer*, 14 October.

1974

'Is Freudian Symbolism a Myth?' *NYRB*, 24 January. See also *Symbols and Sentiments*, ed. Ioan Lewis. London: Academic Press, 1977.

'Folie à Deux'. Review of *The Freud/Jung Letters: The Correspondence between Sigmund Freud and C. G. Jung*, ed. William McGuire. *NYRB*, 18 April.

'Suitable Place for Treatment'. Review of *A Home for the Heart* by Bruno Bettelheim. *NYRB*, 12 May.

'Unhealthy Activities'. Review of *Creative Malady* by George Pickering. *Observer*, 6 October.

1975

*'Freud and the Imagination'. *NYRB*, 3 April. (Published in this volume as 'Psychoanalysis and the Literary Imagination'.)

'A Family and Its Head'. Review of *The Manson Murders* by Vincent Bugliosi. *TLS*, 18 April.

'Ideas of Madness'. Review of *Madness and Morals* by Vieda Skultans. *Observer*, 18 May.

'As the Apple to Its Core'. Review of *Transactional Analysis in Psychotherapy* by Eric Berne. *New Society*, 3 July.

'Miscalculated Risks'. Review of *The St Albans Poisoner* by Anthony Holden. *TLS*, 26 September.

'People before Rats'. Review of *Human Beings* by Liam Hudson. *TES*, 21 November.

1976

'Actions Louder than Words'. Review of *A New Language for Psychoanalysis* by Roy Schafer. *NYRB*, 27 May.

'Warmth, Cant, and Gobbledegook'. Review of *Ordinary Ecstasy* by John Rowan. *TES*, 4 June.

'In Praise of Friendship'. Review of *Friends and Lovers* by Robert Brain. *New Society*, 28 October.

'Sickness of the Mind'. Review of *Breakdown* by Stewart Sutherland. *Observer*, 31 October.

1977

'Psychiatric Gambit'. Review of *Psychiatry on Trial* by Malcolm Lader. *New Society*, 4 August.

*'Freud and His Heirs'. *Listener*, 27 October. (Published in this volume as 'The Present State of Freudian Psychoanalysis'.)

1978

Introduction to *The Dissociation of a Personality: The Hunt for the Real Miss Beauchamp* by Morton Prince. Oxford: Oxford University Press, pp. v–xxi.

'The Way Madness Lies'. Review of *Reasoning about Madness* by J. K. Wing. *Observer*, 18 June.

'Will the Real Miss Beauchamp Please Stand Up?' (Abridgement of Introduction to *The Dissociation of a Personality*.) *New Society*, 9 November.

1979

The Innocence of Dreams. London: The Hogarth Press, 1979, and Oxford: Oxford University Press, 1981.

'Steps to an Ecology of Hope'. *The Sources of Hope*, ed. Ross Fitzgerald. Oxford: Pergamon Press, pp. 3–23.

*'The Psyche and the Senses'. *How Does it Feel?*, ed. Mick Csaky. London: Thames and Hudson.

*'Freud and Timpanaro'. *New Left Review*, 118, November/December. (Published in this volume as 'The Freudian Slip'.)

1980

'How Psychosomatic is Your Illness?' Review of *Social Causes of Illness* by Richard Totman. *NYRB*, 3 April.

*'Knowing the Worst Too Young'. Review of *Attachment and Loss*, vol. 3: *Loss, Sadness and Depression*, by John Bowlby. *New Society*, 13 March. (Published in this volume as part of 'Bowlby: Attachment and Loss'.)

'A Very Rum Fellow Indeed'. Review of *Havelock Ellis: Philosopher of Sex* by Vincent Brome; *Havelock Ellis: A Biography* by Phyllis Grosskurth, and *Olive Schreiner* by Ruth First and Ann Scott. *TES*, 18 July.

'Sensuality from the Start'. Review of *Paedophilia: The Radical Case* by Tom O'Carroll and *The Story of Ruth* by Morton Schatzman. *TLS*, 21 November.

1981

'Back to the Old Adam'. Review of *The Red Lamp of Incest* by Robin Fox. *Observer*, 18 January.

'Not a Science'. Review of *The Case for a Personal Psychotherapy* by Peter Lomas. *New Society*, 16 July.

1982

'Orgone Recital'. Review of *Record of a Friendship: The Correspondence between Wilhelm Reich and A. S. Neill, 1936–1957*, ed. Beverley R. Placzek. *The Times*, 14 January.

'A New Look at Anti-psychiatry'. Review of *Psycho Politics* by Peter Sedgwick. *The Sunday Times*, 7 March.

'Variations on an Archetypal Theme'. Review of *Archetype: A Natural History of the Self* by Anthony Stevens. *New Society*, 20 May.

'Different Premises'. Review of *Freud and Jung: Conflicts of Interpretation* by Robert S. Steele. *THES*, 13 August.

'How a Child Reacts to the Arrival of Baby'. Review of *Siblings: Love, Envy and Understanding* by Judy Dunn and Carol Kendrick. *New Society*, 11 November.

'Twilight States'. Review of *Dreams and How to Guide Them* by Hervey de Saint-Denys. *TLS*, 17 December.

1983

*'Viewpoint: Analysis and the Autobiographer'. *TLS*, 27 May. (Published in this volume as 'On Autobiography'.)

'The Problems of Translating Freud'. Review of *Freud and Man's Soul* by Bruno Bettelheim. *New Society*, 14 July.

'Bedside Book'. Review of *The Oxford Book of Dreams*, ed. Stephen Brook. *New Society*, 20 October.

*'What Analysts Say to Their Patients'. Unpublished lecture. (Published for the first time in this volume.)

1984

'A Case of Hysteria'. Review of *The Assault on Truth: Freud's Suppression of the Seduction Theory* by Jeffrey Moussaieff Masson. *NYRB*, 12 April.

*'Psychoanalysis and Beyond'. Unpublished article. (Published for the first time in this volume.)

*'Where I Came From'. Unpublished article, revised 1984. (Published for the first time in this volume.)

1985

'Symbolism, Imagination and Biological Destiny'. Lecture delivered in 1984 at All Soul's College, Oxford, as one of the Chichele Lectures on 'Psychoanalysis and Its Influence on the Arts and Humanities'. London: Duckworth (forthcoming).

Index

CHATTO TIGERSTRIPE

Chatto Tigerstripe – a unique partnership

Chatto & Windus is collaborating with a group of distinguished writers on a new and promising development in the relationship between authors and publishers.

The name of the association, 'Tigerstripe', was chosen to reflect the mood of the intended list – various, bold, adventurous and memorable. The titles will range across the whole spectrum of fiction and non-fiction, and comprise some of today's most powerful, innovative and controversial writing.

Some new and forthcoming Tigerstripe books are listed overleaf.

New and forthcoming titles in Tigerstripe

G.   John Berger

Solitary and extraordinary witness to Europe before the Great War, G. is at once Don Giovanni and Garibaldi: pursuing sexual and political freedom, he heralds the turbulent new century. *G.* won the 1972 Booker McConnell prize, and is widely regarded as the greatest English novel of the Seventies.

Pig Earth   John Berger

In these magnificent tales John Berger presents compelling portraits of a peasant community. The lives of Catherine, Joseph and the cow Rousa, Marcel and, most movingly, Jean and the dwarf Cocadrille possess extraordinary immediacy and vitality as Berger remakes storytelling, with effortless originality, into something at once traditional and contemporary.

Images of God: The Consolation of Lost Illusions   Peter Fuller

Arguing powerfully for a fresh recognition of the role of religious feeling in art, Peter Fuller ranges from Rouault to Piper, from Ruskin to Roger Scruton, and from the New Expressionism to the crafts. *Images of God* confirms him as one of Britain's most versatile and important critics.

Britain's Royal Romance (*forthcoming*)
Tom Nairn

The United Kingdom lives and breathes monarchy like no other society recorded in history. Tom Nairn's eloquent and brilliantly sustained analysis of this infatuation prescribes a much-needed antidote – an argument for a quiet republicanism – and comes up with some startling conclusions about the nature of British society in the process.

The White Bird
Writings by John Berger (*forthcoming*)

This collection of essays and poems may prove John Berger's most useful and important book to date, the fullest statement of his unique ways of seeing. Essays on travel, on love, on politics, on writing, as well as major statements on painting and the philosophy of art, include the classic 'Moment of Cubism' and the previously unpublished 'The White Bird'.